OXFORD

take off in
Latin American
Spanish

Rosa María Martín

D1450977

OXFORD
UNIVERSITY PRESS

OXFORD
UNIVERSITY PRESS

Great Clarendon Street, Oxford OX2 6DP

Oxford University Press is a department of the University of Oxford.
It furthers the University's objective of excellence in research, scholarship,
and education by publishing worldwide in

Oxford New York

Auckland Cape Town Dar es Salaam Hong Kong Karachi
Kuala Lumpur Madrid Melbourne Mexico City Nairobi
New Delhi Shanghai Taipei Toronto

With offices in
Argentina Austria Brazil Chile Czech Republic France Greece
Guatemala Hungary Italy Japan Poland Portugal Singapore
South Korea Switzerland Thailand Turkey Ukraine Vietnam

Oxford is a registered trade mark of Oxford University Press
in the UK and in certain other countries

Published in the United States
by Oxford University Press Inc., New York

British Library Cataloguing in Publication Data

Data available

Library of Congress Cataloging in Publication Data

Data available

ISBN 978-0-19-953440-1 (Book and CDs)
ISBN 978-0-19-860989-6 (Coursebook)

This coursebook is only available as a component of Take Off In Latin American Spanish

1

Commissioning, development, and project management: Tracy Traynor
Project management (2nd edition): Natalie Pomier
Audio production: Gerald Ramshaw; Richard Carrington;
Daniel Pageon, Actors World Production Ltd
Music: David Stoll
Design: Keith Shaw
Editorial: Brigitte Lee, Lydia Goldsmith
Teaching consultant: Jenny Ollerenshaw

Printed in China through Phoenix Offset

Contents

Introduction

Oxford Take Off In Latin American Spanish is designed to help the beginner develop the basic language skills necessary to communicate in Spanish in most everyday situations. It is intended for learners working by themselves, providing all the information and support necessary for successful language learning.

How to use the course

The book and the recording are closely integrated, as the emphasis is on speaking and listening. The recording contains step-by-step instructions on how to work through the units. The presenter will tell you when to use the recording on its own, when to use the book, and when and how to use the two together. The book provides support in the form of transcriptions of the recording material, translations of new vocabulary, and grammar explanations. You'll find this icon ⓐ in the book when you need to listen to the recording.

1 (recording/book) Read the unit objectives on the first page telling you what you will learn in the unit, and then begin by listening to the **dialogue** on the recording. You may not understand everything the first time you hear it, but try to resist the temptation to look at the transcript in the book. The first activity on the recording will help you develop your listening skills by suggesting things to concentrate on and listen out for. You'll be given the opportunity to repeat some of the key sentences and phrases from the dialogue before you hear it a second time. You may need to refer to the vocabulary list (book) before completing the second activity (book). Listen to the dialogue as many times as you like, but as far as possible try not to refer to the dialogue transcript (book).

2 (book) Once you have listened to all the new language, take some time to work through the **transcript, Vocabulary, Language Building**, and **activities** in the book to help you understand how it works.

3 (recording) Then it's time to practice speaking: first **Pronunciation practice** and then the **Your turn** activity. You will be given all the instructions and cues you need by the presenter on the recording. The first few times you do this you may need to refer back to the vocabulary and language building sections in the book, but aim to do it without the book after that.

4 (book) The fourth learning section, **Culture**, concentrates on reading practice. Try reading it first without referring to the vocabulary list to see how much you can already understand,

making guesses about any words or phrases you are not sure of. The activities which accompany the text will help you develop reading comprehension skills.

5 (recording/book) For the final learning section, return to the recording to listen to the **Story**. This section gives you the opportunity to have some fun with the language and hear the characters in the story use the language you have just learnt in different situations. The aim is to give you the confidence to cope with authentic Spanish. There are activities in the book to help you.

6 (book) Return to the book, and work through the activities in the **Test** section to see how well you can remember and use the language you have covered in the unit. This is best done as a written exercise. Add up the final score and, if it is not as high as you had hoped, try going back and reviewing some of the sections.

7 (recording/book) As a final review, turn to the **Summary** on the last page of the unit. This will test your understanding of the new situations, vocabulary and grammar introduced in the unit. Use the book to prepare your answers, either by writing them down or speaking aloud, then return to the recording to test yourself. You will be given prompts in English on the recording, so you can do this test without the book.

8 (book) At the very end of each unit you will find some suggestions for **revision** and ideas for further practice.

Each unit builds on the work of the preceding units, so it's very important to learn the vocabulary and structures from each unit before you move on. There are review sections after units 3, 7, 10, and 14 for you to test yourself on the material learnt so far.

Other support features
If you want a more detailed grammar explanation than those given in the Language Building sections, you will find a *Grammar Summary* at the end of the book. For a definition of the grammar terms used in the course, see the *Glossary of Grammatical Terms* on page 245.

The *Answers* section at the end of the book will give you the answers to all the book activities. Some activities require you to give information about yourself, so you may also need to check some vocabulary in a dictionary.

At the end of the book you'll find a comprehensive Spanish–English Vocabulary.

For additional practice, your *Take Off In Latin American Spanish* pack contains an extra CD you can listen to while on the go without having to refer to the coursebook. You will also find a travel dictionary and phrasebook that easily slips into your handbag or pocket when you travel around.

The Spanish language

More and more people are choosing to learn Spanish and it is easy to see why. Spanish is spoken by almost 400 million people as their first language and the vast majority of these are in Central and Latin America. It is one of the easier languages to start learning as it is derived from Latin and so a lot of vocabulary will be recognizable to the English speaker. The pronunciation of Spanish is also consistent and relatively straightforward for the English-speaking learner.

This course focuses on the Spanish spoken in Mexico. Each country in Central and Latin America has its own slight variations in pronunciation, vocabulary, and, in some cases, structure, but whether you speak to people from Mexico, Argentina, Chile, Venezuela, Peru, or any of the other Spanish-speaking countries in the Americas, you will be able to communicate effectively using the language taught here. Spanish was introduced in Central America by European colonists from the late 15th century. The indigenous ancient civilizations, such as Maya, Aztec, and Inca, and the Hispanic traditions of the colonists have contributed to a rich and varied culture, which is reflected in the language spoken today throughout the continent.

Learning to communicate in another language may be challenging, but it is also a very rewarding and enriching experience. Most Spanish speakers you come across will be impressed by your attempts and very encouraging. We have made this course as varied and entertaining as possible, and we hope you enjoy it.

Pronunciation

To achieve good pronunciation, there is no substitute for listening carefully to the recording and, if possible, to Spanish native speakers, and trying to reproduce the sounds you hear. Here are a few guidelines for you to keep in mind when doing so. You will find this section most useful if you listen to the Pronunciation section on the recording as you read it.

Pronunciation

Vowels
Vowels in Spanish are pronounced consistently and they are always short. In vowel combinations, each vowel is pronounced separately.

Written as	*Phonetic symbol*	*English approximation*	*Example*
a	/a/	*between* cat *and* arm	casa, camisa
e	/e/	let	escalera, lejos
i	/i/	kit	distinto, primero
o	/o/	lost	nombre, solo
u	/u/	good	uno, fruta
u + e	/we/	wet	bueno
i + e	/je/	yet	tiene
e + i	/ei/	wait	aceite
i + u	/ju/	you	ciudad

Consonants
Most consonants are pronounced as in English. The exceptions are:

Written as	*Phonetic symbol*	*English approximation*	*Example*
v	/b/	bed	vacaciones, viejo
z	/s/	sink	zona, zapato
c + i/e	/s/	sink	centro, cine
h		*not pronounced*	hermano, helado
j	/x/	*Scottish* loch	jamón, jugo
g + i/e	/x/	*Scottish* loch	gente, gigante
ñ	/ɲ/	onion	niño, piña
r beginning of word and after l, n, s	/rr/	*rolled*	rojo, sonrisa
between vowels	/r/	*softer*	pero, era
rr	/rr/	*rolled*	perro

Combinations

qu	/k/	k [u *not pronounced*]	queso, quiero
cu	/kw/	hard c [u *pronounced*]	cuello
ll	/j/	yet	llave, calle
gu + i/e	/g/	hard g [u *not pronounced*]	guerra, guitarra
gu + *other letters*	/gw/	hard g [u *pronounced*]	guapo

Stress

Words in Spanish are stressed as follows:

- word ending in a vowel or **n** or **s** – on the penultimate syllable
  casa, **quie**ren, **co**mes
- word ending in any other consonant – on last syllable
  hab**lar**, sal**ud**
- irregular stress shown by an accent
  pel**í**cula

1

Starting out
En camino

OBJECTIVES

In this unit you'll learn how to:

- ✓ greet people
- ✓ meet people and give your name
- ✓ ask for a drink and something to eat

And cover the following grammar and language:

- ✓ masculine and feminine nouns
- ✓ formal and informal ways of saying 'you'
- ✓ the verb **ser** ('to be')
- ✓ question forms
- ✓ polite requests using **me da** ('I'd like'), **(yo) quiero** ('I'd like'), and **por favor** ('please')

LEARNING SPANISH 1

Spanish is relatively easy to learn, especially at the beginning. Many words are similar to their English equivalents, which means you can build up vocabulary quickly. Spanish is also comparatively easy for English speakers to pronounce.

You can go far with just a little language, so even when you are not sure how to form a correct, complete sentence, try using the words you do know. Don't worry about getting things wrong. Even with some errors, people will still be able to understand you. The more confidence you gain in actually communicating, the more fluent you'll become.

Finally, it's important to work through each unit at your own pace, listening to the recording several times if necessary before going on.

Now start the recording for Unit 1.

1.1 Greetings

Saludos

ACTIVITY 1 is on the recording.

ACTIVITY 2

Match the person with the correct time of day.

1 Señor González   a night
2 Juan   b morning
3 Señora Martín   c afternoon

DIALOGUE 1

○ Buenos días, señor Pérez.
■ Buenos días, señora Martín. ¿Cómo está usted?
○ Bien, gracias. ¿Y usted?
■ Muy bien, gracias. Adiós.

■ Buenas tardes, señorita García.
○ Buenas tardes, señor González. ¿Cómo está?
■ Bien, gracias.

○ Buenas noches, Juan. ¿Cómo estás?
■ Bien, gracias. ¿Y tú?
○ ¡Muy bien!

VOCABULARY	
buenos días	good morning
el señor (Sr.)	Mr
la señora (Sra.)	Mrs, Ms
¿cómo está usted?	how are you? [*formal*]
bien	fine
gracias	thank you
y	and
usted	you [*formal*]
muy bien	very well
adiós	goodbye
buenas tardes	good afternoon
la señorita (Srta.)	Miss
buenas noches	goodnight, good evening
¿Cómo estás?	how are you?
tú	you [*informal*]

If you are uncertain about any of the grammatical terms used in the ***Language Building*** *sections, see the Glossary of Grammatical Terms on page 245.*

✓ Señor, señora

In Spanish, all nouns have a gender: they are either masculine (**señor, amigo**) or feminine (**señora, amiga**). The gender of the noun determines the form of other words used with it, such as the definite article ('the') and the indefinite article ('a'):

un/el amigo	a/the (male) friend
una/la amiga	a/the (female) friend

As a general rule, most nouns ending in **-o** are masculine and most nouns ending in **-a** are feminine. There are some exceptions: for these and words that don't end in **-o** or **-a**, it's best to learn the gender as you go along.

✓ Formal and informal ways of saying 'you'

There are two ways of addressing people in Spanish, depending on the level of formality.

usted is used in formal situations – to people such as waiters or salespeople, in business contexts, or when talking to older people; **tú** is used more informally, with younger people and people you know well.

If in doubt, use **usted** unless you are invited to use **tú** by the person you're speaking to. It's always better to err on the side of caution than to risk giving offense.

✓ Exclamations and questions

Spanish exclamations and questions begin and end with an exclamation or question mark; these are inverted at the beginning (**¡Muy bien! ¿Cómo está usted?**). In questions, the word order is usually the same as in English.

ACTIVITY 3

¿**tú** or **usted**? Choose the correct form for these people.

1 a bank employee
2 your Mexican friend
3 a salesperson
4 the teenage son of your Mexican friend
5 the father of your Mexican friend

Now do activities 4 and 5 on the recording.

1.2 Pleased to meet you!
¡Mucho gusto!

 ACTIVITY 6 is on the recording.

ACTIVITY 7

For all true/false activities, correct the statements which are false.

1 The conversations take place in the afternoon.	T/F
2 Sr. González has met Sra. Yuste before.	T/F
3 Sr. González knows Sr. Gómez.	T/F
4 Sr. Gómez asks Sra. Yuste how she is.	T/F

DIALOGUE 2

○ ¿Es usted la señora Yuste?
■ Sí, soy la señora Yuste.
○ Buenos días, yo soy el señor González. Mucho gusto.
■ Encantada.

○ ¡Señor Gómez! ¡Buenos días, señor Gómez!
▼ ¡Señor González! ¡Buenos días! ¿Cómo está?
○ Muy bien, gracias. Le presento a la señora Yuste. Y él es el señor Gómez.
▼ Encantado, señora … Perdone, ¿cómo se llama?
○ Yuste, me llamo Carmen Yuste.
▼ Mucho gusto, señora Yuste.

VOCABULARY

mucho gusto	pleased to meet you [*literally* much pleasure]
(él/ella; usted) es	(he/she/it) is; (you) are [*formal*]
sí	yes
(yo) soy	(I) am
encantada	pleased to meet you [*said by a woman*]
le presento a	this is
y él	and this [*masc.*]
encantado	pleased to meet you [*said by a man*]
perdone	excuse me
¿cómo se llama?	what's your name?
me llamo …	my name is …

✅ *ser* ('to be')

In Spanish there are two verbs 'to be' – **estar** and **ser**. They are used in different ways: **ser** is used to describe a permanent state; **estar** will be covered in Unit 2.

(yo) **soy**	I am	(nosotros/as) **somos**	we are
(tú) **eres**	you are [*informal*]	(ustedes) **son**	you are [*pl.*]
(él/ella) **es**	he/she/it is	(ellos/as) **son**	they are
(usted) **es**	you are [*formal*]		

Note that the formal words for 'you' (**usted/ustedes**) take the third person singular/plural form of the verb respectively, i.e. **usted es/ustedes son**.

The subject pronoun (**yo**, **tú**, etc.) is usually omitted. It is used mainly for emphasis or to avoid confusion.

> **Soy** la señora Yuste. I'm Sra. Yuste.
> **Yo soy** el señor González. I'm Sr. González.

The subject pronouns **nosotros** ('we') and **ellos** ('they') refer to an exclusively masculine group or a mixed group (e.g. a group of men and women); **nosotras** and **ellas** refer to an exclusively feminine group.

✅ Introductions

To introduce someone, you use **le presento a ...** (or, informally, **te presento a ...**), followed by the person's name. If you are introducing a number of people, you can also use **ella es ...** for a woman and **él es ...** for a man.

> **Ella es** la señora Yuste y **él es** el señor Gómez. This is Sra. Yuste and this is Sr. Gómez.

✅ *Encantado/encantada* and *mucho gusto*

encantado changes form depending on who says it. A man says **encantado**, but a woman says **encantada**. This follows the rule of **-o** as a masculine ending and **-a** as a feminine ending. However, **mucho gusto** doesn't change form, whether it's spoken by a man or a woman.

ACTIVITY 8

Match the Spanish with the correct English translation.

1	¿Es usted la señora Yuste?	a	I'm Sra. Yuste.
2	Yo soy la señora Yuste.	b	This is Sra. Yuste.
3	Le presento a la señora Yuste.	c	Are you Sra. Yuste?

🎧 Now do activities 9 and 10 on the recording.

1.3 At the café
En la cafetería

ACTIVITY 11 is on the recording.

ACTIVITY 12

What did María and Juan order?

María: to drink _____ Juan: to drink _____
to eat _____ to eat _____

DIALOGUE 3

- ■ Buenas tardes, ¿qué les sirvo?
- ○ Me da un café, por favor.
- ■ ¿Y usted, señora?
- ▼ Yo quiero un jugo de naranja.
- ■ Muy bien, un café y un jugo de naranja.

- ■ ¿Algo más?
- ○ Sí, y yo quiero una torta de jamón.
- ■ ¿Algo más?
- ▼ Nada más, gracias.
- ■ Aquí tienen, un café, un jugo de naranja y una torta. ¿La torta es para usted, señor?
- ○ Sí, gracias.

VOCABULARY	
¿qué les sirvo?	what would you like to have? [*formal*]
me da ...	I'd like ...
un café	a coffee
yo quiero	I'd like
por favor	please
un jugo (de naranja)	an (orange) juice
¿algo más?	anything else?
una torta (de queso)	a (cheese) sandwich
nada más	nothing else
aquí	here
aquí tienen	here you are [*literally* here you have]
para	for

✓ Asking for something to eat or drink

To ask for something to eat or drink in Spanish, you can use the following expressions.

> **Me da** una cerveza. I'd like a beer.
> **Y yo quiero** un café negro, **por favor**. And I'd like a black coffee, please.

Or simply:

> Un helado, **por favor**. An ice cream, please.
> Un pastel, **por favor**. A cake, please.
> Una cerveza, **por favor**. A beer, please.
> Un café con leche, **por favor**. A coffee with milk, please.

✓ *un jugo de .../una torta de ...*

To say what kind of fruit juice or sandwich you want, you use **de** ('of') as a link word.

> un jugo **de papaya** a papaya juice [*literally* a juice of papaya]
> un jugo **de piña** a pineapple juice
> una torta **de jamón** a ham sandwich

ACTIVITY 13

You're in a café in Mexico ordering drinks and a snack for yourself and a friend. How would you ask for:

1 a ham sandwich and a cheese sandwich?
2 a papaya juice and a coffee?

ACTIVITY 14

Match the Spanish with the correct English translation.

1	nada más	a	for you
2	para usted	b	I'd like a sandwich, please
3	¿algo más?	c	I'd like
4	un jugo de naranja, por favor	d	nothing else
5	quiero una torta, por favor	e	anything else?
6	yo quiero	f	an orange juice, please

ⓐ Now do activities 15 and 16 on the recording.

1.4 Restaurants, cafés, and bars in Mexico

Cafeterías, cafés, y bares en México

In Mexico, a lot of social and business life takes place in the **cafetería** or the **café**. The **cafetería** is like a self-service restaurant, with an informal atmosphere. You can have breakfast, lunch, or an evening meal: it offers quick meals or **tortas** (a kind of sandwich), as well as other refreshments. They also serve coffee and other drinks as well as **botanas** (bar snacks). You order and pick up your food and drink at the bar, and take it to the table yourself or remain at the bar. People meet friends, read the newspaper, have informal business meetings, or simply take a break during working hours in these **cafeterías**. They are open from early morning until about 8 or 9 o'clock in the evening.

A **café** is more elegant than a **cafetería**, but does not normally sell alcohol. Instead of ordering at the bar, you wait at your table to be served by the waiter (**el mesero**) or waitress (**la mesera**). Note that coffee (**un café**) is not normally served with milk unless you ask for it. Ask for the check (**la cuenta**) when you want to pay. It is common to leave a tip (**una propina**) of around 10%.

Bars (**los bares**) serve mainly alcoholic drinks. They open in the early evening and stay open until the early hours of the morning.

The main meal of the day is lunch (**la comida** in Mexico; **el almuerzo** in some other Latin American countries) and is taken around 2 or 3 p.m. This is either eaten at home or in a **cafetería**. Alternatively, people buy **quesadillas** (a tortilla filled with cheese) from a street vendor (**un puesto callejero**). You can also buy **tortas** from the **tortería**.

ACTIVITY 17

Here's a menu showing drinks and snacks from the Cafetería Coyoacán. Can you identify what they are and sort them into food and drink items? Reading them aloud may help you to recognize what they are.

Using the menu, how would you order a drink and food for the following people? There may be more than one item on the menu that's appropriate. Use **me da, yo quiero**, and **por favor** in your orders.

María – would like a dessert and a hot drink: she doesn't like tea.
Juan – would like a fizzy soft drink and is a vegetarian.
Miguel – would like a fruit juice and a sandwich.

CAFETERÍA COYOACÁN

Té solo

Pastel de chocolate

Té limón

Torta de jamón y queso

Café

Ensalada de fruta

Jugo de naranja

Limonada

Jugo de jitomate

Hamburguesas

Coca cola

Ensalada

Drinks:

Food items:

1.5 Un extraño en la ciudad

EN LA CAFETERÍA COYOACÁN
IN THE CAFETERÍA COYOACÁN

It's mid-morning in the Cafetería Coyoacán. María García is taking her coffee break there and chatting with the owner of the bar, Sr. Herrera, an old family friend, when a stranger enters.

el extraño	stranger
en	in
la ciudad	city
su familia	your family
¿qué vas a tomar?	what would you like to have? [*informal*]
el hombre	man
¿conoce a … ?	do you know … ?
pues	well [*used when thinking how to reply*]
pero	but
esta foto	this photo
¡mire!	look! [*formal imperative*]
allí	there
no está	she isn't here

ACTIVITY 18

Listen to the conversation and put the following events in the correct order.

1 A man calls the waiter.
2 Someone orders coffee.
3 Someone asks about the waiter's family.
4 Someone orders orange juice.
5 Someone asks about a woman.
6 Someone orders a ham sandwich.

ACTIVITY 19

Who says what? Choose between Sr. Herrera (H), María García (M), and the stranger (S).

1 How are you [*formal*]?	H/M/S
2 How are things?	H/M/S
3 Do you know the woman in this photo?	H/M/S
4 This is Srta. García.	H/M/S
5 Nothing else.	H/M/S

STORY TRANSCRIPT

Sr. Herrera	Buenos días, María.
María	Buenos días, señor Herrera, ¿cómo está usted?
Sr. Herrera	Muy bien. ¿Y tú?
María	Bien … bien, gracias. ¿Y cómo está su familia?
Sr. Herrera	Bien, gracias. ¿Qué vas a tomar?
María	Un café, por favor.
Sr. Herrera	¿Algo más?
María	Sí, quiero una torta de… jamón y queso.
Extraño	Buenos días. ¡Por favor!
Sr. Herrera	Sí, señor, ¿qué le sirvo?
Extraño	Un jugo de naranja, por favor.
Sr. Herrera	¿Algo más, señor?
Extraño	No, nada más, gracias. Por favor, ¿conoce a la señorita de esta foto?
Sr. Herrera	Pues … Sí. Es María … ¡María García! … Pero … esta foto … esta foto …
Extraño	¿La … señorita … García?
Sr. Herrera	Sí, ésta es la señorita García … Mire … está aquí en el café … allí, allí … ¡María! ¡María! ¡Ah! No está.

Test

Now it's time to test your progress in Unit 1.

1 Match the words and phrases to their Spanish translations.

1	Good morning	a	Buenas tardes
2	Pleased to meet you	b	Le presento a …
3	Thank you	c	Muy bien, gracias
4	This is …	d	Buenas noches
5	Good afternoon	e	¿Cómo está?
6	Goodnight	f	Encantado
7	How are you?	g	Bien, gracias
8	Very well, thank you	h	Gracias
9	Well/Fine, thank you	i	Buenos días

9

2 How would you ask for these things in a café or a bar?
(Score 2 points for a correct answer, 1 point if you make one error.)

1 A coffee with milk and an ice cream.
2 A cheese sandwich and a beer.
3 A tomato juice and a salad.
4 A tea and a ham sandwich.

8

3 Raymond Castle has to go to the airport to meet a Mexican business colleague, Francisco Santillana. They haven't met before and Sr. Santillana doesn't speak English. Complete their conversation below.

Castle   ¿1_____ _____ el Sr. Santillana? Yo 2___ el Sr. Castle.
Santillana Sí, soy yo. (shaking hands) ¡3_____!
Castle   (shaking hands) ¡4_____ _____!
Santillana ¿5_____ _____?
Castle   6_____, gracias.

9

Answers to the activities are in the Answer section on page 213.

4 How would you say the following in Spanish? (2 points for each correct answer, 1 point if you make one error.)

1 Are you Sra. Martín?
2 How are you?
3 Good morning!
4 This is Sra. Martín.
5 I'd like a coffee with milk.

10

5 Take the part of the customer in the following dialogue. (Deduct 1 point for each error.)

Mesero	¿Qué va a tomar?	
Cliente	(Order a coffee.)	(3 points)
Mesero	¿Algo más?	
Cliente	(Say yes and order a ham and cheese sandwich and a salad.)	(4 points)
Mesero	¿Algo más?	
Cliente	(Say nothing more and thanks.)	(3 points)

10

6 Write the Spanish for each of the following words, using the correct form of the definite article **el** or **la**.

Example: Mr   **el señor**

1 Mrs
2 Miss
3 waiter
4 waitress
5 male friend

5

TOTAL SCORE **51**

If you scored less than 41, look at the Language Building sections again before completing the Summary on page 14.

Summary 1

 Now try this final test, summarizing the main points covered in this unit.

How would you:
1 greet someone in the morning? in the afternoon or early evening? at night?
2 ask a business acquaintance how he is?
3 ask a friend how she is?
4 say you're very well, thanks?
5 introduce Sra. Martín?
6 say 'pleased to meet you'?
7 order a coffee and an orange juice?
8 say 'thank you'?

REVIEW

Before moving on to Unit 2, play Unit 1 through again and compare what you can say and understand now with what you knew when you started. Make a note of any vocabulary you still feel unsure of.

Remember that it will also be useful to come back and listen to Unit 1 again after working through the next few units, in order to reinforce what you've learned here.

▷ ▷ ▷ ▷ ▷ ▷ ▷ ▷ ▷ ▷ ▷ ▷ ▷ ▷ ▷

Out and about
En la ciudad

OBJECTIVES

In this unit you'll learn how to:

- ✓ ask for and understand simple directions
- ✓ say what places are in a town and where they are located
- ✓ talk about distances

And cover the following grammar and language:

- ✓ the verb **estar** ('to be')
- ✓ simple questions and negative statements
- ✓ numbers 1–20
- ✓ the plural of nouns
- ✓ ordinal numbers – **primero**, **segundo**, **tercero**, etc. ('first', 'second', 'third', etc.)
- ✓ the impersonal construction **hay** ('there is/there are')
- ✓ the plural forms of the articles **unos/unas** ('some') and **los/las** ('the')
- ✓ prepositions of location

LEARNING SPANISH 2

Don't try to do too much at once. You will learn more effectively if you study for half an hour or so at regular intervals. It also helps if you can learn with someone else. If you can persuade a friend or family member to study with you, it will give you an extra impetus to keep working. Agree on times to meet and goals for the week, and test each other regularly.

🎧 Now start the recording for Unit 2.

2.1 Directions

Direcciones

ACTIVITY 1 is on the recording.

ACTIVITY 2

Match the places with the correct location and distance.

the cathedral   in a square   15 minutes away
Frida Kahlo's house   in a suburb   5 minutes away

DIALOGUE 1

○ Disculpe, señorita. ¿Dónde está la catedral, por favor?
■ Está en la plaza de la Constitución.
○ ¿Está lejos?
■ No, está muy cerca, a cinco minutos.

○ Por favor, ¿dónde está la casa de Frida Kahlo?
■ Está en una colonia que se llama Coyoacán.
○ ¿Está lejos?
■ No, no está lejos; en carro a quince minutos. Está al sur de la ciudad.
○ ¿Está en el mapa?
■ Sí, mire … Aquí.

VOCABULARY

¡disculpe!	excuse me! [*literally* hear me; *formal*]
¿dónde está … ?	where is … ?
la catedral	cathedral
la plaza	square [*in a town/village*]
lejos	far
muy cerca	very near
a cinco minutos	five minutes away [*literally* at five minutes]
la casa	house
una colonia	suburb
que se llama	which is called
en carro	by car [*literally* in car]
a quince minutos	15 minutes away
al sur	to the south
de la ciudad	from the city [*literally* of the city]
el mapa	map

✅ *estar* ('to be')

There are two verbs meaning 'to be' – **ser** (see Unit 1) and **estar**. One use of **estar** is to state where someone or something is located: **está en la plaza** ('it's in the square'). Other uses are covered in Units 5, 7, and 9.

(yo) **estoy**	I am	(nosotros/as) **estamos**	we are
(tú) **estás**	you are	(ellos/as; ustedes) **están**	they are;
(él/ella; usted) **está**	he/she/it is; you are		you are

In words with an irregular stress pattern, an accent is used to indicate a stressed vowel.

✅ Forming simple questions and negative statements

A simple statement is made into a question by a change in intonation: the voice rises at the end of the sentence instead of falling.

> **¿Está lejos? No, no está lejos.** Is it far? No, it isn't far.

To form a negative statement, add **no** before the verb: <u>no</u> está lejos.

✅ Numbers from 0 to 20

0	cero						
1	uno/una	6	seis	11	once	16	dieciséis
2	dos	7	siete	12	doce	17	diecisiete
3	tres	8	ocho	13	trece	18	dieciocho
4	cuatro	9	nueve	14	catorce	19	diecinueve
5	cinco	10	diez	15	quince	20	veinte

uno drops the **-o** when it occurs before a noun: **un kilómetro** ('one kilometer'); **una** doesn't change: **está a una hora** ('it's an hour away').

✅ The articles in the plural

	singular		plural	
	masculine	feminine	masculine	feminine
a/an some	un	una	unos	unas
the	el	la	los	las

✅ The plural of nouns

To make a noun ending in **-o** or **-a** plural, simply add **s**: **el kilo → los kilo<u>s</u>, la casa → las casa<u>s</u>**. Nouns ending in **-l**, **-n**, or **-s** add **-es** to form the plural. If the last syllable is accented in the singular, the accent is dropped in the plural: **el melón → los mel<u>ones</u>** ('melons'); **el ingl<u>és</u> → los ingl<u>eses</u>** ('Englishmen').

🎧 Now do activities 3 and 4 on the recording.

2.2 In the street

En la calle

ACTIVITY 5 is on the recording.

ACTIVITY 6

1 Calle Cinco de Mayo is a long walk.   T/F
2 Calle Estrella Errante is at the end of avenida
   Canal de Miramontes on the right.   T/F
3 The house is the third house on the right.   T/F
4 It's next to a bank.   T/F

DIALOGUE 2

○ ¿Dónde está la calle Cinco de Mayo, por favor?

■ La calle Cinco de Mayo … está lejos. La tercera calle a la izquierda, todo derecho hasta el final y la segunda a la derecha.

○ ¿Puede repetirlo, por favor?

■ La tercera a la izquierda, todo derecho hasta el final de la calle y la segunda calle a la derecha.

○ ¡Taxi! A la calle Estrella Errante, por favor. Está cerca de la avenida Canal de Miramontes.

■ Sí, señor. … ¿Está aquí?

○ No. Es todo derecho, al final de la avenida a la izquierda. El número diecinueve.

■ ¿Aquí?

○ Es la tercera puerta a la izquierda. Al lado del banco.

VOCABULARY	
la calle	street
a la izquierda	on the left
(todo) derecho	straight on
a la derecha	on the right
hasta	until
el final	end
¿puede repetirlo?	can you repeat that?
la avenida	avenue
el número	number
es	it is [from ser]
la puerta	door
al lado de	next to
el banco	bank

⊘ Directions

In directions, the words for 'left' and 'right' are always given in the feminine form: **la izquierda, la derecha**. To say something is on the left or on the right, you use the preposition **a** [*literally* 'at', 'to']:

a la izquierda   on the left   **a** la derecha   on the right

When **a** is followed by the masculine definite article **el**, the words combine to become **al**, but when **a** is followed by the feminine definite article **la**, the words do not change:

a + el → al   **al** final   to the end
a + la is unchanged   **a la** derecha   on the right

The preposition **de** ('of', 'from') also follows this pattern:

de + el → del   al lado **del** banco   next to the bank
de + la is unchanged   **de la** ciudad   from the city

⊘ Ordinal numbers

In directions involving streets, ordinal numbers ('first', 'second', 'third', etc.) are given in the feminine form because **la calle** is feminine.

la primera (calle) a la derecha   the first (street) on the right
la segunda (calle) a la izquierda   the second (street) on the left

The masculine form is **el primero, el segundo, el tercero**, etc. Note that the **-o** is dropped for **primero** and **tercero** when they are used in front of a noun.

el primero	the first	**el primer equipo**	the first team
el segundo	the second	**el segundo tren**	the second train
el tercero	the third	**el tercer edificio**	the third building

A full list of ordinal numbers is given in the Grammar Summary on page 230.

ACTIVITY 7

Match the Spanish with the correct English translation.

1 Todo derecho hasta el final, la segunda a la derecha.
2 Es la tercera calle a la izquierda.
3 Es la primera calle a la derecha.
4 Es la tercera puerta a la derecha.

a It's the first street on the right.
b It's the third house on the right.
c It's the third street on the left.
d Straight on to the end, the second on the right.

⊛ Now do activities 8 and 9 on the recording.

19

At the tourist information office
En la oficina de turismo

🎧 **ACTIVITY 10** is on the recording.

ACTIVITY 11

The hotel is E: what are the other buildings?

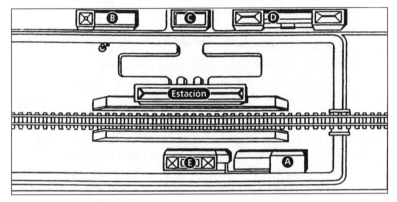

DIALOGUE 3

○ ¿Hay un hotel por aquí?

■ Sí, hay un hotel detrás de la estación, El Hotel Oriente.

○ Gracias. ¿Hay un supermercado por aquí?

■ Sí, hay un supermercado al lado del Hotel Oriente.

○ ¿Y, dónde está el restaurante El Virrey?

■ Está al lado del banco, enfrente de la estación, entre el banco y el hospital.

VOCABULARY	
la oficina de turismo	tourist information office
¿hay ... ?	is there ... ?
por aquí	around here
hay ...	there is ...
detrás de	behind
la estación	station
el supermercado	supermarket
el restaurante	restaurant
enfrente de	opposite
entre	between
el hospital	hospital

⊘ *hay* ('there is/there are')

hay is the impersonal form of the verb **haber** ('to have') and is used to mean 'there is/there are'. Its form does not change.

Hay un restaurante cerca de aquí. There is a restaurant near here.
¿**Hay** cafeterías en esta calle? Are there (any) bars in this street?
No **hay** un hospital por aquí. There isn't a hospital around here.

⊘ Prepositions and prepositional phrase of location

Prepositions are words which are used to indicate where something is in relation to something else. Remember that **de + el → del**.

Hay un hotel **al lado de** la estación. There is a hotel next to the station.
Hay un supermercado **enfrente del** hotel. There is a supermarket opposite the hotel.
Hay un hotel **detrás de** la estación. There is a hotel behind the station.
Hay una parada de autobús **delante del** museo. There is a bus stop in front of the museum.
Hay un estacionamiento **debajo del** hotel. There is a parking lot underneath the hotel.
Hay una oficina **encima del** banco. There is an office above the bank.

ACTIVITY 12

Match the Spanish with the English translation.

1	al lado de …	a	opposite
2	enfrente de …	b	the station
3	por aquí	c	between
4	delante de	d	around here
5	detrás de	e	next to
6	entre	f	behind
7	¿hay … ?	g	in front of
8	la estación	h	is there … ?

ACTIVITY 13

You're in the tourist information office and want to find out where things are.

1 How would you ask if the following facilities are nearby?
   a a bank   b a hotel   c a supermarket
2 You know there is a station and a restaurant.
   How do you ask where they are?

⊙ Now do activities 14 and 15 on the recording.

2.4 A stroll in Mexico City
Un paseo en la Ciudad de México

Mexico has a vibrant culture and many Mexican cities have a wealth of monuments (**monumentos**) and other important and interesting buildings (**edificios importantes e interesantes**) worth visiting. Read the following text about Mexico City and follow the guide on the map.

Un paseo para una mañana de domingo
La Ciudad de México es una ciudad histórica. Hay muchos monumentos y edificios importantes e interesantes en la ciudad. Mire el mapa y siga las direcciones.

1 El Museo Mural Diego Rivera es el museo del famoso pintor del siglo veinte.
2 Siga todo derecho por la avenida Juárez. A la derecha está el Museo Nacional de Arte Popular.
3 A la izquierda está el Monumento Juárez. Siga derecho al final de la calle. A la izquierda está el Palacio de Bellas Artes.
4 Enfrente está la Torre Latino Americana. Tome la calle de la izquierda y siga derecho. Tome la segunda calle a la izquierda. El Teatro Blanquita está a la derecha.
5 Siga derecho. A la izquierda está el Museo Nacional de la Estampa.

el paseo	stroll
la mañana	morning
el domingo	Sunday
una ciudad histórica	a historic city
muchos monumentos	many monuments
seguir (sigo)	to follow
¡siga!	follow/carry on [*formal imperative*]
el siglo	century
por	along
tomar	to take
¡tome!	take [*formal imperative*]
el palacio	palace
la torre	tower

ACTIVITY 16

Look at the map again. Can you find the monuments mentioned in the text?

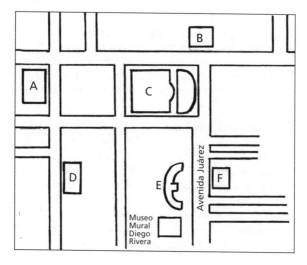

ACTIVITY 17

Using the map, give directions in Spanish.

1. You are at the Museo Nacional de Arte Popular.
   ¿Dónde está la Torre Latino Americana?
2. You are at the Teatro Blanquita.
   ¿Dónde está el Monumento Juárez?
3. You are at the Museo Nacional de la Estampa.
   ¿Dónde está el Palacio de Bellas Artes?

ACTIVITY 18

Now look at the instructions below. Which building are you being directed to?

1 You are at la Torre Latino Americana. It's on your right.
   Siga derecho, la segunda a la izquierda. Está a la derecha.
2 You are at the Museo Nacional de la Estampa. It's on your right.
   Tome la primera a la derecha. Siga derecho. Tome la segunda a la derecha. Siga derecho. Está a la izquierda, enfrente del Monumento Juárez.
3 You are at el Monumento Juárez. It's on your left.
   Siga derecho al final. Está enfrente.

2.5 Un extraño en la ciudad

 ### ¿HAY UN HOTEL POR AQUÍ?
IS THERE A HOTEL AROUND HERE?

María has left the Cafetería Coyoacán. The stranger is talking with Sr. Herrera, who gives him some directions. Where is he going?

la biblioteca municipal	local library
en camión	by bus
a ver	let's see
conozco a (María)	I know (María)
la sección de periódicos	newspaper section
¡silencio!	silence!
los documentos antiguos	old documents
de nada	not at all, it's a pleasure
la terminal de autobuses	bus station

ACTIVITY 19

Listen to the recording again and put the events in the correct order.

1 The stranger asks where there is a hotel.
2 The stranger asks where the newspaper section is.
3 Sr. Herrera tells the stranger his name.
4 Sr. Herrera tells the stranger where there is a hotel.
5 The librarian tells the stranger to keep quiet.
6 The stranger asks Sr. Herrera where the local library is.

ACTIVITY 20

Which of these statements is true (**verdadero**) and which is false (**falso**)?

1 El hotel está lejos.   V/F
2 El hotel está enfrente de la estación.   V/F
3 La biblioteca está lejos.   V/F
4 El hotel está cerca de la casa de María.   V/F
5 En la biblioteca hay periódicos antiguos.   V/F

ACTIVITY 21

Can you find the Spanish for these questions in the story transcript? Write the questions down and then give the answers in Spanish.

1 Are there any old newspapers?
2 What's it called?
3 Is there a newspaper section?
4 Is there a hotel round here?
5 Where's the public library?
6 You know María, don't you?
7 Where is it?
8 Here?

STORY TRANSCRIPT

Extraño	Disculpe, señor …
Sr. Herrera	Señor Herrera. Me llamo Juan Herrera.
Extraño	¿Hay un hotel por aquí?
Sr. Herrera	Sí, señor. Hay un hotel muy cerca, está enfrente de la terminal de autobuses.
Extraño	¿Cómo se llama?
Sr. Herrera	Se llama Hotel Oriente. Está a cinco minutos. Siga esta calle todo derecho y tome la segunda a la izquierda. El hotel está allí.
Extraño	Muchas gracias. Disculpe … señor … Herrera …
Sr. Herrera	Sí, señor.
Extraño	¿Dónde está la biblioteca municipal?
Sr. Herrera	Pues … a ver … ¡está lejos! A quince o veinte minutos en camión. Hay una parada al lado de la cafetería. Está cerca de la casa de María, la señorita de la foto. Usted conoce a María, ¿no?
Extraño	No, a María no, pero conozco a … Bueno, perdone, adiós.
	…
Extraño	Por favor, ¿hay una sección de periódicos?
Librarian	Sí.
Extraño	¿Dónde está?
Librarian	Está aquí, a la derecha … Silencio, por favor.
Extraño	Perdone. ¿Hay periódicos antiguos?
Librarian	Sí. Hay periódicos y documentos muy antiguos allí, a la izquierda.
Extraño	Gracias. ¿Aquí?
Librarian	Sí, aquí, enfrente de la oficina.
Extraño	Muchas gracias.
Librarian	De nada.

Test

Now it's time to test your progress in Unit 2.

1 Match these words and phrases to their Spanish translations.

1 Is there a bank round here? a Está muy cerca.
2 Is it far? b ¿Dónde está el banco?
3 It's next to the bank. c No hay bancos por aquí.
4 Where is the bank? d Está detrás del banco.
5 There aren't any banks around here. e Está al lado del banco.
6 It's opposite the bank. f Está enfrente del banco.
7 It's behind the bank. g ¿Hay un banco por aquí?
8 It's very near. h ¿Está lejos?

8

2 How would you give these directions in Spanish? (Score 2 points for each correct answer and 1 point if you make one error.)

1 Second on the right and all the way to the end of the street.
2 Third street on the left and it's on the right.
3 All the way to the end of the street, left, and it's on the left.
4 First on the right, second on the left, and it's on the right.

8

3 Raymond Castle is in Mexico on business. He needs to buy some things and to visit a bank, so he asks the hotel receptionist for information. Fill in the blanks in the conversation.

Raymond   1_____. ¿2_____ un supermercado por 3_____ ?
Recepcionista Sí, señor. Siga todo derecho, al 4_____ de la calle. La 5_____ a la izquierda.
Raymond   Gracias. Y ¿6_____ hay un banco?
Recepcionista Hay un banco al 7_____ del supermercado.
Raymond   ¿8_____ lejos?
Recepcionista No, no. Está 9_____ cinco minutos.

9

4 Write down the following numbers in Spanish.

1	16	3	7	5	13	7	11	9	5
2	17	4	20	6	3	8	12	10	8

10

5 Complete the following dialogue. Deduct 1 point for each error.

A: ¿Dónde está el museo?
B: Say it's in the Plaza del Virrey.

_____ (2 points)

A: ¿Está muy lejos?
B: Say it's five minutes away on the bus.

_____ (4 points)

A: ¿Qué número?
B: Say number fourteen.

_____ (1 point)

A: ¿Dónde está la parada?
B: Say it's the first street on the left.

_____ (3 points)

10

6 Write the plural forms of these words.

1 la casa
2 el melón
3 el pastel
4 el jitomate
5 la plaza

5

TOTAL SCORE **50**

If you scored less than 40, look at the Language Building sections again before completing the Summary on page 28.

Summary 2

 Now try this final test, summarizing the main points covered in this unit.

How would you:
1 ask if there is a museum in the area?
2 ask where the bank is?
3 ask where avenida Canal de Miramontes is?
4 say that the cathedral is ten minutes away?
5 say it's the second street on the left?
6 tell someone to go straight on to the end of the street?
7 say that the hotel is opposite the station?

REVIEW

Before moving on to Unit 3, play Unit 2 through again and listen out for the three main question forms introduced in this unit: **¿hay … ?** and **¿dónde hay … ?**/**¿dónde está … ?** Imagine you're on holiday and want to find out about various facilities: practice how you would ask what there is and where to find it, using these phrases and the vocabulary you have learned in the unit.

Shopping
De compras

OBJECTIVES

In this unit you'll learn how to:

✓ ask for items when shopping for food

✓ ask prices

✓ ask for items at the post office

And cover the following grammar and language:

✓ the formal imperative

✓ numbers up to 1,000

✓ more polite requests using **querer** ('to want')

✓ adjectives

✓ the direct object pronoun **lo/la/los/las** ('him', 'her', 'it', 'them')

LEARNING SPANISH 3

When you're attempting an activity, always try listening to the recordings several times before looking at the transcript in your book. When you first listen, it may feel as though you haven't understood very much, but try doing the activities anyway. The activities are structured to help you to understand the dialogues and to work out what's happening for yourself. Write down some kind of answer, and don't look at the answer key until you've had a go, even if you consider it only to be a guess. Guesswork is an important strategy in learning a new language and you'll probably be pleasantly surprised at how often you're right.

Now start the recording for Unit 3.

En la tienda

(🎧) **ACTIVITY 1** is on the recording.

ACTIVITY 2

Match the product with the correct quantity.

A potatoes / onions / tomatoes / milk / oil /
B a kilo / a bottle / two kilos / two liters / half a kilo

DIALOGUE 1

○ ¿Qué desea?
■ Quiero un kilo de papas.
○ Un kilo de papas. ¿Algo más?
■ Sí. Quiero dos kilos de cebollas y medio kilo de jitomates.
○ Muy bien. ¿Algo más?
■ Nada más, gracias.

○ ¿Qué desea?
■ ¿Podría darme una botella de aceite, por favor?
○ ¿Algo más?
■ Ummm, sí. Dos litros de leche.
○ Aquí tiene.
■ Muchas gracias.

VOCABULARY	

¿qué desea?	what would you like?
un kilo	a kilo
la papa	potato
la cebolla	onion
medio kilo	half a kilo
el jitomate	tomato
cien gramos	100 grams
¿podría darme...?	could I have ... ?
un litro	a liter
el aceite	oil
la botella	bottle
el vino	wine

✅ The formal imperative

The formal imperative is used in many everyday transactions, such as asking for things in stores and giving directions. Learn these useful phrases by heart. There will be more on the imperative in Units 13 and 14.

Deme un paquete de papas fritas. Could you give me a pack of potato chips? (from **dar**, 'to give')
Deme una lata de sardinas. Could you give me a can of sardines?
Siga … Follow …/Carry on … (from **seguir**, 'to follow')
Mire … Look … (from **mirar**, 'to look')
Tome … Take … (from **tomar**, 'to take')

✅ Weights and measures

Grams or kilos are used for weights and liter(s) for liquid.

Quiero **cien gramos de** queso. I'd like 100 grams of cheese.
Quiero **dos kilos de** zanahorias. Could you give me two kilos of carrots?
¿Podría darme **un litro de** leche? I'd like a liter of milk.

Note that the indefinite article is used for **un cuarto** ('a quarter'), but not with **medio** ('half'). The word **kilo** can be included or omitted.

Quiero **un cuarto de** jamón. I'd like a quarter of ham.
Deme **medio kilo de** queso. Could you give me half a kilo of cheese?

✅ Numbers: 20 to 1000

20	**veinte**	50	**cincuenta**	80	**ochenta**
30	**treinta**	60	**sesenta**	90	**noventa**
40	**cuarenta**	70	**setenta**		

100	**cien**	500	**quinientos/as**	900	**novecientos/as**
200	**doscientos/as**	600	**seiscientos/as**	1.000	**mil**
300	**trescientos/as**	700	**setecientos/as**		
400	**cuatrocientos/as**	800	**ochocientos/as**		

There is no word for 'and' in numbers over 100: **ciento noventa** – 190. Note how **cien** changes to **ciento** when followed by another number.

ACTIVITY 3

Match the item with the correct container/quantity.

A jitomates / cebollas / queso / jugo de naranja / aceite
B cien gramos / botella / kilo / lata / litro

🎧 Now do activities 4 and 5 on the recording.

3.2 At the post office
En la oficina de Correos

ACTIVITY 6 is on the recording.

ACTIVITY 7

1	A postcard costs five pesos.	T/F
2	The first customer buys five postcards.	T/F
3	He buys a small envelope.	T/F
4	It costs eighty pesos to send the package.	T/F
5	The second customer buys stamps for a package.	T/F

DIALOGUE 2

○ ¿Cuánto cuesta una tarjeta, por favor?

■ Cinco pesos.

○ Quiero cinco tarjetas, por favor.

■ Son veinticinco pesos. ¿Algo más?

○ Sí. Un sobre grande, por favor. ¿Cuánto es?

■ Tres pesos.

○ Disculpe, quiero mandar este paquete a Estados Unidos.

■ Un momento … a ver … treinta pesos.

○ ¿Y una carta para Inglaterra?

■ Diez pesos.

○ ¿Y una tarjeta?

■ Ocho pesos.

○ Gracias. ¿Podría darme timbres para el paquete, cinco tarjetas y una carta?

VOCABULARY

la oficina de Correos	post office
¿cuánto cuesta?	how much is it?
la tarjeta	postcard
el sobre	envelope
grande	large
¿cuánto es?	how much is it?
mandar	to send
el paquete	package
Estados Unidos	US
Inglaterra	England
un momento	one moment
la carta	letter
el timbre	(postage) stamp

✅ More on numbers

The word **y** ('and') is used to link numbers above 30. In the numbers 16–19 and 21–29, **y** changes to **i** and the two numbers form one word:

16 **dieciséis**	37 **treinta y siete**	73 **setenta y tres**
24 **veinticuatro**	44 **cuarenta y cuatro**	86 **ochenta y seis**
25 **veinticinco**	55 **cincuenta y cinco**	99 **noventa y nueve**
31 **treinta y uno**	62 **sesenta y dos**	

The words for the hundreds actually change ending depending on the gender of what they refer to.

    quinientas personas 500 people

This is because the hundreds function like adjectives (see section 3.3).

✅ Asking how much something costs

These are two different ways of asking how much something costs:

    ¿Cuánto es? How much is it (altogether)?
    ¿Cuánto cuesta? How much does it cost (altogether)?

Note that **¿cuánto cuesta?** takes a verb in the plural when it is used for more than one thing:

    ¿Cuánto cuestan los timbres? How much are the stamps?

The verb **ser** is used in response to the question **¿cuánto es?**

    ¿Cuánto es? **Son** ochenta y cinco pesos.
    How much is it? It is [*literally* they are] 85 pesos.

The plural form (**son**) is used because it refers to the number of pesos.

ACTIVITY 8

Without looking at Dialogue 2, fill in the blanks, using words from the list below.

para/son/grande/más/cuánto/cuesta/quiero/mandar

- ■ Un sobre 1_____, por favor.
- ○ ¿Algo 2_____?
- ■ Sí. ¿Cuánto 3_____ un timbre 4_____ los Estados Unidos?
- ○ Ochenta pesos.
- ■ 5_____ cinco timbres, por favor. ¿6_____ es?
- ○ 7_____ cuatrocientos pesos.
- ■ Quiero 8_____ este paquete a Inglaterra.

 Now do activities 9 and 10 on the recording.

3.3 At the grocery
En la frutería

🔊 **ACTIVITY 11** is on the recording.

ACTIVITY 12

1　What costs 15 pesos?
2　What costs 25 pesos?
3　What costs 40 pesos?
4　What weighs 3 kilos?

DIALOGUE 3

○　¿Qué desea?
■　Un melón.
○　¿Lo quiere grande o pequeño?
■　Lo quiero grande, por favor. ¿Cuánto es?
○　Quince pesos. ¿Algo más?
■　Sí. ¿Tiene piñas?
○　Sí, las tengo muy baratas, a veinticinco pesos. Dos por cuarenta pesos. Mire, estas dos están muy buenas. ¿Las quiere?
■　Sí, sí, las quiero. Ummm … ¿Cuánto cuesta la sandía?
○　A doce el kilo. Ésta pesa tres kilos. ¿La quiere?
■　No, no, la quiero pequeña. Ésta.
○　Tenga. ¿Algo más?
■　Nada más, gracias.

VOCABULARY	
el melón	melon
lo/la	it
pequeño	small
¿tiene … ?	do you have … ?
la piña	pineapple
los/las	them
tengo …	I have …
barato	cheap
bueno	good
la sandía	watermelon
pesar	to weigh
tenga	here you are [*literally* have; *formal imperative*]

✓ Adjectives

Adjectives agree in number (singular or plural) and gender (masculine or feminine) with the noun they describe. They usually come after the noun:

	masculine	*feminine*
singular	un melón **pequeño**	una manzana **pequeña**
plural	dos melones **pequeños**	cuatro manzanas **pequeñas**

There is more on adjectives in Units 4, 5, and 9.

✓ More on introductions

To introduce a group of people, you use **éstos** for men and **éstas** for women. For a mixed group you use **éstos**:

> **Éstos** son mis hermanos. These are my brothers.
> **Éstas** son mis hermanas. These are my sisters.

✓ Direct object pronouns *lo/la* ('him', 'her', 'it'), *los/las* ('them')

The direct object of a verb is the noun, pronoun, or phrase which is directly affected by the action of the verb. In Spanish, the form of the direct object pronouns for 'it' and 'them' is affected by gender as well as number:

	sing.	*pl.*
masc.	**lo**	**los**
fem.	**la**	**las**

Do you want …	¿Quiere …	
the melon?	**el melón**?	sí, **lo** quiero
the meat?	**la carne**?	sí, **la** quiero
the peaches?	**los duraznos**?	no, no **los** quiero
the strawberries?	**las fresas**?	sí, **las** quiero

Note that they come before the verb. There is more on direct object pronouns in 4.2

ACTIVITY 13

Ask for the following items using **quiero** and the correct form of the direct object pronoun **lo, la, los,** or **las**.

Example: Cheese. **El queso. Lo quiero**.

1 A pack of potato chips. 4 Two bottles of beer.
2 A can of sardines. 5 Ham.
3 A liter of oil. 6 Stamps.

(⌓ฦ) Now do activities 14 and 15 on the recording.

3.4 Mexican markets
Los mercados mexicanos

ACTIVITY 16

Match these two lists. List A is the name of the shop and list B, in English, is the name of the produce they sell. Can you work out what the products are in Spanish?

A	B
la tortillería	fruit
la carnicería	cakes
la frutería	fish
la verdulería	bread
la pastelería	ham
la panadería	flowers
la pescadería	tortilla
la florería	vegetables
la salchichonería	meat

ACTIVITY 17

Read the text, study the vocabulary, and then do the cross-word without referring to the vocabulary list.

En México, como en muchos países, hay muchos supermercados muy grandes e hipermercados. Pero los mercados también son muy importantes. El mercado es una tradición mexicana muy antigua. En los mercados mexicanos hay tiendas pequeñas que se llaman puestos. Hay muchas clases de puestos. En la carnicería hay carne como por ejemplo, salchichas, res, y cerdo. En la frutería hay fruta: naranjas, guayabas, mangos, zapotes, duraznos, etc. En la verdulería hay verduras, como papas , cebollas o zanahorias. En las pastelerías y panaderías hay pasteles, galletas y pan. En la pescadería hay muchas clases de pescado como huachinango y mojarra. Y en los puestos de abarrotes hay sal, azúcar, o aceite. También hay tortillerías que venden las típicas tortillas de maíz, y neverías que venden helados y nieves. Los helados son de leche y las nieves son de agua. A veces venden aguas frescas hechas de frutas, por ejemplo de sandía.

el mercado	the market
un puesto	a market stand
la salchichonería	delicatessen
la carnicería	butcher's store
las salchichas	sausages
la res	beef

el cerdo	pork
la frutería	grocery
la guayaba	guava fruit
el mango	mango
el zapote	sapote [*type of fruit*]
el durazno	peach
la papa	potato
la verdura	vegetables
la pastelería	cake store
la panadería	baker's
el pastel	cake
el pan	bread
la pescadería	fish store
el pescado	fish
el huachinango	red snapper
la mojarra	*Mexican fish*
la sal	salt
el azúcar	sugar
el puesto de abarrotes	grocery stand
la tortillería	*store selling Mexican tortillas*
la tortilla	Mexican corn tortilla
la nevería	ice cream store
la nieve	sherbet

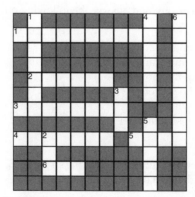

Across
1 Where you buy fish.
2 This is sweet and can be bought in the same stand as 6 Across.
3 This is made of corn.
4 The Spanish for peach.
5 The Spanish for potato.
6 Put this on food to season it.

Down
1 The Spanish for market.
2 Buy this in the butcher's.
3 Buy this in 6 Down.
4 Buy this in 6 Down or a cake store.
5 Tropical fruit.
6 A store for bread and cakes.

3.5 Un extraño en la ciudad

 ## MARÍA EN EL MERCADO
MARÍA AT THE MARKET

María leaves home to go to the market. Although she doesn't see him, the stranger from the cafeteria is waiting outside her house. He follows her as she goes into the butcher's.

el filete	a fillet of beef
la chuleta de cerdo	a chop (pork)
el dinero	money
¿Me conoce?	Do you know me?
creo que sí	I think so
la cartera	wallet
¡qué hombre tan raro!	what a strange man!
el empleado/la empleada	employee
quiero mandar esta carta certificada	I'd like to send this as a registered letter

ACTIVITY 18

Listen to the recording and answer the following questions in English.

1 Who buys some meat?
2 Who drops some money?
3 Who picks up the money?
4 Who drops the wallet?
5 Who knows who?
6 Who wants to send a letter?

ACTIVITY 19

Who says the following: María (M), the stranger (S), the butcher (B), or the post office employee (P)?

1 Quiero un kilo de filetes.   M/S/B/P
2 ¿Quiere algo más?   M/S/B/P
3 ¿Me conoce?   M/S/B/P
4 ¡Qué hombre tan raro!   M/S/B/P
5 Quiero mandar esta carta certificada. M/S/B/P
6 Son dieciocho pesos.   M/S/B/P

ACTIVITY 20

Here are the answers to some of the questions in the dialogue.
What are the questions?

1 Quiero un kilo de filetes y medio kilo de chuletas de cerdo.
2 No gracias.
3 Creo que sí.
4 Son dieciocho pesos.

STORY TRANSCRIPT

María	Buenos días, don José.
Butcher	Buenos días, señorita María. ¿Qué desea?
María	Quisiera un kilo de filetes y medio kilo de chuletas de cerdo.
Butcher	Aquí tiene. ¿Desea algo más?
María	No gracias. Oh, el dinero …
Extraño	Aquí tiene, señorita …
María	Oh, muchas gracias …
Extraño	De nada, señorita … María.
María	Oh … ¿Me conoce? Señor …
Extraño	Creo que sí … sí … Adiós, señorita María …
María	¡Disculpe, señor! ¡Disculpe! … un momentito … ¿Su cartera?
Butcher	¡Qué hombre tan raro!
María	Adiós, don José.
Butcher	¡Señorita, señorita … su carne!
María	¡Ah! Sí. Perdone. Gracias.
Extraño	Por favor … quiero mandar esta carta certificada. ¿Cuánto cuesta?
PO clerk	A ver … Son dieciocho pesos.
Extraño	Muy bien, … un momento … ¡La cartera! ¿Dónde está la cartera? Un momento … un momento, por favor.

Test

Now it's time to test your progress in Unit 3.

1 Match the words and phrases to their Spanish translations.

1	¿Qué desea?	a	Here you are. (2 answers)
2	¿Los quiere?	b	How much is a postcard?
3	¿Quiere algo más?	c	Do you want them?
4	Aquí tiene.	d	I want them.
5	¿Cuánto cuesta una tarjeta?	e	Do you have any pineapples?
6	Nada más.	f	Do you want anything else? (2 answers)
7	¿Tiene piñas?		
8	Las quiero.	g	What would you like?
9	¿Algo más?	h	That's all.
10	Tenga.		

10

2 How would you ask for these things in Spanish? (Score 2 points for every correct answer and 1 point if you make a mistake.) Start your request with **Quiero ...**

1 Two kilos of potatoes and half a kilo of onions.
2 A liter of wine and a can of oil.
3 100 grams of ham and 200 grams of cheese.
4 Two packs of potato chips and two bottles of beer.
5 Four postcards and five stamps for the US.

10

3 Give the Spanish for these numbers.

1	18	3	35	5	100	7	500	9	440
2	27	4	59	6	250	8	370	10	99

10

4 In which stores would you buy the following food items? Give your answers in English and Spanish.

1 jamón 6 huachinango
2 queso 7 sal
3 carne 8 sandías
4 mangos 9 pasteles
5 zanahorias 10 pan

`10`

5 Take the part of the customer in the following dialogue with a salesperson (**dependienta**).

Cliente: (Ask how much the watermelons are.)
_____

Dependienta: Cuestan cincuenta pesos. ¿Cuántas quiere?
Cliente: (Ask for two.)
_____

Dependienta: ¿Las quiere grandes?
Cliente: (Say no, you want small ones.)
_____

Dependienta: ¿Algo más?
Cliente: (Say you don't want anything else.)
_____

(Ask for the price.)
_____

`10`

TOTAL SCORE `50`

If you scored less than 40, look at the Language Building sections again before completing the Summary on page 42.

Summary 3

 Now try this final test, summarizing the main points covered in this unit.

How would you:
1 say you want half a kilo of tomatoes?
2 say you want a bottle of oil?
3 say you want a litre of milk?
4 say you don't want anything else?
5 say you want 100g of cheese?
6 ask how much a stamp for the US costs?
7 say that something costs 45 pesos?
8 say 'here you are' as you hand your money over to the assistant?

REVIEW

Before moving on to the first Review, play this unit through again and check that you know the food vocabulary. A good way of remembering the items is to make a shopping list in Spanish. Classify each food item into categories such as vegetables, fish, meat, and so on. Then practice writing down in Spanish which stores you'd go to in order to buy each item. If you don't know the word for what you need, look it up in your dictionary.

Review 1

VOCABULARY

1 Look at the Spanish expressions below and group them according to what they mean. Which ones are for:

   a greeting people?   c asking how someone is?
   b saying goodbye?   d saying how you are?

   1 ¿Cómo estás?   5 Adiós.
   2 Buenos días.   6 Buenas tardes.
   3 ¿Cómo está usted?   7 Muy bien.
   4 Bien, gracias.   8 Buenas noches.

2 Match the phrases on the left with those on the right to complete the food and drink items.

   un café   de queso
   un té   de naranja
   un jugo   limón
   una torta   de chocolate
   un pastel   con leche

3 Follow each plan and choose the right directions from a–e.

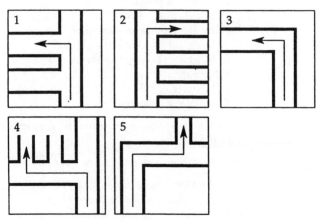

Answers to the activities can be found in the Answer section on page 213.

a Todo derecho hasta el final y la primera a la izquierda.
b La primera a la izquierda y la segunda a la derecha.
c La segunda a la izquierda.
d Todo derecho hasta el final, la primera a la derecha y la primera a la izquierda.
e La tercera a la derecha.

4 Possible or impossible? Put a check or a cross next to each phrase.

1 Una lata de jitomates.   4 Un paquete de papas fritas.
2 Un litro de zanahorias.   5 Cien gramos de leche.
3 Un kilo de queso.

GRAMMAR AND USAGE

5 Choose the best response to each of the following questions.

1 ¿Cómo está usted?
   A Muy bien, gracias.
   B Mucho gusto.
2 ¿Es usted la señora Martínez?
   A Sí, es la señora Martínez.
   B Sí, soy la señora Martínez.
3 ¿Dónde está el museo?
   A Está en la plaza.
   B Sí, está muy cerca.
4 ¿Hay una parada en esta calle?
   A Sí, delante del supermercado.
   B Sí, está en la calle Domínguez.
5 ¿Qué quería?
   A La quiero grande.
   B Quiero una sandía.

6 Complete these sentences, using the appropriate words from the list.

está / las / deme / cuesta / a / de / al / hay

1 ¡Señor González! Buenos días. ¿Cómo _____ usted?
2 _____ un café con leche, por favor.
3 La casa está _____ diez kilómetros _____ la ciudad, _____ norte.
4 _____ un hotel detrás de la estación.
5 ¿Cuánto _____ un timbre para los Estados Unidos?
6 Tengo dos naranjas. ¿_____ quiere?

7 Choose the most appropriate word to complete the sentences.

1 Quiero un timbre (**para/de**) los Estados Unidos.
2 El hospital está detrás (**del/de la**) banco.
3 (**Es/Está**) la tercera casa a la izquierda.
4 Yo (**soy/es**) el señor González.
5 La torta (**es/está**) para usted.

🎧 LISTENING

8 Your Mexican business colleague has left a message on your answering machine giving you instructions about how to get to his house this evening. Listen to the message and answer the questions in English.

1 How long does it take to get to your friend's house from the Plaza de las Flores?
2 Which direction do you turn at the end of the Avenida de la Independencia?
3 What number is the house?
4 What is next to the house?
5 What is in front of the house?

9 Listen to this conversation in a store. There are five differences between what you hear and the transcript here. Underline the differences.

A: ¿Qué desea?
B: ¿Tiene latas de sardinas?
A: Sí. ¿Cuántas quiere?
B: ¿Las tiene grandes?
A: No. Las tengo pequeñas. ¿Las quiere pequeñas?
B: Sí. Quiero cinco.
A: Aquí tiene. ¿Algo más?
B: Sí. Deme dos kilos de naranjas.
A: ¿Algo más?
B: Sí. ¿Cuánto cuestan las sandías?
A: Veinte pesos. ¿Quiere una?
B: Deme dos.
A: ¿Algo más?
B: Nada más. ¿Cuánto es?
A: Son ochenta y cinco pesos.

10 Practice saying each of these names, and then listen to the recording to check your pronunciation.

1 Señor Pérez   3 Señorita María García
2 Señora Martín   4 Señor Juan Gómez

11 You're in Mexico on business. Complete the conversation you have with a Mexican colleague.

Juan Gómez: Buenas tardes. Me llamo Juan Gómez.
You: (Say you're pleased to meet him and tell him your name.)
             _____.

Juan Gómez: ¿Cómo está usted?
You: (Tell him you're well and ask how he is.)
             _____.

Juan Gómez: Bien. ¿Quiere un café?
You: (Say yes. Ask if there's a bar in the area.)
             _____.

Juan Gómez: Sí, hay uno al final de la calle.

12 You're going to hear some questions on the recording. The questions will be about the following topics, but in a different order. You'll be asked about:

- your name
- how you are feeling
- if you'd like tea or coffee
- if your house is in a city
- where your home town is
- if there is a museum in your city

Use this list to prepare what you're going to say, then test yourself using the recording.

4

Personal information
Información personal

OBJECTIVES

In this unit you'll learn how to:

- ✓ say where you live and where you're from
- ✓ say what job you do
- ✓ give your address and telephone number
- ✓ spell your name and address

And cover the following grammar and language:

- ✓ the present tense of regular verbs ending in -ar, -er, and -ir
- ✓ the verb ser ('to be') for nationalities and professions
- ✓ nouns and adjectives of nationality
- ✓ nouns of profession
- ✓ review of numbers

LEARNING SPANISH 4

A wide vocabulary is the key to successful language learning, but don't try to learn too much at once. It's best to study frequently, for short periods of time. Take six or seven items of vocabulary as a maximum and learn them. Put them into sentences to fix them in your mind, then come back to them later. Much of the vocabulary in this book is presented by topic – for example, buildings in a town, methods of transport. Learning vocabulary in this way is usually very effective.

It is important to get a good Spanish–English dictionary to support your learning. While you may feel you don't need a large dictionary at this stage, make sure it is comprehensive enough to illustrate the word in use in sample phrases.

Now start the recording for Unit 4.

47

4.1 Where are you from?

¿De dónde es usted?

ACTIVITY 1 is on the recording.

ACTIVITY 2

	¿De dónde es?	¿Dónde vive?
Paco García Margarita Herrero Jorge Martínez El hermano de Paco García		

DIALOGUE 1

- Buenas tardes. Soy Paco García.
- ○ Encantada. Margarita Herrero. Y él es el señor Jorge Martínez.
- Mucho gusto.
- ▼ Encantado.
- ¿Ustedes no son mexicanos?
- ▼ No, yo soy argentino y Margarita es de España.
- ¡Ah! Hay muchos españoles en mi trabajo. Y mi hermano trabaja en España. ¿Ustedes viven en México?
- ▼ Yo vivo en México. Margarita vive en España.
- ¿Dónde vive usted?
- ▼ Yo vivo en Guadalajara.
- ¡Yo también! ¡Qué casualidad! ¿Cenamos juntos y platicamos?

VOCABULARY

¿de dónde es?	where are you from?
vivir	to live
argentino	Argentinian
México	Mexico
España	Spain
mexicano	Mexican
el trabajo	job
el hermano	brother
trabajar	to work
¡qué casualidad!	what a coincidence!
cenar	to have dinner
juntos/as	together
platicar	to talk, speak

✓ The present tense of regular verbs: -ar verbs

There are three different types of regular Spanish verbs. Their infinitives end in **-ar** (e.g. **trabajar**, 'to work'), **-er** (e.g. **comer**, 'to eat, to have lunch'), or **-ir** (e.g. **vivir**, 'to live').

All the verbs in each regular group have the same endings in the present tense, which are added to the stem of the verb (**trabaj-**, **viv-**, **com-**). The endings for regular **-ar** verbs are as follows:

trabaj**o**   trabaj**amos**
trabaj**as**   trabaj**an**
trabaj**a**

Other **-ar** verbs: **llamar** ('to call'), **viajar** ('to travel'), **cenar** ('to have dinner'), **estudiar** ('to study'), **manejar** ('to drive'). For **-ir** and **-er** verbs see pages 51 and 53.

✓ Nationalities

Words describing nationality usually change ending according to whether a man or woman is being described, although there are a few exceptions: **estadounidense** ('American'), **canadiense** ('Canadian'). Nationalities do not begin with a capital letter and can be used either as an adjective or noun: **un irlandés** ('an Irishman'), **es irlandés** ('he's Irish').

Country	El país	[masc. sing.]	[fem. sing.]
Colombia	Colombia	colombiano	colombiana
England	Inglaterra	inglés	inglesa
Spain	España	español	española

In the plural, **-s** is added to all feminine forms and to masculine forms ending in **-o** in the singular. Other masculine forms take the ending **-es**.

Mis padres son **españoles**. My parents are Spanish.
Las mujeres son **inglesas**. The women are English.

ACTIVITY 3

Complete the story with the correct form of the verbs in brackets. New vocabulary: **a veces** ('sometimes').

Mi hermano y yo (1 **estar**) en Guadalajara. La casa (2 **estar**) en el centro de la ciudad. Yo (3 **trabajar**) y mi hermano (4 **estudiar**) en la universidad. A veces nosotros (5 **viajar**) a la Ciudad de México. Mis padres (6 **estar**) allí. A veces nosotros (7 **cenar**) en un restaurante cerca de mi trabajo. (8 **Hablar**) de la universidad y del trabajo.

🎧 Now do activities 4 and 5 on the recording.

¿Quién es quién?

(🎧) **ACTIVITY 6** is on the recording.

ACTIVITY 7

1 What is Rosita Blasco's profession?
2 What is the name of the accountant?
3 Who is the head of personnel?
4 Where is Señorita Vázquez?
5 Who is a neighbor of Rosita?
6 How many drivers are there?

DIALOGUE 2

■ Buenos días a todos. Les presento a la señorita Rosita Blasco, la nueva secretaria bilingüe de la empresa.
○ Buenos días.
■ Y ella es Carmen Soto. Carmen es contadora en la empresa. Y él es Javier Montero, jefe de personal, y a su lado está Ana Vázquez, gerente de ventas.
○ Ana me conoce. Vivimos en la misma calle.
■ ¡Qué casualidad! Bueno … Toño Espinosa es diseñador y a su lado está Sara Gil, ingeniera. Paco Salas y Jaime Vargas son los choferes.
○ Encantada de conocerlos.

VOCABULARY

todos	everyone
les presento	I'd like to introduce you to
la empresa	company, firm
nuevo	new
el secretario/la secretaria	secretary
bilingüe	bilingual
el contador/la contadora	accountant
el jefe/la jefa (de personal)	head (of personnel)
el/la gerente de ventas	sales manager
mismo	same
el diseñador/la diseñadora	designer
el ingeniero/la ingeniera	engineer
el/la chofer	driver
encantada de conocerlos	I'm very pleased to meet you

✅ The present tense of regular verbs: -ir verbs

Endings for regular **-ir** verbs in the present tense are as follows:

vivir ('to live')

viv**o**	viv**imos**
viv**es**	viv**en**
viv**e**	

Other regular **-ir** verbs: **escribir** ('to write'), **permitir** ('to permit'), **dirigir** ('to manage'). Note that **dirigir** has a **j** in the first person singular (**dirijo**), but is otherwise regular.

✅ Preposition *a* with people

In Spanish, when the object of the verb is a person, the preposition **a** must be used.

> Le presento **a los empleados**. I'd like to introduce you to the staff.
> Conozco **al empresario**. I know the company director.

✅ Direct object pronouns 2

The direct object pronouns **me** ('me'), **te** ('you'), and **nos** ('us') are used in the same way as **lo/la/los/las** (see 3.3).

> Ana **me** conoce. Ana knows me.
> **Los** llamamos todos los domingos. We call them every Sunday.

✅ Describing professions

Note that the article is not used when you say what someone's job is:
Miguel es profesor ('Miguel is a teacher').

ACTIVITY 8

Complete the story by supplying the correct form of the verbs.

A veces mi hermano y yo (1 **escribir**) a mis padres en la Ciudad de México. A veces, ellos (2 **llamar**) por teléfono. (3 **Hablar**) de la familia, de mi trabajo y de los estudios de mi hermano. Tengo un carro pero no (4 **manejar**) a mi trabajo. Yo (5 **salir**) de casa a las ocho y mi hermano (6 **salir**) a las nueve. Los amigos (7 **vivir**) cerca de nuestra casa y (8 **salir**) juntos.

🔊 Now do activities 9 and 10 on the recording.

How do you spell it?

¿Cómo se escribe?

🎧 **ACTIVITY 11** is on the recording.

ACTIVITY 12

1	Which building does María live in?	A/E/I
2	In which year was she born?	1955/1965/1975
3	What is her phone number?	329 5568/ 329 5678/ 329 5579
4	On which day in February was she born?	11/12/13
5	What is the number of her home?	16/17/18

DIALOGUE 3

○ ¿Cuál es su apellido, por favor?

■ Cauich.

○ ¿Cómo se escribe?

■ C-A-U-I-C-H.

○ ¿Su nombre?

■ María.

○ Su dirección, por favor.

■ Calle Central, número diecisiete, edificio A, departamento 101; Mérida.

○ ¿Fecha de nacimiento?

■ El doce de febrero, de mil novecientos setenta y cinco.

○ ¿Podría darme su número de teléfono también?

■ Tres, veintinueve, cincuenta y cinco, sesenta y ocho.

VOCABULARY	

el apellido	surname
¿cómo se escribe?	how do you spell it?
el nombre	(first) name
la dirección	address
la fecha de nacimiento	date of birth
febrero	February
necesitar	to need
el número de teléfono	telephone number

⊘ The present tense of regular verbs: -er verbs

comer ('to eat')   como   comemos

                        comes   comen

                        come

Other examples of regular -**er** verbs are: **responder** ('to respond'), **leer** ('to read'), **correr** ('to run'), **ver** ('to see, to watch'), **creer** ('to believe'), **prometer** ('to promise').

⊘ The alphabet

Note that there is one letter which does not appear in the English alphabet: **ñ** (**eñe** – pronounced 'enyeh'). Until the early 1990s, **ch** and **ll** were also considered separate letters in Spanish, appearing in dictionaries after **C** and **L** respectively. They now appear as part of the **C** and **L** entries. Check your dictionary to see if you have an old or a new version.

⊘ Addresses and telephone numbers

Mexican addresses start with the street name, followed by the number:

    Calle Central, diecisiete 17 Main Street

Mexicans live in apartments or houses often grouped together in **colonias** or **urbanizaciones**. So a typical address gives the street and number followed by the name of the **colonia**. If they live in an apartment (**departamento**), the number is also included: Depto. $1°2$ – first floor, second door. e.g.

Calle Barlovento, 410
Edificio 22, Depto. $2°3$
Col. Bosque Residencial
México D. F. C. P 03900

Telephone numbers are given in pairs where possible:

    12 34 56   doce, treinta y cuatro, cincuenta y seis

    623 4567   seis, dos, tres ... cuarenta y cinco, sesenta y siete

---

ACTIVITY 13

Write down the numbers in words.

1 2468583
2 Calle Central, 26
3 238 9963
4 Avenida de la Independencia, 35
5 245 5428
6 Paseo de La Reforma, 153

🎧 Now do activities 14 and 15 on the recording.

4.4 Mexico's popular culture
La cultura popular de México

ACTIVITY 16

Read the questions about music and television in Mexico. From the information given in the text, find the answers and write them in Spanish if you can. Use the vocabulary list to help you.

1 What is the name of the traditional music popular in the north of Mexico?
2 What is the name of the traditional music popular in Mexico City?
3 Where is the **mariachi** popular?
4 Which country influences Mexican pop music?
5 How do some Mexican artists change American pop songs?
6 What is the most popular form of television program?
7 Where do most of the other programs come from?

La música es muy popular en México. La música tradicional es diferente en las distintas regiones. En el norte se llama norteña. En la ciudad de México el estilo se llama música ranchera. Otro estilo popular por todo el país es el mariachi. La música pop de los Estados Unidos es muy popular en el radio. Muchos artistas mexicanos cantan canciones de los Estados Unidos y cambian la letra y el ritmo. También hay grupos de pop de México que son muy populares y venden muchos discos.

Las telenovelas de México son muy famosas en la televisión de muchos países hispano-hablantes. Se emiten cada día y duran mucho tiempo. También hay muchos programas de los Estados Unidos que son muy populares. Muchos de estos programas están doblados al español.

distinto	different
el estilo	style
cantar	to sing
le canción	song
la letra	lyrics
el ritmo	rhythm
el grupo	music group
vender	to sell
el disco	record
la telenovela	television soap
hispano-hablante	Spanish-speaking
emitir	to broadcast
durar	to last
doblado	dubbed

ACTIVITY 17

Complete these sentences without looking at the text, if you can. Then read through the text to check your answers.

1 La música es muy _____ en México.
2 El mariachi es una música tradicional que es popular por todo el _____.
3 La música pop de los Estados Unidos es muy popular en el _____.
4 Los grupos de pop de México venden muchos _____.
5 Las telenovelas de México son muy _____ en la televisión de muchos países hispano-hablantes.

ACTIVITY 18

Look at these two lists of words and match the words from each list.

1 una telenovela   a a collection of people who play music
2 doblado   b used to describe a country where Spanish is spoken
3 grupo   c to broadcast through radio or television
4 hispano-hablante   d a television story in many parts
5 emitir   e a foreign film translated into your own language

4.5 Un extraño en la ciudad

UN VIEJO AMIGO
AN OLD FRIEND

Después de la escena en el mercado, el extraño regresa a la cafetería Coyoacán y empieza a hablar con el señor Herrera.

After the scene in the market, the stranger returns to the Cafetería Coyoacán and strikes up a conversation with Sr. Herrera.

viejo	old
la compañía	company, firm
la tarjeta	(business) card
bonito	nice, pretty
mucho	much, a great deal
la oficina de seguros	insurance firm
creer	to believe
la esquina	the corner
hablar (por teléfono)	to call [*on the telephone*]
cuando	when
hábleme cuando venga María	call me when María comes

ACTIVITY 19

¿Verdadero o falso?

1 Jorge habla mucho con el señor Herrera.   V/F
2 El señor Herrera conoce a María muy bien. V/F
3 Jorge no conoce a María.   V/F
4 Jorge no es de la Ciudad de México.   V/F
5 No tiene tarjeta.   V/F
6 María trabaja en una tienda.   V/F
7 Trabaja en el centro de la ciudad.   V/F
8 Vive cerca de la cafetería Coyoacán.   V/F

ACTIVITY 20

Complete these questions taken from the dialogue and then match them with the answers.

1 ¿Cómo _____?
2 Usted conoce a María, ¿_____?
3 ¿De _____ es usted?
4 ¿____ ____ trabaja?
5 ¿Vive _____?

a Bueno, vive cerca de aquí.
b Soy de Chihuahua.
c Trabaja en una oficina de seguros en el centro.
d Muy bien, gracias.
e Sí, la conozco muy bien.

ACTIVITY 21

Who ...

1 ... works in a bar?
2 ... works as a salesperson?
3 ... works in an office?
4 ... works in the center of town?
5 ... lives in Chihuahua?
6 ... is staying in a hotel?
7 ... visits the cafeteria regularly for coffee?
8 ... lives near the cafeteria?

STORY TRANSCRIPT

Jorge	¡Buenas tardes!
Sr. Herrera	Buenas tardes, señor. ¿Cómo está?
Jorge	Muy bien gracias, ¿y usted?
Sr. Herrera	Muy bien.
Jorge	Usted conoce a María, ¿verdad?
Sr. Herrera	Sí, la conozco muy bien.
Jorge	Yo soy un viejo amigo de la familia. Me llamo Jorge Jimeno.
Sr. Herrera	Pero ella no lo conoce a usted.
Jorge	Sí, sí, me conoce. Soy amigo de la familia.
Sr. Herrera	¿De dónde es usted?
Jorge	Soy de Chihuahua. Soy gerente de ventas de una compañía. Mire usted ... aquí tiene mi tarjeta.
Sr. Herrera	Gracias. Chihuahua es una ciudad muy bonita, ¿verdad?
Jorge	Sí, muy bonita.
Sr. Herrera	¿Usted viaja mucho en su trabajo?
Jorge	Sí, mucho. Sr. Herrera, ... ¿María trabaja?
Sr. Herrera	Sí, trabaja.
Jorge	¿En qué trabaja?
Sr. Herrera	Creo que trabaja en una oficina de seguros en el centro ... en la plaza de Santo Domingo.
Jorge	¿Y vive cerca?
Sr. Herrera	Pues ...
Jorge	Sr. Herrera, soy amigo de la familia.
Sr. Herrera	Bueno, vive cerca de aquí ... en la calle Rincón del Sur ... en la esquina.
Jorge	Mire, señor, estoy en este hotel. Aquí está el número de teléfono. Hábleme cuando venga María.
Sr. Herrera	Sí, señor. Ella toma café aquí.

Test

Now it's time to test your progress in Unit 4.

1 Introduce these people to a friend, giving their nationality.
(Score 2 points for each question, 1 point if you make one
mistake.)

Example: Señor Giménez/Argentina. **Le presento al** señor
Giménez. Es **argentino**.

1 Señora Campos/España.
2 Jorge Ballesteros/México.
3 Señorita Tomás/Argentina.
4 Madame Deschamps/Francia.
5 Dieter Müller/Alemania.
6 Peter Jones and Barry Wright/Estados Unidos.

12

2 Complete this short biography by supplying the verbs in
the correct form. (Score 1 point for each correct answer.)

Me (1 llamar) Paco y (2 ser) de México. (3 vivir) en Miami
en los Estados Unidos con mi hermano. (4 Trabajar) juntos
en una empresa internacional. Yo (5 trabajar) en la oficina,
(6 ser) secretaria bilingüe, y mi hermano (7 ser) chofer.
Cuando (8 estar) juntos en la oficina (9 comer) juntos.
Nosotros (10 vivir) en un departamento en el norte de
Miami.

10

3 Write down in Spanish what these people do for a living.

1 El señor Rodríguez _____. (teacher)
2 La señorita Martín _____. (student)
3 El señor Ortega y la señora Sánchez _____.
(engineers)
4 La señora Serrano y la señorita Moreno _____.
(secretaries)
5 El señor Carrasco _____. (receptionist)

5

4 Write down these addresses and telephone numbers in words. (Score 2 points for each correct answer, 1 point if you make one mistake.)

1 Calle Barlovento, 25. Tel: 533 1237.
2 Avenida Los Insurgentes, 143. Tel: 418 9558.
3 Paseo de Acapulco, 76. Tel: 348 6894.
4 Calle Seguro Social, 97. Tel: 976 2992
5 Plaza Hildago, 15. Tel: 456 3284.

| 10 |

5 Complete your side of the conversation below. (Deduct 1 point for each mistake.)

You: (Introduce yourself to Sr. Giménez.) (2 points)
Sr. G: Mucho gusto. ¿En qué trabaja usted?
You: (Tell him you are a sales manager.) (2 points)
Sr. G: ¡Ah! Yo también. Pero usted no es mexicano/a, ¿verdad?
You: No. (Tell him your nationality but that you live and work in Mexico City.) (2 points)
Sr. G: Yo vivo en la Ciudad de México también. ¿En qué calle vive?
You: (Tell him you live in a street called Rivera.) (1 point)
Sr. G: ¿Qué número?
You: (Tell him number 17.) (1 point)
Sr. G: ¡Mi hermano vive en el número veinte!

| 8 |

6 Complete the sentences using the appropriate verb with the correct endings.

conoc-/habl-/viv-/trabaj-/com-

1 (Nosotros) _____ en un banco.
2 ¿(Ustedes) _____ en un restaurante?
3 (Yo) _____ en una plaza.
4 Mis papás _____ por teléfono.
5 Él no _____ a María.

| 5 |

TOTAL SCORE | 50 |

If you scored less than 40, look at the Language Building sections again before completing the Summary on page 60.

Summary 4

 Now try this final test, summarizing the main points covered in this unit.

How would you:
1 say 'I'd like to introduce you to Sra. Martínez'?
2 ask someone you have just met if he is Argentinian?
3 say you live in Guadalajara?
4 ask some colleagues if they work in Colombia?
5 say you're a teacher?
6 say you know María?

REVIEW

Think of the jobs that your family and friends do, and practice answering the question ¿en qué trabaja? by saying what their professions are. Use your dictionary to find out what the jobs are in Spanish, and how they change according to gender and number. This is a useful method of extending your vocabulary of jobs and professions.

You can adopt the same approach for addresses and telephone numbers. Practice saying the addresses and telephone numbers of friends and family in Spanish. Notice telephone numbers wherever you go and practice saying them in Spanish as well. Remember, practice makes perfect. You'll soon be saying numbers without thinking about it.

5

Home and family
La casa y la familia

OBJECTIVES

In this unit you will learn how to:

- ✓ talk about your family
- ✓ give ages
- ✓ describe different parts of the house
- ✓ talk about different kinds of accommodation
- ✓ give dates

And cover the following grammar and language:

- ✓ the verb **tener** ('to have')
- ✓ possessive adjectives **mi**, **tu**, **su**, etc. ('my', 'your', 'his/her', etc.)
- ✓ position of adjectives
- ✓ prepositions **de**, **para**, **por**

LEARNING SPANISH 5

Buy a notebook and divide it into alphabetical sections. Every time you learn a new item of vocabulary, write it in the correct section. You may also want to reproduce the same vocabulary in another part of the book, this time by topic, as recommended in Unit 4.

It's often useful to put the item of vocabulary into a sample sentence. This will help you to remember it. Take your notebook with you wherever you go, or you could make a recording of new vocabulary to listen to in the car or bath. If you practice regularly, you can learn a great deal of vocabulary in a short time. If you're not sure of the pronunciation of a word, include a pronunciation guide.

🎧 Now start the recording for Unit 5.

5.1 Are you married?

¿Está usted casada?

ACTIVITY 1 is on the recording.

ACTIVITY 2

Using the Vocabulary below and on page 63, fill in the details of Pepe and Margarita's families.

Óscar es _____ de Margarita. Margarita es _____ de Óscar. Pablo es _____ de Margarita. El papá de Pepe es _____ de Carmen. Carmen es _____ de José.

DIALOGUE 1

- ■ ¿Está usted casada?
- ○ Sí. Estoy casada. Mi esposo se llama Oscar.
- ■ ¿Tiene hijos?
- ○ Sí, tenemos tres hijos. ¿Y usted?
- ■ Sí, yo también estoy casado. Tengo dos hijos.
- ○ Mire; aquí tengo una foto. ¡Les tomamos muchas fotos! Éste es mi hijo, Pablo, y ésta es su hermana, Patricia. Y ésta es la pequeña, Claudia.
- ■ Ah, sí. ¡Qué bonita!
- ○ ¿Cuántos años tienen sus hijos?
- ■ Mi hija, Carmen, tiene doce y mi hijo, José, tiene ocho.
- ○ Mi hijo tiene diez años, Patricia tiene ocho y Claudia tiene cinco. Me escriben todos los días.

VOCABULARY	
casado	married
el esposo	husband
la esposa	wife
tener (tengo)	to have
el hijo	son
la hija	daughter
los hijos/los niños	children
la hermana	sister
tomar fotos	to take photographs
¡qué bonita!	how pretty, beautiful!
¿cuántos años tienen?	how old are they? [*literally* how many years do they have?]

✅ *tener* ('to have')

tener ('to have') is also used to give a person's age. It is irregular:

tengo tienes tiene tenemos tienen

Tengo tres hijos – un muchacho y dos muchachas. I have 3 children – a boy and 2 girls.
Tiene quince años. He/She is 15. [*literally* He/She has 15 years.]

✅ *¿cuánto ... ?* ('How many ... ?')

¿cuánto? is an adjective, which means that it changes ending to agree with the noun it refers to:

¿**Cuántos hermanos** tiene? How many brothers have you got?
¿**Cuánta gente** hay? How many people are there?

✅ Indirect object pronouns

Indirect object pronouns are used to replace nouns which are indirectly affected by the action of the verb: **me, te, le, nos, les**. Like direct object pronouns, they come before the verb.

¡**Les** tomamos muchas fotos! We take lots of photographs of them.
Me escriben todos los días. They write to me every day.

✅ Possessive adjectives: *mi, tu, su, nuestro, suyo*

In Spanish, the possessive adjectives ('my', 'your', 'his', etc.) take a different form depending on the gender and number of the noun described. For mixed groups, the masculine form is used.

mi hermano my brother	**mis hermanos** my brothers and sisters
tu papá your father	**tus papás** your parents
su hijo your/his/her/their son	**sus hijos** your/his/her/their children
nuestro abuelito our grandfather	**nuestros abuelitos** our grandparents
su tío your uncle	**sus tíos** your aunts and uncles

ACTIVITY 3

Choose the correct form of **cuántos/cuántas** for a–c and the correct possessive adjective for d–f.

a ¿_____ hermanos tienes?
b ¿_____ abuelitos tienes?
c ¿_____ mujeres hay?
d Tengo un hermano. ____ hermano se llama Pedro.
e Pedro tiene un abuelito. ____ abuelito se llama Alberto.
f ¡Hola, María! ¿Es ésta ____ hermana?

🔊 Now do activities 4 and 5 on the recording.

5.2　Do you live in an apartment?
¿Vive usted en un departamento?

ACTIVITY 6 is on the recording.

ACTIVITY 7

¿Pepe o María? ¿Quién …

1 vive en un departmento viejo?
2 vive en el décimo piso?

3 tiene una cocina pequeña?
4 tiene una casa en el pueblo?
5 tiene un baño muy grande?

DIALOGUE 2

■ ¿Vive usted en el centro de la ciudad?

○ Sí. Vivo en un departamento. También tenemos un departamento en la playa.

■ Tenemos un departamento en el centro y una casa en el pueblo de mis papás. ¿Cómo es su departamento?

○ Es grande y moderno. Está en el décimo piso. Hay un recibidor ancho. Tiene una sala, un comedor y una cocina y tres recámaras. La cocina es pequeña …

■ Mi departamento no es grande. Está en el centro de la ciudad y es viejo. Está en el tercer piso. La cocina es estrecha. La casa del pueblo es grande y vieja. Tiene un baño muy grande. Es de mi mamá.

VOCABULARY	
el departamento	apartment
la playa	beach
¿cómo es … ?	what's … like? [*literally* how is … ?]
moderno	modern
décimo	tenth
el piso	floor (of a building)
el recibidor	entrance
ancho	wide
la sala	living room
el comedor	dining room
la cocina	kitchen
la recámara	bedroom
estrecho	narrow
el (cuarto de) baño	bathroom

✅ ¿Cómo es ... ?

¿cómo es ... ? is used to ask people to describe something, such as their house, or to describe someone's appearance or character (see Unit 9).

¿Cómo es el departamento? What's the apartment like?
¿Cómo es? What's it/he/she like?

As these are permanent characteristics, the verb **ser** is used. Note the use of **estar** in the following example to inquire how someone is feeling (a temporary state):

¿Cómo está? How are you?; How is he/she?

✅ Position of adjectives

Adjectives agree in gender and number with the noun they describe and normally follow the noun:

un departamento **viejo** an old apartment
una vista **bonita** a pretty view
una cocina **moderna** a modern kitchen
una habitación **pequeña** a small room

A few adjectives precede the noun: see Grammar Summary, page 226.

✅ Preposition *de*

de is used to show possession (the equivalent of the English 's). Note that the word order is different from English.

la madre **de** Juan Juan's mother [*literally* the mother of Juan]
La casa es **de** mi madre. The house is my mother's.

ACTIVITY 8

Complete the sentences with the appropriate adjective from the list, making sure you use the correct form.

moderno/pequeño/bonito/ancho/antiguo

1 El niño tiene dos años. Es muy _____.
2 El hotel tiene dos años. Es muy _____.
3 Las vistas del hotel son _____.
4 La avenida en el centro de la ciudad es _____.
5 El centro de la ciudad tiene mucha historia; tiene muchos edificios _____.

🎧 Now do activities 9 and 10 on the recording.

I'd like a room
Quiero una habitación

ACTIVITY 11 is on the recording.

ACTIVITY 12

1 La habitación es para tres personas.	V/F
2 La habitación es para dos noches.	V/F
3 La habitación cuesta 1000 pesos la noche.	V/F
4 Hoy es el trece de julio.	V/F
5 La habitación está en el tercer piso.	V/F

DIALOGUE 3

■ Buenos días. Quiero una habitación, por favor.

○ Sí, señor. ¿Para cuántas personas?

■ Una doble, para dos personas. Y tenemos un niño de dos años.

○ Está bien ¿Para cuántas noches la quiere?

■ Para tres noches.

○ ¿Podría darme el pasaporte, por favor? Gracias.

■ ¿Cuánto cuesta la noche?

○ Mil pesos la noche.

○ A ver, una habitación para tres noches, para el trece, catorce y quince de julio. Es la número doscientos treinta y cinco. Está en el segundo piso. ¿Tiene equipaje?

■ Sí. Está en el carro. ¿Puedo pagar con tarjeta de crédito?

○ Sí, señor.

VOCABULARY	
para	for
la persona	person
una (habitación) doble	a double (room)
el niño/la niña	little boy/girl
de dos años	aged two [*literally* of two years]
la noche	night
el pasaporte	passport
julio	July
el equipaje	luggage
poder (puedo)	to be able to
pagar	to pay
la tarjeta de crédito	credit card

✓ *por* and *para*

These two prepositions are frequently confused by learners of Spanish: both can be translated 'for', but which is used depends on the situation. They correspond to a range of different prepositions in English.

para is used to describe a purpose, intention, or destination.

> La medicina es **para** la tos. The medicine is for your cough.
> El regalo es **para** mi madre. The gift is for my mother.
> Este tren es **para** Guadalajara. This train is for Guadalajara.

por is used to describe cause or motive.

> No podemos ir **por** el mal tiempo. We can't go because of the bad weather.
>
> No puedo ir en tren **por** la huelga. I can't go by train because of the strike.

por can also be used to describe movement through, time during, approximate location, or means by which something is done.

> ¿Hay un banco **por** aquí? Is there a bank around here?
> Vamos **por** el parque y **por** la avenida. We'll go through the park and along the avenue.
> Le mandé un mensaje **por** fax. I sent him a message by fax.

✓ Dates: *las fechas*

enero	January	**mayo**	May	**septiembre**	September
febrero	February	**junio**	June	**octubre**	October
marzo	March	**julio**	July	**noviembre**	November
abril	April	**agosto**	August	**diciembre**	December

Unlike English, the months in Spanish do not take a capital letter. Apart from the first, dates are given as cardinal numbers and precede the month:

> **el primero de** mayo May 1st
> **el veinte de** agosto August 20th

ACTIVITY 13

What are these dates? Write them in full in Spanish.

a 3-31   b 6-3   c 11-10   d 12-12   e 5-23   f 9-5

🎧 Now do activities 14 and 15 on the recording.

En venta

Americans sometimes buy second homes, usually **departamentos** or **casas**, on or near the coast in Mexico. They either rent out their properties to other people during the year, or stay there themselves during the summer holidays, and sometimes at weekends too.

ACTIVITY 16

You're looking for somewhere to buy on the coast. Read the newspaper advertisements opposite, then decide which ones match your requirements in a–h. Here's what you're looking for:

a something just for you but with a pool if possible.
b somewhere with more than one bathroom because you have a young family.
c a fairly cheap apartment just for you.
d an unfurnished apartment with two bedrooms near the beach but also near the center of town.
e somewhere with a separate garage and a separate kitchen.
f somewhere with a good view of the sea.
g somewhere just for you with a garden and maybe a pool.
h somewhere in a quiet area for the whole family.

céntrico	central
los muebles	furniture
amueblado	furnished
la oferta	bargain
perfecto estado	perfect condition
el jardín	garden
la cochera	garage
la alberca	swimming pool

1

Departamento céntrico, muy cerca de la playa, 2 recámaras, sala, comedor, cocina y terraza. Sin muebles. Precio: 400.000. Ref 852

2

Departamento 3 recámaras, cocina independiente, amueblado, gran terraza, cochera independiente. Precio 440.000

3

Departamento con maravillosas vistas al mar, edificio de calidad y de tres pisos, tres recámaras, sala, comedor, cocina, baño, terraza, amueblado, lugar para estacionamiento incluido. 990.000

4

Departamento 1 recámara, sala-comedor, cocina, baño, terraza. 270.000

5

Campo de Golf Las Flores. Departamento, 1 recámara, alberca. 340.000

6

Oportunidad, departamento de tres recámaras, gran terraza, en perfecto estado, zona muy tranquila. Precio 420.000 Ref 454

7

Departamento cerca del mar, una recámara, cocina equipada, jardín y alberca. Precio 320.000

8

Casa, en zona muy tranquila, 3 recámaras y un estudio, dos baños, cochera, jardín de 600m^2. Precio 1.170.000. Ref 441

5.5 Un extraño en la ciudad

 JORGE CAMBIA DE HOTEL
JORGE CHANGES HOTEL

Jorge está en la biblioteca con los periódicos. Luego, cambia de hotel. No quiere una habitación tranquila. Quiere una habitación con vista a la calle. ¿Por qué?

Jorge is in the library with the newspapers. Then he changes his hotel. He doesn't want a quiet room – he wants a room with a view of the street. Why?

luego	then, afterwards
¿por qué?	why?
la información	information
sobre	about
la fotocopia	photocopy
el artículo	(newspaper) article
quisiera	I'd like
la llave	key
el parque	park
atrás	behind
la vista	view
bonito	nice, pretty
tranquilo	quiet, peaceful
el ruido	noise
el tráfico	traffic
no importa	it's not important

ACTIVITY 17

Answer the following questions in English.

1 What is Jorge looking for in the library?
2 What does he ask the librarian?
3 How far from the library is his new hotel?
4 Why does the receptionist at the new hotel offer him the first room?
5 Why doesn't he accept this room?
6 What is perfect about the second room?

ACTIVITY 18

Put these phrases in the order you hear them.

1 Es una habitación muy tranquila.
2 Ésa es la casa de María.
3 Está a cinco minutos a pie.
4 Quiero una fotocopia de este artículo.
5 Aquí está la información sobre María y la familia.

ACTIVITY 19

¿Verdadero o falso?

1 En el artículo hay una foto de la familia de María.	V/F
2 Quiere una habitación para una noche.	V/F
3 Jorge Jimeno está en la habitación 220.	V/F
4 La habitación tiene una vista muy bonita.	V/F
5 La casa de María está enfrente del hotel.	V/F
6 María no está en la calle.	V/F

STORY TRANSCRIPT

Jorge	A ver … sí … aquí está la información sobre María y la familia. Y también hay una foto de toda la familia. Disculpe, quiero una fotocopia de este artículo.
Librarian	Sí, señor. Pase por aquí.
Jorge	¿Qué tan lejos está el Hotel Corona?
Librarian	Está a cinco minutos a pie.
Jorge	Buenos días. Quisiera una habitación, por favor.
Receptionist	¿Para cuántas noches?
Jorge	Dos o tres.
Receptionist	Bueno … la habitación número 211. Aquí tiene la llave.
Jorge	¿Esta habitación es con vista a la calle?
Receptionist	No, señor. Es con vista al parque, atrás. Es una habitación muy tranquila con una vista muy bonita.
Jorge	No, necesito una habitación con vista a la calle. Es muy importante.
Receptionist	De acuerdo. Pero hay ruido del tráfico.
Jorge	No importa.
Receptionist	Pues la habitación número doscientos veinte está libre. ¿La quiere?
Jorge	Sí, gracias.
Jorge	A ver. Sí. Esa es la casa de María. Está enfrente. Esta habitación es perfecta. Y allí está María en la calle.

Test

Now it's time to test your progress in Unit 5.

1 Write down in Spanish the following information about your family. (Score 2 points for each correct answer, 1 point if you make one mistake.)

   1 Say you have three brothers and one sister.
   2 Say you have two children, a boy aged eight and a girl aged six.
   3 Say your father is sixty and your mother is fifty-eight.
   4 Say you are married and your wife's/husband's name is Josefina/José.

8

2 Match the sentences 1–5 with a suitable response from a–e.

   1 Ésta es una foto de mi casa.
   2 Usted está casada, ¿verdad?
   3 ¿Cuántos años tiene su hijo?
   4 ¿Cuántos hijos tiene usted?
   5 Ésta es la pequeña, María.

   a Tiene ocho.
   b Tengo dos.
   c ¡Qué bonita!
   d Sí, mi esposo se llama Óscar.
   e ¡Es grande!

5

3 Study the family tree and complete the sentences.

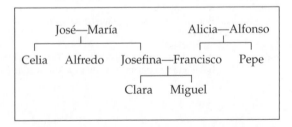

1 José es _____ de Clara y Miguel.
2 Alfredo es _____ de Clara y Miguel.
3 Miguel es _____ de Clara.
4 Miguel es _____ de Francisco.
5 Clara es _____ de Miguel.
6 Francisco es _____ de Clara.
7 Josefina es _____ de Miguel.
8 Alicia es _____ de Clara.

8

4 Fill the gaps with either **por** or **para**.

1 Estas manzanas son ___ mi madre.
2 ¿Cuánto cuesta la habitación ___ noche?
3 Mi papá trabaja ___ la noche.
4 Siga ___ esta calle hasta el final.
5 ___ mí, la sopa.
6 Hablo a mi amigo ___ teléfono.

6

5 You're reserving a hotel room in Mexico City. Write your requirements in Spanish. (2 points for each correct answer, 1 point if you make one mistake.)

1 A double room for three nights.
2 You want the room on February 14th.
3 Ask how much it costs.
4 Ask if the room is on the third floor.
5 Say you have luggage.

10

6 Write these dates in full in Spanish.

1 6-23   2 2-13   3 9-19   4 7-30   5 5-1

5

TOTAL SCORE **42**

If you scored less than 32, look at the Language Building sections again before completing the Summary on page 74.

Summary 5

 Now try this final test, summarizing the main points covered in this unit.

How would you:
1 ask someone if she's married?
2 say you have three children?
3 say María is your sister?
4 say she's three years old?
5 ask how old José is?
6 ask someone what her apartment's like?
7 say you'd like a double room for three nights?

REVIEW

Draw your own family tree and make sentences about the various relationships. Then construct sentences giving the ages of the various members of your family.

Now practice saying where your house is and what it's like. How many rooms are there and what are they? You can use your dictionary to add to the vocabulary you have already learned in this unit.

Practice dates, making sure you know the names of the days and months. Every day say what date it is. Pick out key dates in your family calendar (for example, birthdays) and practice saying them in Spanish.

What time is it?
¿Qué hora es?

OBJECTIVES

In this unit you'll learn how to:

✓ ask and tell the time

✓ ask and say what time stores and other facilities open and close

✓ ask and say what time events start and finish

✓ talk about working hours and daily routines

✓ talk about the days of the week

And cover the following grammar and language:

✓ time expressions **de … a** and **desde … hasta** ('from … until')

✓ reflexive verbs

✓ radical-changing verbs

LEARNING SPANISH 6

Confidence is so important when speaking a language. A good way of overcoming any inhibitions you may feel is to practice saying the words and sentences you learn on your own when no one can hear you. Exaggerate the pronunciation and enjoy yourself. If you get the opportunity, through movies or with Spanish speakers, listen carefully to how they speak and try to reproduce their speaking style with your own voice. Use a tape recorder to record yourself speaking and play it back as often as you like. Little by little you will gain confidence when you are speaking with other people.

🎧 Now start the recording for Unit 6.

What's your schedule?
¿Qué horario tienes?

ACTIVITY 1 is on the recording.

ACTIVITY 2

Which is the odd one out in each group?

1 Jobs:
    a salesman   c sales manager
    b office worker   d accountant

2 Workplace:
    a insurance office c furniture store
    b electrical   d sales office
       appliances store

3 Finish work:
    a 6 p.m.   c 8.15 p.m.
    b 5 p.m.   d 8 p.m.

4 For lunch:
    a 1 hour   c 2 hours
    b 3 hours   d 2 1/2 hours

DIALOGUE 1

■ ¿Qué haces? ¿Trabajas?

○ Sí, trabajo en una tienda de electrodomésticos. Soy dependiente. ¿Y tú?

■ Yo trabajo en una compañía de seguros, en una oficina.

○ ¿Qué horario tienes?

■ Trabajo de nueve a seis. Tengo una hora a mediodía para comer, a la una y media.

○ Yo trabajo de nueve a una y de cuatro a ocho. Tengo tres horas a mediodía para comer.

■ ¿En qué trabaja usted?

▼ Soy gerente de ventas de una compañía de muebles.

■ ¿Qué horario tiene?

▼ Mi horario es de nueve a una y media y por la tarde de cuatro a ocho y cuarto.

■ ¿Viaja mucho?

▼ Sí. Viajo mucho. Cuando viajo, no tengo horario.

VOCABULARY

hacer (hago)	to do
la tienda de electrodomésticos	electrical appliances store
el dependiente/la dependienta	salesman, saleswoman
el horario	timetable
el mediodía	midday

✓ Telling the time

In Spanish, times are given using the verb **ser**:

¿Qué hora **es**? What time is it?   **Son** las cuatro. It's four o'clock.

The definite article and the verb are both used in the plural – **son las cuatro** – except for **es la una** ('it's one o'clock'). The 24-hour clock is used mainly at stations and airports: **las catorce horas** ('14.00'), **las catorce treinta** ('14.30').

For half hours add **y media**. To give times with quarter hours, you use **cuarto** ('quarter') with **y** or **para**:

Son las ocho **y media**. It's half past eight.
las once **y cuarto** a quarter past eleven [*literally* eleven and quarter]
cuarto para las once a quarter to eleven

y and **para** are also used with minutes:

las ocho **y** diez ten past eight   cinco **para** las nueve five to nine

To specify what time something happens the preposition **a** is used:

a las ocho de la mañana   at eight o'clock in [*literally* of] the morning
a las ocho de la noche   at eight o'clock in the evening
a las once de la noche   at eleven o'clock at night
a medianoche/**a** mediodía   at (around) midnight/at (around) midday

✓ *de ... a* ('from ... to'), *desde ... hasta* ('from ... until')

There are two ways of saying what hours you work or when a store is open: these are interchangeable.

Trabajo **de** nueve **a** seis. I work from nine until six.
Trabajo **desde** las nueve **hasta** las seis. I work from nine until six.

The definite article is dropped with **de ... a**, but kept with **desde ... hasta**.

ACTIVITY 3

1 Give the Spanish for the following times.
   a 10 o'clock   b 11.30   c 3 o'clock   d 6.30
2 What do you do? Use **Soy ...** or **Trabajo en ...**
   a sales manager   c head of personnel
   b furniture company   d grocery store
3 Write down these hours using **de ... a**.
   a from 10 to 1 and from 4 to 7   c from 9 to 1 and 4 to 8
   b from 9 until 5   d from 2 until 10 o'clock

🎧 Now do activities 4 and 5 on the recording.

6.2 | What time do you get up?
¿A qué hora te levantas?

ACTIVITY 6 is on the recording.

ACTIVITY 7

What time does Bernardo …

1 get up?
2 leave home in the morning?
3 start work in the morning?
4 finish work in the evening?
5 have dinner?
6 go to bed?

DIALOGUE 2

- ¿A qué hora te levantas?
- Me levanto a las siete de la mañana.
- ¿A qué hora sales de tu casa?
- Desayuno a las siete y media y salgo de mi casa a las ocho. Llego a mi trabajo a las ocho y media.
- ¿Acabas a la una?
- Sí. A mediodía voy a casa para comer con la familia. Después tomamos café y hablamos. Descanso, veo la tele, leo el periódico …
- ¿A qué hora regresas a trabajar?
- Por la tarde trabajo de cuatro y media a ocho. Regreso a casa y ceno a las nueve y media.
- ¿Y a qué hora te acuestas?
- A las once y media o a las doce.

VOCABULARY

levantarse	to get up
durante	during
desayunar	to have breakfast
llegar	to arrive
ir	to go
voy	I go
después	afterward
descansar	to relax
la tele	television
regresar	to return
la tarde	afternoon
cenar	to have dinner
acostarse (me acuesto)	to go to bed

✅ Reflexive verbs

A reflexive verb is one whose subject performs the action of the verb upon himself or herself. In Spanish this idea is conveyed by a reflexive pronoun ('myself', 'yourself', etc.): the pronoun is not normally used in English, e.g. **levantarse**, 'to get up' [*literally* 'to raise oneself']:

(yo) **me** levanto	(nosotros/as) **nos** levant**amos**
(tú) **te** levant**as**	(ellos/as/ustedes) **se** levant**an**
(él/ella/usted) **se** levant**a**	

In the infinitive (**levantarse**) and the imperative (**levántate**), the reflexive pronoun is added to the end of the verb. Note the accent in the imperative form.

Other reflexive verbs:

acostarse	to go to bed	**bañarse**	to take a shower
peinarse	to comb one's hair	**vestirse**	to get dressed
lavarse	to wash oneself		

✅ Radical-changing verbs

Radical-changing verbs are verbs in which the vowel in the stem ('radical' = stem) changes in the singular forms and in the third person plural. In all other ways they follow the pattern of regular -**ar**, -**er**, and -**ir** verbs. The verb **acostarse** ('to go to bed') is a radical-changing verb. In the singular and third person plural forms, **o** changes to **ue**:

acostarse: me ac<u>ue</u>sto, te ac<u>ue</u>stas, se ac<u>ue</u>sta, nos acostamos, se ac<u>ue</u>stan

The verb **tener** ('to have') is also a radical-changing verb, as well as being irregular (see p. 63).

In vocabulary lists from now on, the first person singular of such verbs will be shown in brackets after the infinitive.

ACTIVITY 8

Complete this account of Pepe's day. Here's his timetable:

Pepe gets up at 7 o'clock and works from 9.15 until 1.15. He eats at 2 o'clock and returns to work at 4. He works until 7.45. He goes to bed at 11.30.

Pepe se levanta a las siete …

 Now do activities 9 and 10 on the recording.

What time does the movie start?
¿A qué hora empieza la película?

🎧 **ACTIVITY 11** is on the recording.

ACTIVITY 12

What happens at each of these times?

Example: 4.30 p.m. El cine abre a las cuatro y media.

a 6.15 p.m.   b 8 p.m.   c 10 a.m.

DIALOGUE 3

■ ¿Vamos al cine esta tarde?
○ Sí, pero yo quiero visitar el museo también.
■ Está bien. ¿A qué hora empieza la película?
○ La película empieza a las seis y cuarto.
■ ¿Cuánto dura?
○ Dos horas más o menos. Termina a las ocho.
■ ¿El museo está abierto los domingos?
○ Sí, está abierto todos los días menos los lunes.
■ ¿A qué hora abre en las mañanas?
○ A las diez. Y en la noche cierra a las ocho.
■ Comemos en un restaurante cerca del museo y en la tarde vamos al museo y luego vamos al cine a las seis.
○ Nos vemos en la puerta del museo a las dos.

VOCABULARY	
empezar	to start, begin
la película	movie
¿vamos ... ?/vamos	shall we go ...?/let's go
el cine	the movies, movie theater
visitar	to visit
durar	to last
más o menos	more or less
terminar	to finish
abierto	open
todos los días	every day
menos	except
abrir	to open
cerrar	to close
nos vemos	we'll meet

⊘ More radical-changing verbs

empezar ('to begin'), **cerrar** ('to close'), and **pensar** ('to think') are all **-ar** verbs which are radical-changing: in the singular and the third person plural, the **e** in the stem changes to **ie**:

empiezo, empiezas, empieza, empezamos, empiezan

querer ('to want') is an **-er** verb which behaves in the same way:

quiero, quieres, quiere, queremos, quieren

It is followed by a verb in the infinitive:

Quiero **visitar** el museo. I'd like to visit the museum.

⊘ Days of the week

All days of the week in Spanish are masculine and are not capitalized:

los días de entre semana: lunes, martes, miércoles, jueves, viernes
weekdays: Monday, Tuesday, Wednesday, Thursday, Friday
el fin de semana: sábado, domingo
the weekend: Saturday, Sunday

To say 'on Monday' etc. or 'on the weekend' in Spanish, you use the definite article, with no preposition:

El lunes tengo clase. On Monday I have a class.
Los sábados no trabajo. On Saturdays I don't work.
Los fines de semana descanso. On the weekend I relax.

ACTIVITY 13

Use the following information to write eight sentences.

Example: La Máscara del Zorro empieza a las cinco y termina a las siete.

La Máscara del Zorro: **tarde** 4–6, 6–8, 8–10, 10–12
Pastelería: **mañana** 9.30–1.30; **tarde** 4.30–8 (**sábados**: 10–2)
Museo: **lunes**: cerrado; **martes–sábado** 10–7, **domingo** 11–5

ACTIVITY 14

Write a short dialogue using Dialogue 3 as a model:

A: ¿el cine/esta tarde?
B: ¿a qué hora/empezar/película?
A: empezar/7/terminar/9.
B: cenar/después

🎧 Now do activities 15 and 16 on the recording.

6.4 A typical day in Mexico
Un día típico en México

ACTIVITY 17

Read the letter from Miguel describing his typical day and find out the following information:

1 what time he gets up.
2 what he does in the middle of the morning.
3 where he has lunch.
4 what time he has dinner.
5 what he does on Sundays.

Hola David,

¿Cómo estás? Me preguntas cómo son los horarios típicos en México. Me levanto a las seis y media y empiezo a trabajar a las ocho. Desayuno muy rápido: café o leche, jugo de naranja, pan dulce, pan tostado. A media mañana mucha gente toma un café en una cafetería cerca de su trabajo. Yo almuerzo una torta de milanesa o de jamón.

Normalmente termino el trabajo a la una y regreso a casa para comer. Después tomo un café, platicamos. Ésta es la costumbre de sobremesa. Regreso a trabajar a las cuatro y trabajo hasta las ocho. A media tarde tomo un café con un pastel. Después, en casa, a las nueve y media ceno algo ligero.

Los fines de semana es distinto. Como a las dos y media. Los domingos todos se reúnen con la familia o en casa de los abuelitos. Comen todos en familia y la gente da un paseo con la familia. Hablan y toman. Las comidas de domingo son más especiales y comemos en casa o en un restaurante.

Un abrazo,
Miguel

me preguntas	you ask(ed) me
pan dulce	Danish pastry
pan tostado	toast
la gente	people
el almuerzo	mid-morning snack
la costumbre	custom
sobremesa	*the period immediately after lunch when people sit around the table chatting* [*literally* over the table]
ligero	light
distinto	different
dar un paseo	to take a walk, a stroll
un abrazo	best wishes

ACTIVITY 18

Now describe your own daily routine, using the letter as a model. Use the verbs that appear in the letter and add times and activities to describe your own situation. Use the vocabulary section to help you.

ACTIVITY 19

Find eight words which have something to do with meals or food.

A	P	A	N	D	U	L	C	E	O
Z	K	L	F	C	J	I	A	P	Q
Y	L	M	E	E	K	H	F	M	N
A	I	U	G	N	D	P	E	U	T
B	D	E	S	A	Y	U	N	O	O
B	X	R	H	S	S	R	Q	P	R
C	T	Z	I	E	F	G	X	C	T
U	S	O	B	R	E	M	E	S	A
D	W	V	U	T	N	K	O	M	L
P	A	N	T	O	S	T	A	D	O

6.5 Un extraño en la ciudad

UNA INVITACIÓN A CENAR
AN INVITATION TO DINNER

Cuando María sale del trabajo, va a la Cafetería Coyoacán.
Jorge la sigue. Se presenta como el hombre del mercado, y le
ofrece algo de tomar. Hablan …

When María leaves work, she goes to the Cafetería Coyoacán.
Jorge, who has been waiting for her, follows her. In the bar he
introduces himself as the man in the market, and offers to buy
her a drink. They get talking …

para mí	for me
bastante	quite
largo	long
fijo	fixed
el sueldo	salary
las vacaciones	vacation
de vacaciones	on vacation
exactamente	exactly
de viaje	(traveling) on business
conmigo	with me
así	therefore, that way
continuar	to continue
la conversación	conversation
de acuerdo	fine
hasta luego	see you later [*literally* until then]

ACTIVITY 20

Who …

1 offers whom a drink?
2 has an orange juice?
3 works very long hours?
4 doesn't have a very interesting job?
5 has a good salary?
6 invites whom to dinner?
7 suggests which restaurant to go to?
8 suggests they meet in the cafetería?

ACTIVITY 21

Match these questions to the correct answers from the dialogue.

1 ¿Lo conozco?
2 ¿Quieres tomar algo?
3 Trabajas muchas horas, ¿verdad?
4 ¿Es interesante tu trabajo?
5 ¿Quiere cenar conmigo?

a Una limonada, por favor.
b Sí, es un día bastante largo, pero normal.
c Soy el señor del mercado.
d Está bien. Pero primero voy a mi casa.
e No es muy interesante pero el sueldo es bueno.

STORY TRANSCRIPT

Jorge	Buenas tardes. Me llamo Jorge Jimeno.
María	¿Lo conozco?
Jorge	Soy el señor del mercado ... la cartera ...
María	¡Ah sí! Mucho gusto. Soy María.
Jorge	¿Quieres tomar algo?
María	Bueno, una limonada, por favor.
Jorge	Para mí un jugo de naranja. Gracias.
Jorge	¿A qué hora terminas el trabajo?
María	A las ocho.
Jorge	Trabajas muchas horas, ¿verdad?
María	Bueno. Trabajo de nueve a una y media y de cuatro y media a ocho. Sí, es un día bastante largo, pero normal. ¿Y usted? ¿Trabaja muchas horas?
Jorge	Yo no tengo horario fijo pero trabajo muchas horas. ¿Es interesante tu trabajo?
María	Bueno, no mucho. Trabajo en una oficina. No es muy interesante pero me pagan muy bien. ¿Está usted de vacaciones?
Jorge	No exactamente. Estoy de viaje.
María	¡Oh! Son cuarto para las nueve. Muchas gracias por la limonada. Voy a cenar. Es muy tarde.
Jorge	¿Quieres cenar conmigo en un restaurante y así continuamos la conversación?
María	Mmm ... De acuerdo. Pero primero voy a mi casa. Hay un restaurante aquí al lado de la cafetería ... se llama Corregidora. ¿Nos vemos aquí a las nueve y media y vamos al restaurante?
Jorge	De acuerdo ... Hasta luego. Sr. Herrera, otro jugo, por favor.

Test

Now it's time to test your progress in Unit 6.

1 **¿Qué hora es?** Write the following times in full in Spanish, using the phrases **de la mañana**, **de la tarde**, or **de la noche.** (2 points for a correct answer, 1 for one mistake).

1 7.15 a.m.   4 11 p.m.
2 1.30 p.m.   5 4.45 p.m.
3 6.30 p.m.

> **10**

2 **¿Qué horario tienen?** Write down in words the hours these people work, using **desde ... a**. (2 points for a correct answer, 1 for one mistake).

1 Jaime: 9 a.m.–1 p.m.; 4 p.m.–8 p.m.
2 Carmen: 8.30 a.m.–1.30 p.m.; 4.30 p.m.–7.30 p.m.
3 Jorge: 8 p.m.–6 a.m.
4 Puri: 8 a.m.–5 p.m.
5 Alfonso: 2.45 p.m.–8.30 p.m.

> **10**

3 Write nine sentences about your day, saying what time you usually do things. Use the following verbs:

levantarse / desayunar / salir / llegar / comer / terminar / regresar / cenar / acostarse

> **9**

4 Use the correct verb in the correct form to complete these sentences.

1 La tienda _____ a la una del mediodía.
2 La película _____ tres horas.
3 El cine _____ a las once de la noche.
4 La película _____ a las ocho y _____ a las once.
5 El museo _____ a las diez de la mañana.

> **6**

5 **¿Qué quieres hacer?** Complete the dialogue. (2 points for a correct answer, 1 for one mistake).

A: ¿Quieres ir al cine?
Tú: (No, you don't want to go to the cinema.)
A: ¿Qué quieres hacer?
Tú: (You want to have supper in a restaurant.)
A: ¿A qué hora nos vemos?
Tú: (You'll meet him at 7.30 at the restaurant.)

_____ | 6 |

6 Replace the infinitive in brackets with the correct form of the verb (all are irregular).

1 En la mañana yo (**salir**) de casa a las ocho.
2 María (**regresar**) a casa a mediodía.
3 Yo (**tener**) dos hermanos.
4 Mis padres no (**querer**) café.
5 Yo (**conocer**) a tu amigo, Juan.

_____ | 5 |

7 Make sentences using **querer** + another verb. (2 points for a correct answer, 1 for one mistake).

1 You want to have dinner.
2 You want to go out.
3 You want to visit your parents.
4 You want to go home.

_____ | 8 |

8 Complete the following sentences by translating the words in brackets. Note that some of them are reflexive verbs: you will need to include the correct reflexive pronoun.

1 (**I get up**) a las siete.
2 (**I eat dinner**) a las nueve de la noche.
3 (**I go to bed**) a las once.
4 (**I take a shower**) por la mañana.
5 (**I relax**) después de comer.
6 (**I go out**) a las ocho.

_____ | 6 |

TOTAL SCORE | 60 |

If you scored less than 50, look at the Language Building sections again before completing the Summary on page 88.

Summary 6

Now try this final test, summarizing the main points covered in this unit.

How would you:
1 ask the time?
2 say it's a quarter to nine in the morning?
3 say you work from nine to five?
4 say the movie starts at six and finishes at eight?
5 say the store opens at ten and closes at six?
6 say 'let's meet at the restaurant at eight'?

REVIEW

Practice saying the time to yourself in Spanish. Get into the habit of practicing the different structures for saying the time: **cuarto para las dos**, etc. Look at timetables and practice saying complete sentences: **abre a las diez**, etc. What is your daily routine? Work through it in Spanish.

Review your vocabulary for jobs by identifying the jobs done by your friends and family in Spanish. Extend the vocabulary by using your dictionary to look up the Spanish for jobs you don't know. Practice your own details whenever you get the chance: **Me llamo...**, **trabajo en ...**, **me levanto a las ...** **trabajo de ... a ...**, etc. Do this for other people as well to improve your fluency.

This unit is full of new verbs, some of them irregular. It's important to practice saying them over and over. Pay particular attention to the reflexive verbs and the radical-changing verbs.

Eating out
En el restaurante

OBJECTIVES

In this unit you'll learn how to:

✅ talk about different kinds of food and drink

✅ order items from the menu in a restaurant

✅ complain about things in a restaurant

✅ ask for the check

And cover the following grammar and language:

✅ the disjunctive pronouns **mí**, **ti**, etc.

✅ the verb **poder** ('to be able') followed by the infinitive

✅ more irregular verbs

✅ **se** in passive constructions

LEARNING SPANISH 7

Use a tape recorder to record yourself speaking Spanish and to help you improve your pronunciation. First of all, listen to the stress, intonation, and rhythm of people speaking Spanish on the recording, then try to reproduce it yourself. Don't underestimate the value of simply listening to sentences and copying them as exactly as you can. It's all good practice. Start by doing this with individual words, and then build up to longer sentences.

🔊 Now start the recording for Unit 7.

7.1 What's on the menu?

¿Qué hay en el menú?

 ACTIVITY 1 is on the recording.

ACTIVITY 2

Sort the items: **appetizer, entrée, dessert**, or **drink**?

fruta	sopa	mojarra	agua	flan
pollo	ensalada	cerveza	pescado	

DIALOGUE 1

○ ¿Qué hay en el menú del día?

▼ Para empezar, hay sopa o ensalada. Luego hay pollo o pescado, y de postre hay flan o fruta.

■ Para empezar, quiero la ensalada y el pollo de plato fuerte.

○ Para empezar, quiero sopa y luego pescado. ¿Qué pescado es?

▼ Es mojarra a la plancha.

○ Bueno. Pues quiero la mojarra.

▼ Muy bien. ¿Y de beber?

○ Agua de limón, por favor.

▼ ¿Qué van a tomar de postre?

○ Pues el flan.

■ Para mí también, por favor.

VOCABULARY

el menú (del día)	menu (of the day)
para empezar	to begin
el postre	dessert
la sopa	soup
la ensalada	salad
el pollo	chicken
de plato fuerte	as an entrée
luego	then
la mojarra	*type of fish*
el flan	crème caramel
a la plancha	grilled
el agua (de limón)	(lemon) water
para beber	to drink

⊘ Disjunctive pronouns after a preposition

After prepositions, such as **para** ('for'), **con** ('with'), **sin** ('without'), **de** ('of, from'), an emphatic form of the pronoun, known as the disjunctive pronoun, is used:

para <u>mí</u> for me	**con <u>nosotros/as</u>** with us
para <u>ti</u> for you	**sin <u>ustedes</u>** without you
con <u>él/ella</u> with him/her	**sin <u>ellos/as</u>** without them

El anillo es **para ti**. The ring is for you.

con + mí becomes **conmigo** and **con + ti** becomes **contigo**. Note that **mí** has an accent to distinguish it from the possessive pronoun **mi** ('my'), but **ti** has no accent.

⊘ *para* + infinitive

para is frequently used for the English equivalent of 'to'. It is followed by the infinitive: **para empezar** ('to begin').

ACTIVITY 3

Complete the sentences using the appropriate word or phrase from the list below.

empezar / beber / cómo / quiero / qué

1 Para _____ quiero la sopa.
2 ¿_____ es la mojarra? A la plancha.
3 ¿_____ es pollo al ajillo? Es pollo con ajos.
4 ¿El pescado o el pollo? _____ el pescado.
5 ¿Qué quiere _____? Agua mineral, por favor.

⊙ Now do activities 4 and 5 on the recording.

7.2 There's a knife missing

Falta un cuchillo

ACTIVITY 6 is on the recording.

ACTIVITY 7

¿Alfonso o Carmen? Quién …

1 ¿… toma café negro?
2 ¿… toma un café con leche?
3 ¿… no tiene cuchara?
4 ¿… no tiene cuchillo?

DIALOGUE 2

○ ¿Qué hay de postre?
▼ Hay flan, fruta, helado, coctel de frutas, pastel.
○ Para mí, fruta, una manzana. Estoy satisfecho.
■ Para mí, pastel.
▼ Sí. Se toma con crema.
■ Muy bien.
▼ ¿Toman cafés?
■ Un café negro, por favor.
○ Y para mí un café con leche.

■ No tengo cuchara. Disculpe, ¿podría traer una cuchara?
▼ Sí, señorita. Ahorita la traigo.
○ Y falta un cuchillo para la fruta. ¿Puede traer uno también, por favor?
▼ Sí, señor, ahorita lo traigo.
■ Falta un café. ¿Puede traerlo?
▼ Sí, en seguida lo traigo.

○ Disculpe, por favor. ¿Puede traer la cuenta?
▼ Sí, ahorita la traigo.

VOCABULARY	
faltar	to lack, to be missing
el cuchillo	knife
la cuchara	spoon
la fruta del tiempo	seasonal fruit
el pastel	tart, cake
satisfecho	full
se toma	it is eaten [*from* tomarse]
la crema	cream
traer (traigo)	to bring
en seguida	immediately
la cuenta	check

✅ *poder* + infinitive

poder ('to be able') is an irregular verb (see page 95 and Unit 8 for more on its uses). It is followed by an infinitive. When **poder** is used in a request, the conditional form is often used.

> No **puedo acabar** el pollo. I can't finish the chicken.
> ¿**Podría traer** la cuenta? Could you bring the check?
> ¿**Podría limpiar** la mesa? Could you clean the table?

Note that the direct object pronoun is added to the infinitive:

> La mesa está sucia. ¿**Podría limpiarla?** The table is dirty. Could you clean it?

✅ More irregular verbs

traer is an irregular **-er** verb which adds **g** in the first person singular and changes the **e** to **i**:

> Ahora **traigo** la cuenta. I'll bring the check now.
> Ahora **trae** la copa. He's bringing the wine glass now.

The rest of the verb is regular. The following verbs also add **g** in the first person singular: **hacer**, 'to do' (**hago, haces**, etc.), **tener**, 'to have' (**tengo, tienes**, etc.), **venir**, 'to come' (**vengo, vienes**, etc.), **salir**, 'to leave' (**salgo, sales**, etc.), **poner**, 'to put' (**pongo, pones**, etc.)

✅ *faltar* ('to be missing, lacking')

This verb is used in the following way:

> **Falta** un cuchillo. There's a knife missing. [*literally* A knife is missing.]
> **Faltan** dos vasos. There are two glasses missing.

✅ *se* in passive constructions

se is often used in passive constructions or where there is no specific subject. It is followed by a verb in the third person singular or plural:

> **Se toma** con crema. You eat it [*literally* it is eaten] with cream.
> **Se puede** comer frío. You can eat it/It can be eaten cold.

ACTIVITY 8

Write these sentences in Spanish.

1 What is there for dessert?
2 There isn't a fork.
3 Could you bring some coffee?
4 They'll bring the check now.
5 I can't finish my dessert.
6 You eat it cold.

🔊 Now do activities 9 and 10 on the recording.

The soup is cold

La sopa está fría

ACTIVITY 11 is on the recording.

ACTIVITY 12

What's the problem with each of the following?

1 the table   4 the check
2 the soup   5 the restaurant
3 the fish

DIALOGUE 3

○ ¡Disculpe! La mesa está sucia. ¿Podría limpiarla, por favor?
■ En seguida.

○ Por favor … La sopa está fría. Disculpe, ¿podría calentarla, por favor?
■ Sí, señora.

○ El pescado está quemado. ¿Podría cambiarlo?
■ Sí, señora.

○ Disculpe, señor. La cuenta está mal. ¿Podría checarla?
■ A ver. Sí, sí, tiene razón.
○ Este restaurante es muy malo. Las mesas están sucias, la sopa está fría, el pescado está quemado y yo estoy muy enojada.
■ Lo siento mucho, señora.

VOCABULARY	
la mesa	table
sucio	dirty
limpiar	to clean
frío	cold
calentar	to heat up
quemado	burnt
cambiar	to change
mal	wrong, mistaken
tener razón	to be right
malo	bad
enojado	angry, annoyed
lo siento (mucho)	I'm (very) sorry

✅ More uses of *estar* and *ser*

estar is used to describe where someone or something is located. It can also be used to describe a temporary state:

La mesa **está** sucia. The table is dirty.
La sopa **está** fría. The soup is cold.

In these examples the temporary state can be remedied (by cleaning, heating, or replacing). Compare this with the following example:

El restaurante **es** muy malo. The restaurant is very bad.

This statement describes a more permanent state, which would take some time to change, so the verb **ser** is used.

✅ More on ¿podría ...? + the infinitive and direct object pronouns

When ¿**podría** ...? + the infinitive is used with a direct object pronoun in the plural, the forms **los** and **las** are used.

dos cuchillos – ¿Podría traer**los**? Could you bring them?
estas cucharas – ¿Podría cambiar**las**? Could you change them?

ACTIVITY 13

Complete this story, using the correct form of **ser** or **estar** and the correct form of the adjective.

El restaurante Cuatro Estaciones _____ muy (**bueno**). _____ enfrente del cine Alameda. La comida _____ (**bueno**) también. Pero hoy hay un problema. Hay dos meseros (**nuevo**). _____ (**malo**). La sopa _____ (**frío**) y la carne _____ (**quemado**). Los clientes _____ (**enojado**). La señora Martínez _____ (**muy importante**). Ella _____ (**enojado**). La comida _____ (**malo**) y su cuenta _____ (**equivocado**).

ACTIVITY 14

Add the correct form of the direct object pronoun to the infinitive.

Example: la sopa – ¿Puede cambiarla?

1 la carne – cambiar
2 el flan – cambiar
3 las cucharas – cambiar
4 los platos – cambiar
5 el pollo – cambiar
6 la cuenta – mirar
7 la mesa – limpiar

Now do activities 15 and 16 on the recording.

7.4 Mexican cuisine
La cocina mexicana

ACTIVITY 17

Read the following text about some of Mexico's famous dishes and study the new vocabulary. Then identify which dish is described in each of the statements below.

1　This dish is a type of pancake.
2　This dish is from Puebla.
3　You can fry these.
4　This is a rice dish.
5　This is served as a starter.
6　This has carrots in it.
7　You need peanuts for this dish.
8　You can eat these with cream.

Los tacos son una de las comidas más populares. Consisten en una tortilla, de maiz o trigo, enrollada con algún guisado como contenido. Pueden ser fritas también. Se les puede poner salsa picante y crema.

El mole poblano es originario de la Ciudad de Puebla. Consiste en una combinación de varios chiles, cacahuates, tortilla frita, caldo de pollo y chocolate (entre otros ingredientes). Todo ello conforma una salsa espesa de color café muy oscuro. En ella se hierven piezas de pollo o guajolote (pavo) y se sirve caliente.

Arroz a la mexicana

Es un plato muy popular que se sirve para empezar: consiste en arroz cocido con chícharos, pedacitos de zanahoria y puré de tomate que le dan un color rojizo.

el maíz	maize, corn
el trigo	wheat
enrollar	to roll
el guisado	stew
frito	fried
la salsa picante	spicy sauce
el cacahuate	peanut
caldo de pollo	chicken broth
espeso	thick
el guajolote	turkey
el arroz	rice
la zanahoria	carrot
los chícharos	peas

ACTIVITY 18

1 ¿Qué tiene el mole?
2 ¿Cómo se hace el mole?
3 ¿Qué se puede hacer con pollo y chocolate?
4 ¿Qué se puede comer frito?
5 ¿Qué tiene el arroz a la mexicana?

ACTIVITY 19

How do you make burgers and French fries? Use the following vocabulary to help you.

se calienta(n)	se corta(n)	se sirve(n)	las papas
la salsa	se fríe(n)	la hamburguesa	

ACTIVITY 20

Choose another simple recipe and write down the instructions in Spanish. Use your dictionary to find any words you don't know.

7.5 Un extraño en la ciudad

🔊 LA CENA
DINNER

Jorge y María están en el restaurante. Pero María está muy nerviosa. ¿Qué le pasa?

estás comiendo	you are eating
nervioso	nervous
tener hambre	to be hungry
de verdad	really
pedir	to ask for
¿qué te pasa?	what's the matter (with you)? [*informal*]
entender (entiendo)	to understand
realmente	really
el / la turista	tourist
decir	to say
no entiendo nada	I don't understand at all
complicado	complicated
quizás	perhaps
hasta mañana	see you tomorrow [*literally* until tomorrow]
explicar	to explain

ACTIVITY 21

¿Verdadero o falso?

1 María no termina el pollo porque está quemado.   V / F
2 María quiere helado de postre.   V / F
3 María no quiere pedir la cuenta.   V / F
4 María quiere más información de Jorge.   V / F
5 Jorge no puede decir la verdad.   V / F
6 Salen del restaurante juntos.   V / F

ACTIVITY 22

The following lines are taken from the dialogue, but they are in the wrong order. Rearrange them so that they make sense.

a No, de verdad, no quiero nada más. ¿Pedimos la cuenta?
b ¿Quieres café?
c ¿Qué tienes?
d ¿No te acabas el pollo?
e No importa. ¿Quieres postre?
f No. Lo siento. No tengo mucha hambre. No puedo acabármelo.

g Sí, de la Cafetería Coyoacán.
h No, gracias.
i ¿Quién es usted? Lo conozco, ¿verdad?
j Eres muy importante para mí.

ACTIVITY 23

Complete this account of the story by filling the gaps with the appropriate form of the verb from the list below. Use the present tense. Some verbs may be used more than once.

querer / tener / comer / entender / irse / conocer / estar / poder

Jorge y María (1) _____ en el restaurante. María no (2) _____ porque no (3) _____ hambre. No (4) _____ postre ni café. (5) _____ pedir la cuenta. María no (6) _____ problemas en el trabajo. El problema es Jorge. María (7) _____ a Jorge. Jorge dice que conoce a María pero no (8) _____ decirle nada. María no (9) _____ y (10) _____ del restaurante.

STORY TRANSCRIPT

Jorge	María. No estás comiendo. ¿No te acabas el pollo? Está muy bueno.
María	No. Lo siento. No tengo mucha hambre. No puedo acabármelo.
Jorge	No importa. ¿Quieres postre? ¿Quieres helado?
María	No, gracias.
Jorge	¿Quieres un café?
María	No, de verdad, no quiero nada más. ¿Pedimos la cuenta?
Jorge	Estás muy nerviosa, ¿verdad? ¿Qué te pasa?
María	Nada. No tengo mucha hambre.
Jorge	¿Tienes problemas en el trabajo?
María	No. Trabajo mucho, pero no tengo problemas. El problema es usted.
Jorge	No entiendo. ¿Qué pasa?
María	¿Quién es usted? Lo conozco, ¿verdad?
Jorge	Sí, de la Cafetería Coyoacán.
María	No, no. De antes.
Jorge	Mira. Me llamo Jorge Jimeno. Soy gerente de ventas y vivo en Chihuahua.
María	Sí, pero ¿quién es usted realmente?
Jorge	Soy turista en la ciudad, nada más.
María	¿Por qué está aquí? ¿Por qué no me dice la verdad? ¿Por qué?
Jorge	María, yo te conozco, sí. Eres muy importante para mí. Pero ahora no puedo decirte nada más. Lo siento.
María	No entiendo nada. Ya me voy. ¡Adiós!
Jorge	Por favor, ¡María! La situación es muy complicada. Ahora no puedo decirte quién soy. Mañana quizás.
María	No entiendo nada. ¡Adiós!
Jorge	Bueno. Hasta mañana.

Test

Now it's time to test your progress in Unit 7.

1 Give the Spanish for:

1 the appetizer
2 two appetizer dishes
3 the entrée
4 two entrée dishes

5 dessert
6 two dessert dishes
7 the check

`10`

2 Complete the questions about food on the menu.

1 ¿___ ___ en el menú?
2 ¿___ ___ el pescado?
3 ¿___ ___ la sopa?

`3`

3 Complete this dialogue using the words below.

estoy quiero beber luego para
hay nada empezar vas bueno

A: ¿Qué _____ a tomar para empezar?
B: Para _____ quiero la sopa.
A: Yo _____ la ensalada
B: ¿Y _____?
A: El pollo, por favor.
B: _____ mí, el pescado. ¿Y para _____?
A: Agua mineral.
A: ¿Qué _____ de postre?
B: El helado es _____. ¿Y para usted?
A: No quiero _____. _____ satisfecho.

`10`

4 Using **faltar**, tell the waiter what's missing.

Example: no plate – Falta un plato.

1 no knife.
2 no spoon.
3 no glass.
4 no glasses.
5 no plates at all.
6 no fork.

`6`

5 Read the dialogues and complete your part. (Score 2 points for a correct answer, 1 point if you make one mistake.)

1 You: (Call the waitress. Ask her to bring the soup.)
   Mesera: Sí, sí, lo siento. Ahorita la traigo.
2 You: (Tell the waitress that your chicken is cold.)
   Mesera: Lo siento.
   You: (Ask her to change it.)
   Mesera: Sí, en seguida.
3 You: (Ask the waitress to bring the check.)
   Mesera: Ahorita la traigo.
   You: (Tell her the check is wrong.)

9

6 Choose between **ser** and **estar** to complete the following sentences.

1 El restaurante (**es/está**) muy bueno.
2 La casa (**es/está**) grande.
3 El vino blanco no (**es/está**) frío.
4 La cuenta (**es/está**) equivocada.

4

7 Complete the following sentences, choosing the appropriate verb from list A and the appropriate direct object pronoun from list B:

A cambiar / calentar / traer / limpiar / mirar
B lo / la / los / las

1 El pollo está quemado. ¿Podría _____, por favor?
2 La sopa está fría. ¿Podría _____ ,por favor?
3 Las copas están sucias. ¿Podría _____, por favor?
4 La mesa está sucia. ¿Podría _____, por favor?
5 Faltan dos cafés. ¿Podría _____, por favor?
6 Falta un plato. ¿Podría _____, por favor?
7 La cuenta está mal. ¿Podría _____, por favor?
8 Quiero la carne con papas, no con ensalada. ¿Podría _____, por favor?

16

TOTAL SCORE **58**

If you scored less than 48, look at the Language Building sections again before completing the Summary on page 102.

Now try this final test, summarizing the main points covered in this unit.

How would you:
1 say you want salad to start?
2 complain that the fish is burnt and ask the waiter to change it?
3 say there are two knives missing?
4 and ask the waiter to bring them?
5 say the restaurant is bad?
6 ask for the check?

REVIEW

If you're eating out, see if you can translate the dishes into Spanish. How would you order in Spanish? Use constructions you have learned in this unit: **para mí, para empezar, para beber**, etc. Think about the other questions you would use when eating out in Mexico: **¿cómo es el pollo? ¿qué tiene la sopa? ¿qué es el cocido?** Can you answer the questions yourself?

Go through the verbs in this unit. Practice the impersonal form when you talk about something: **se toma, se hierve, se sirve**, etc. Look at the irregular and radical-changing verbs, for example **traer, poder**, and practice them in any spare moment you have. Then make up sentences using them.

Finally, practice the difference between **estar** and **ser** by noting different situations as you go through the day. Think about how you would describe things, such as a store – **es bonito** ('it's nice') and **está abierta** ('it's open') – or a street – **la calle es ancha** ('the street is wide') and **está sucia** ('it's dirty'), and so on.

Review 2

VOCABULARY

1 Give the appropriate adjective of nationality.

1 una mujer de Francia
2 un muchacho de los Estados Unidos
3 dos muchachas de Escocia
4 dos hombres de México
5 un señor de Canadá

2 Match the jobs and translate the English sentences, making sure you give the correct form [masc., fem., sing., or pl.].

1 José is a journalist.
2 María is a teacher.
3 Señora Gil is an accountant.
4 Gustavo and Javier are engineers.
5 Alicia and Celia are receptionists.
6 Alfonso is a secretary.

a secretario
b contador
c periodista
d recepcionista
e profesor
f ingeniero

3

Sr. Suárez — Sra. Suárez
Juan   Josefina

Le presento a la familia Suárez. El Sr. Suárez es el
_____ de Juan y Josefina y el _____ de la señora
Suárez. La señora Suárez es la _____ de Juan y
Josefina. Josefina es la _____ de Juan y Juan es el
_____ de Josefina.

4 Unscramble the words to identify these rooms in a house.

R O R D E I C B I   A N C C O I   R A M C A E R A
A L A S   R O M E C D O

5 Complete this description using the following verbs

me acuesto me baño   ceno   regreso a termino
llego a   salgo de   desayuno descanso me levanto

_____ a las siete de la mañana. _____ y _____ cereales a las
siete y media. _____ casa a las ocho y _____ mi trabajo a las
ocho y media de la mañana. _____ mi trabajo a las seis de la
tarde y _____ mi casa. _____ a las nueve de la noche, _____
después de cenar. _____ a las once de la noche.

6 Insert the correct word: **éste, ésta, éstos, éstas**.

   1 _____ es mi esposo.
   2 _____ son mis hijos.
   3 _____ es mi mamá.
   4 _____ es mi hermano.
   5 _____ son las muchachas.

7 Write down the correct form of the verb.

   1 Nosotros (**trabajar**) en una empresa juntos.
   2 Mi hermano (**vivir**) en Guadalajara.
   3 Mis padres (**comer**) en un restaurante los viernes.
   4 Yo (**viajar**) de la Ciudad de México a Cuernavaca los sábados.
   5 ¿Tú (**escribir**) a tus padres?
   6 Yo (**querer**) sopa para empezar.
   7 ¿Cuántos años (**tener**) tú?

8 Translate into Spanish.

   1 We get up at seven o'clock.
   2 He goes to bed at eleven.
   3 She gets dressed at eight.
   4 Do you [*sing.*] shower at seven?

9 Choose an appropriate verb in the correct form for each of the following sentences.

   1 La mesa está sucia. ¿Podría _____ la, por favor?
   2 La carne está fría. ¿Podría _____ la, por favor?
   3 Falta el cuchillo. ¿Podría _____ lo, por favor?
   4 Faltan los vasos. ¿Podría _____ los, por favor?

10 These things are dirty. Ask questions choosing the correct direct object pronoun: **¿Podría limpiarlo/la/los/las?**

   1 la mesa   3 los platos
   2 el coche   4 las cucharas

11 **estar** or **ser**? Choose the appropriate verb and write it down in the correct form.

   1 La mesa (**ser/estar**) grande.
   2 El café (**ser/estar**) bueno.
   3 El hospital (**ser/estar**) malo.
   4 La comida (**ser/estar**) fría.
   5 El pollo (**ser/estar**) pequeño.

12 You'll hear some messages from three people inviting you to go out. For each message write down the correct time and information mentioned.

Time: 1.30 / 5.00 / 7.00 / 7.45 / 8.00 /9.30 / 10.00 / 12.00

Information: have a drink before / have dinner before / have dinner after

	Message 1	Message 2	Message 3
Time			
Information			

13 Listen to the conversation in the restaurant and decide: **¿verdadero o falso?**

1 The man chooses a salad.   V / F
2 The chicken comes with potatoes and salad.   V / F
3 The woman wants salad with her chicken.   V / F
4 They both want beer.   V / F
5 The spoon is dirty.   V / F
6 The woman's chicken comes with potatoes.   V / F
7 She eats it anyway.   V / F

14 María is asking you about your family. Prepare your side of the conversation first, then listen to her questions on the recording and answer in the pauses.

María: ¿Usted tiene familia?
You: (Say you have two boys and a girl.)
María: ¿Cuántos años tienen?
You: (Say the girl is twelve and the boys are eight and six.)
María: ¿En qué trabaja?
You: (Tell her you're an engineer.)
María: Usted no es mexicano, ¿verdad?
You: (Tell her you're English and ask her where she's from.)
María: Soy mexicana.
You: (Tell her you have an uncle in Mexico. He lives in Guadalajara.)
María: ¡Qué interesante!

15 Practice saying the following in Spanish. You may prefer to write your answers down before checking them against the recording.

In the restaurant order soup to start, then chicken. Ask for a pineapple juice to drink.
Order an ice cream, say you don't have a spoon, and ask the waiter to bring you one.
Order a coffee. The waiter brings you tea. Tell him, say you want coffee and ask him to change it.
Ask for the check.
Complain that the check is wrong.

Getting around
El transporte público

OBJECTIVES

In this unit you'll learn how to:

- ✓ ask about train and bus times
- ✓ buy a ticket
- ✓ reserve tickets
- ✓ talk about different modes of transport

And cover the following grammar and language:

- ✓ the prepositions **a** and **para** to describe going to and being in or at a place
- ✓ the prepositions **a** and **de** to express distance
- ✓ the prepositions **en** and **a** used with modes of transport
- ✓ verbs followed by the infinitive (**poder**, **querer**, **necesitar**, **desear**)
- ✓ **hay que** + infinitive and **tener que** + infinitive to express obligation
- ✓ possessive pronouns **el mío, el tuyo, el suyo, el nuestro**

LEARNING SPANISH 8

Check the television program listings for Spanish-language films. They are usually shown in the original version and carry subtitles. You'll find that you'll pick up a lot of vocabulary by making use of the subtitles, especially for words and expressions that occur regularly. If you have satellite television, try watching other programs in Spanish. Don't worry about trying to understand everything, but get used to hearing everyday Spanish spoken at normal speed.

Now start the recording for Unit 8.

The next bus for Guadalajara

El próximo autobús para Guadalajara

🔘 **ACTIVITY 1** is on the recording.

ACTIVITY 2

1	The bus is on time.	V/F
2	Josefina wants a roundtrip ticket.	V/F
3	Josefina smokes.	V/F
4	The bus leaves from platform 3.	V/F

DIALOGUE 1

○ Por favor, ¿a qué hora sale el próximo autobús para Guadalajara?

■ Hay uno dentro de una hora, a las tres. Está retrasado.

○ Está bien. Un boleto, por favor.

■ ¿De ida y vuelta?

○ Sí. Quiero regresar el miércoles.

■ ¿Fumadores o no fumadores?

○ No fumadores, por favor. ¿A qué hora llega a Guadalajara?

■ A las seis. Son trescientos pesos.

○ Aquí tiene. ¿De qué andén sale?

■ Del andén dos.

VOCABULARY	
el autobús	bus
próximo	next
dentro de	within, inside
estar retrasado	to be delayed
el boleto	ticket [*for travel*]
(el boleto) de ida	one-way (ticket)
(el boleto) de ida y vuelta	roundtrip (ticket)
reservar	to reserve
fumadores/no fumadores	smoking/non-smoking
aquí tiene	here you are [*formal*]
el andén	bay [*at a bus station*]
¿de qué andén sale?	which bay does it leave from?

✓ *a* ('to, in, at') and *para* ('for')

The preposition **a** is used for *going* to a place, or *arriving in* or *at* a place:

Vamos **a** Guadalajara. We're going to Guadalajara.
¿A qué hora llegamos **a** Cuernavaca? What time do we arrive in Cuernavaca?
El autobús llega **a** la estación. The bus arrives at the station.

However, in the following situations **para** is used:

¿A qué hora sale el autobús **para** Acapulco? What time does the Acapulco train [*literally* the train for Acapulco] leave?
Un boleto **para** Guadalajara, por favor. A ticket to/for Guadalajara, please.

✓ *estar retrasado*

To talk about delays, the construction **estar retrasado** is used:

¿Está retrasado? Is it late?

El autobús **está retrasado** veinte minutos. The bus is 20 minutes late.

✓ Verbs followed by the infinitive

When **poder** ('to be able') and **querer** ('to want') are followed by another verb, that verb is in the infinitive:

¿Puedo comprar un boleto? Can I buy a ticket?
¿Quiere reservar el regreso? Do you want to reserve the return journey?

necesitar ('to need to') and **desear** ('to wish') are also followed by the infinitive in this construction:

Necesito cambiar el boleto. I need to change the ticket.
¿Desea cambiar la habitación? Do you wish to change the room?

The constructions **hay que** + infinitive and **tener que** + infinitive are covered in this unit on pages 111 and 113.

ACTIVITY 3

Complete the following sentences using **a** or **para**.

1 ¿____ qué hora llega el autobús?
2 Ahora llegamos ____ la Ciudad de México.
3 Quiero un boleto ____ Cuernavaca, por favor.
4 El autobús llega ____ las tres.

(🎧) Now do activities 4 and 5 on the recording.

Shall we go by car or by bus?
¿Vamos en carro o en autobús?

🔊 **ACTIVITY 6** is on the recording.

ACTIVITY 7

	Advantages	Disadvantages
Car		
Bus		

DIALOGUE 2

○ ¿Vamos a la Ciudad de México en carro o en autobús?
■ El carro es más rápido.
○ Pero no quiero manejar.
■ Yo puedo manejar, si quieres.
○ ¿A cuántos kilómetros está la Ciudad de México?
■ A seiscientos. Está muy lejos. ¿Cuánto tardamos en el carro?
○ Siete horas. Hay que comer en la cafetería de la autopista.
■ En el autobús podemos leer, descansar, es más cómodo.
○ Pero el carro es más rápido y más barato.
■ Pero no podemos llevar mucho equipaje si vamos en el autobús.
○ Es verdad. Podemos dejar las cosas dentro del carro.

VOCABULARY

rápido	fast
tardar	to take (time)
¿cuánto tarda?	how long does it take?
hay que ...	it's necessary to ...
la autopista	freeway
leer	to read
cómodo	comfortable
llevar	to take, carry
el equipaje	luggage
dejar	to leave (something)

✓ Prepositions *a* and *de* to express distance

The preposition **a** is used in questions or statements about how far away something is, either in distance or time:

> ¿**A** cuántos kilómetros está la Ciudad de México? How far away is Mexico City?
> Está **a** cien kilómetros. It's 100 kilometers away.
> El museo está **a** diez minutos. The museum is 10 minutes away.

To say how far one place is from another, **de** is used:

> Guadalajara está a seiscientos kilómetros **de** la Ciudad de México. Guadalajara is 600 km from Mexico City.

✓ *¿cuánto tardas?*

The verb **tardar** is used to say how long something takes. Unlike English, which uses an impersonal construction ('it takes …'), the form of **tardar** used is determined by the person(s):

> **Tardo / Tardan** media hora. It takes (me / them) half an hour.

✓ *hay que* + infinitive

hay que is an impersonal construction used to express an obligation. It is always followed by an infinitive:

> **Hay que** preparar el carro. We have to prepare the car.
> **Hay que** descansar en la autopista. It's necessary to have a break on the freeway.

✓ Prepositions *en* and *a* with modes of transport

en is used for most modes of transport, with one exception:

> Voy a mi trabajo **en carro/en tren/en motocicleta**. I go to work by car /by train/by motorbike.
> Mi hermano va al instituto **a pie**. My brother goes to school on foot.

ACTIVITY 8

Translate the following sentences into Spanish.

1 How far away is Mexico City?
2 It takes half an hour by bus.
3 It takes me 15 minutes to get to work.
4 It's 300 km to Guadalajara.

(🎧) Now do activities 9 and 10 on the recording.

🎧 **ACTIVITY 11** is on the recording.

ACTIVITY 12

¿Carmen o Juan?

1	Le toma más tiempo ir a su trabajo.	C/J
2	No tiene que cambiar.	C/J
3	Trabaja cerca de su casa.	C/J
4	No puede ir en carro.	C/J
5	A veces tarda diez minutos en llegar a su trabajo.	C/J

DIALOGUE 3

○ Trabajas en la Ciudad de México, ¿verdad? ¿Cómo vas a tu trabajo?

■ Voy en camión y en metro.

○ ¿Cuánto tardas?

■ Tardo dos horas más o menos. Tengo que cambiar de línea en el metro. ¿Cómo vas tú?

○ Voy a pie o en el autobús o en el carro de mi vecino. Trabajamos juntos.

■ ¿Y cuánto tardas en llegar?

○ Si voy a pie tardo veinte minutos. En el carro tardo diez o quince minutos. ¿Por qué no vas en carro?

■ Porque no hay lugar para estacionarse.

○ Mi trabajo sólo está a dos kilómetros de mi casa.

■ El mío está a quince kilómetros por lo menos.

VOCABULARY

el metro	subway
tener que	to have to
la línea	line
el vecino/la vecina	neighbor
en llegar	to get there
¿por qué no (vas) ... ?	why don't you (go) ... ?
	[*used as a suggestion*]
el lugar	(parking) space
estacionarse	to park
sólo	only
el mío	mine
por lo menos	at least

✓ *tener que* + infinitive

tener que followed by the infinitive is used to express a personal obligation, often in excuses for not being able to do something:

No puedo. **Tengo que ir** a Querétaro. I can't. I have to go to Querétaro.

Tengo que llevar el carro al garaje. I have to take the car to the repair shop.

Note the contrast between **tener que**, indicating something that *you personally have to do*, and **hay que**, indicating *an external obligation*:

Tengo que hacer la tarea. I have to do my homework.

Hay que descansar en la autopista. It's necessary to have a break on the freeway.

✓ Possessive pronouns

Possessive pronouns ('mine', 'yours', etc.) always agree in gender and in number with the nouns they refer to:

Mi trabajo está cerca de mi casa. My work is near my house.

El mío está lejos de mi casa. Mine is a long way from my house.

	sing.		pl.	
	masc.	fem.	masc.	fem.
mine	**el mío**	**la mía**	**los míos**	**las mías**
yours [*informal*]	**el tuyo**	**la tuya**	**los tuyos**	**las tuyas**
his/hers /yours [*formal*]	**el suyo**	**la suya**	**los suyos**	**las suyas**
ours	**el nuestro**	**la nuestra**	**los nuestros**	**las nuestras**
theirs/yours	**el suyo**	**la suya**	**los suyos**	**las suyas**

ACTIVITY 13

Complete the sentences by inserting the correct form of **tener que** + an appropriate verb from the following list:
ir, visitar, comer, hacer.

1 A: ¿Dónde están tus hermanos?
  B: _____ _____ _____ la tarea.
2 A: ¿Por qué te vas?
  B: _____ _____ _____ a mi abuelita.
3 A: ¿Podemos ir a un restaurante?
  B: No. _____ _____ _____ en casa.
4 A: ¿_____ _____ ___?
  B: Sí, tenemos que ir ahora.

🔊 Now do activities 14 and 15 on the recording.

8.4 Traveling in Mexico City
Viajar en la Ciudad de México

ACTIVITY 16

The text below describes the ways of traveling around the huge expanse of Mexico City. Read through the passage and answer the following questions, using the context to guess the meanings of the words you don't know before checking with the list of vocabulary. Write your answers in Spanish if you can.

1 There are four names for different kinds of buses. What are they?
2 When was the Metro system constructed?
3 Approximately how many people travel on the Metro system every day?
4 Write down two more pieces of information about the Metro system.
5 If you buy an **abono**, what does it entitle you to do?
6 Why are there two cards?
7 What do you do if the metro does not take you all the way to your destination?

Los ciudadanos de la Ciudad de México tienen la posibilidad de usar muchos medios de transporte para viajar por la ciudad. Pueden ir en un pesero o un camión (también se llaman micros o colectivos) o pueden viajar en un taxi.

También, desde los años 1960, tienen el metro. El metro de la capital de México tiene nueve líneas. Los trenes llegan con mucha frecuencia, es rápido, y los boletos son muy baratos. Lleva cinco millones de personas cada día.

La gente que viaja con frecuencia en camión o en metro puede comprar un abono de ahorro de transporte. Estos abonos consisten en dos tarjetas, una azul para el metro y una morada para los camiones. Con estos abonos, los habitantes de México D.F. pueden utilizar el transporte sin límite durante quince días. Están en venta al principio de cada mes y durante los quince días siguientes. Al final de las líneas del metro hay trenes ligeros que conectan con las otras lineas y que llevan a la gente a los barrios.

andar	travel
la línea	line
con frecuencia	frequently
el pesero	*name for city bus*
el camión	*name for city bus*
el micro	*name for city bus*
el colectivo	*name for city bus*
un abono de ahorro	a 'saver' season ticket
morado	purple
en venta	for sale
quince días	two weeks
ligero	light

ACTIVITY 17

Choose **hay que** + infinitive or the correct form of **poder** to complete the following sentences.

1 Si quieres llegar antes _____ tomar el metro.
2 Si vas en metro y en camión cada día _____ comprar un abono.
3 Si quieres un abono _____ comprarlo al principio del mes o durante los quince días siguientes.
4 Si vives más lejos del final de la línea del metro _____ tomar un tren ligero.
5 Si compras un abono y tomas el metro _____ utilizar la tarjeta azul.
6 Si no quieres ir en el camión _____ tomar un taxi.

Un extraño en la ciudad

TENGO MUCHA PRISA
I'M REALLY IN A HURRY

María explica al Sr. Herrera que va a visitar a su madre porque quiere hablar con ella.

preocupado (por algo)	worried (about something)
tener prisa	to be in a hurry
siempre	always
enfermo	ill, sick
ya	now
mayor	old (person)
difícil	difficult
¿tardas ...?	does it take you ...?
el tren	train
urgentemente	urgently
irse	to go, leave
el viaje	trip
un secreto	a secret
no diga nada	don't say anything

ACTIVITY 18

These questions are taken from the story. Listen again and write down the replies.

1 Tu madre vive sola, ¿verdad? _____.
2 ¿Vas en tren? _____.
3 ¿Tardas mucho en llegar? _____.
4 ¿Vas por mucho tiempo? _____.
5 ¿Tienes un problema, María? _____.

ACTIVITY 19

¿Quién …

1 está preocupado/a?
2 tiene prisa?
3 no está bien?
4 vive solo/a?
5 vive cerca de Cuernavaca?
6 va en tren?
7 viene a la cafetería?
8 sale de la cafetería?

ACTIVITY 20

¿Verdadero o falso?

1 María looks worried.	V / F
2 It takes a long time to get to the village.	V / F
3 There is a bus service to the village.	V / F
4 Her boss has given her time off.	V / F
5 She doesn't want Sr. Jimeno to know about her journey.	V / F

STORY TRANSCRIPT

Sr. Herrera ¡Hola, María! ¿Qué te pasa? ¿Estás preocupada por algo?

María Sí, tengo que visitar a mi mamá y no tengo mucho tiempo. Tengo mucha prisa.

Sr. Herrera ¿Tu mamá no está bien?

María Bueno … está siempre un poco enferma. Y ya es muy mayor. Pero tengo que hablar con ella. Es muy importante.

Sr. Herrera Tu mamá vive sola, ¿verdad?

María Sí, vive sola en un pueblo cerca de Cuernavaca.

Sr. Herrera No está muy lejos de aquí.

María No está muy lejos … a ciento cincuenta kilómetros más o menos, pero es difícil llegar.

Sr. Herrera ¿Vas en tren?

María Voy en tren hasta Cuautla; luego hay un autobús a un pueblo que está cerca. Tengo que ir en carro desde ese pueblo. No hay servicio de autobús.

Sr. Herrera ¿Te tardas mucho en llegar?

María Sí, bastante.

Sr. Herrera ¿Vas por mucho tiempo?

María Voy desde el viernes hasta el lunes. Tengo que pedir dos días de vacaciones a mi jefe y tengo mucho trabajo.

Sr. Herrera ¿Tienes un problema, María?

María Sí, señor. Tengo un problema. Tengo que hablar urgentemente con mi mamá.

Sr. Herrera ¡Ah! Mira quién viene. El señor Jimeno.

María Bueno … me voy. No puedo hablar con él ahora. Tengo que irme. Adiós, Señor Herrera. Hasta el lunes. Mi viaje es un secreto.
No diga nada.

Test

Now it's time to test your progress in Unit 8.

1 Give the Spanish for these questions.

    1 What time is the next bus to Mexico City?
    2 Can I buy a roundtrip ticket?
    3 What time does it arrive?
    4 Is it delayed?
    5 Which bay does it leave from?

10

2 Complete the following by inserting the appropriate word in each of the gaps.

andén / equipaje / cómodo / ida y vuelta / próximo / dentro / retrasado / rápido / comprar

El _____ autobús para la Ciudad de México sale del _____ dos _____ de diez minutos. Está _____ cinco minutos. ¿Usted quiere _____ un boleto de _____? Es un viaje muy _____ y el autobús es muy _____. ¿Tiene mucho _____?

10

3 Look at the grid below and write five sentences giving the distance between each city. (Score 2 points for a correct answer, 1 point if you make one mistake.)

Córdoba to Acapulco	709 km
Guadalajara to Acapulco	907 km
Córdoba to Cuernavaca	384 km
Guadalajara to Aguas Calientes	251 km
Acapulco to Mérida	1853 km

    1 Córdoba _____ Acapulco.
    2 Guadalajara _____ Acapulco.
    3 Córdoba _____ Cuernavaca.
    4 Guadalajara _____ Aguas Calientes.
    5 Acapulco _____ Mérida.

10

4 **¿Cómo vas a tu trabajo?** Reply in Spanish.

1 You go by motorbike. Sometimes you walk.
2 You go by train and then by bus.
3 You go by car but sometimes you go on foot.
4 You go by subway and bus.
5 You go on foot to the bus stop and then by bus.

10

5 Make excuses to decline your friend's suggestions using **tener que**. (Score 2 points for a correct answer, 1 point if you make one mistake.)

A: ¿Quieres ir al cine esta tarde?
You: (You can't because you have to work at home.)
A: ¿Quieres ir mañana?
You: (You can't. You have to visit your mother.)
A: ¿Vamos a la alberca?
You: (You can't. You have to take the car to the repair shop.)
A: ¿Quieres venir a mi casa el sábado?
You: (You are sorry, but you have to clean the house.)
A: Voy a la playa dentro de una semana. ¿Por qué no vienes conmigo?
You: (You can't. You have to go to work.)

10

6 Replace the underlined possessive adjective and noun with the correct possessive pronoun in the following sentences.

1 <u>Mis hijos</u> son mayores.
2 <u>Nuestro carro</u> es nuevo.
3 <u>Los libros de mi esposo</u> son muy interesantes.
4 <u>Mis clases</u> son buenas. ¿Cómo son <u>tus clases</u>?
5 ¿Estos platos son <u>de ustedes</u>?
6 <u>La casa de Alfonso</u> es muy bonita.
7 <u>Tus hermanos</u> son pequeños.
8 <u>Nuestro departamento</u> en la playa es muy bonito.
9 <u>Tus abuelos</u> son buenos.
10 <u>Tu carro</u> es nuevo.

10

TOTAL SCORE **60**

If you scored less than 50, look at the Language Building sections again before completing the Summary on page 120.

Summary 8

 Now try this final test, summarizing the main points covered in this unit.

How would you:
1 ask what time the next bus to Querétaro leaves?
2 say you want to come back on Friday?
3 ask 'What time do we arrive in Guadalajara?'
4 say you have to work?
5 ask how far Guadalajara is from Mexico City?
6 say it takes you half an hour to get to work by bus?

REVIEW

Learn the different modes of transport and practice saying them with the appropriate preposition. Remember that **en** is used except when you go on foot: **a pie**. Also practice talking about distances: first asking how far something is: **¿a cuántos kilómetros está …?**, and then replying using distances that you know, for example, how far your town is from another: **está a cincuenta kilómetros de …** or how far the bus stop is: **está a diez minutos de aquí**, and so on.

Every day, run through the things you have to do and practice saying what they are in Spanish using **tengo que**; for example **tengo que trabajar**, **tengo que comprar comida**, **tengo que llamar a mis papás**, and so on.

Practice saying what you can do when you have free time, using **poder** followed by the infinitive: **puedo leer el periódico hoy, puedo cenar en un restaurante**.

Finally, practice using the possessive pronouns from this unit: **el mío, la mía, los míos, las mías**, etc. Refer to your friends' or family's possessions as well so that you practice other possessive pronouns apart from 'mine'.

People
Gente

OBJECTIVES

In this unit you'll learn how to:

- ✓ describe people physically
- ✓ describe people's personalities
- ✓ describe clothes and gifts

And cover the following grammar and language:

- ✓ the verb **ser** with adjectives of physical description
- ✓ the verb **ser** with adjectives of personality
- ✓ comparatives
- ✓ demonstrative pronouns and adjectives

LEARNING SPANISH 9

Although speaking and understanding spoken Spanish is important, don't underestimate the value of writing in Spanish. The activities in this book provide plenty of written practice, but you may also find it helpful to write your own sentences, even keep a simple diary, using the Spanish you already know.

Writing is a useful consolidation exercise, since you can take your time to consider what you want to say. Start off simply, concentrating on verb endings and choosing appropriate vocabulary. Think about gender and number agreement. Use your dictionary to look up any words you don't know. As you learn more vocabulary and grammar your writing will become more fluent.

🎧 Now start the recording for Unit 9.

Sus hijos son muy guapos

🔊 **ACTIVITY 1** is on the recording.

ACTIVITY 2

	tall	short	slim	plump	dark	fair
Carmen						
Claudia						
José						
Pablo						
Patricia						

DIALOGUE 1

○ Sus hijos son muy guapos. Patricia es como usted.

■ Ésa es Claudia. Patricia lleva un suéter.

○ Ah sí. Perdón.

■ Sí, y Pablo es como su papá.

○ Es muy alto. Y los tres tienen el pelo negro, Patricia, Pablo y Claudia.

■ Sí, es verdad. Todos tenemos el pelo negro. ¿Y sus hijos?

○ José, el pequeño, tiene el pelo oscuro, es bajito y un poco gordo.

■ Sí, y Carmen es alta, delgada y muy rubia. ¡Muy diferentes!

○ Carmen es como mi esposa. Es rubia y alta también. Son muy parecidas.

VOCABULARY

guapo	beautiful, pretty, handsome
como	like, similar to
llevar	to wear
alto	tall
el pelo	hair
oscuro	dark
bajito	short [*stature*]
gordito	fat, plump
delgado	thin, slim
rubio	blond
diferente	different
parecido	similar

✓ *ser* and *estar* in physical descriptions

The verb **ser** is used to describe permanent physical characteristics:

José es **bajito**. Patricia **es alta**. José is short. Patricia is tall.
Pepe **es de estatura mediana**. Pepe is (of) average height.

estar is only used if a characteristic is temporary: for example, if a man has put weight on since you last saw him, you might say: **estás gordito.**

✓ Adjective agreement

Remember that the adjectives agree in number and gender with the person or people being described. Note the use of **ser** and **estar** in the examples:

Juan y Pablo son guapos. Juan and Pablo are handsome.
Carmen es rubia. Carmen is blond.
Somos altos. We are tall.
Estoy delgada. I'm slim [*at the moment*].
Estás muy gorda. You've put on weight [*you're plump at the moment*].
Gustavo tiene los ojos azules. Gustavo has blue eyes.

ACTIVITY 3

Complete the sentences below, by supplying the appropriate opposite. Make sure you make the adjective agree.

Example: María es **bajita**, pero su hermano es **alto**.

1 Raúl es alto, pero su hermana es _____.
2 Regina es delgada, pero su papá es _____.
3 Mis papás son altos, pero los tuyos son _____.
4 Ustedes son muy bajitos. Nosotras somos muy _____.
5 El hermano de Alfonso es gordito, pero su hermana es _____.

Now choose the correct form of the verb **ser**.

6 Beatriz y su hermana _____ muy bajitas.
7 Javier _____ alto.
8 Mi padre y yo _____ altos.
9 Yo _____ delgado, pero mi hermana _____ gordita.

Now do activities 4 and 5 on the recording.

🔊 **ACTIVITY 6** is on the recording.

ACTIVITY 7

1 Sr. Blasco works with Juan.	V/F
2 Juan is very hardworking.	V/F
3 The job involves working alone.	V/F
4 Juan is a popular member of staff.	V/F
5 Sra. Muñoz needs a calm person for this job.	V/F

DIALOGUE 2

○ ¿Usted cree que Juan tiene la personalidad adecuada para este trabajo?

■ Bueno. Creo que sí. Trabajo con él. Es muy trabajador y muy honrado.

○ ¿Trabaja bien con sus compañeros?

■ Sí, sí, es muy simpático.

○ Pero necesitamos una persona tranquila.

■ Juan es muy tranquilo y tiene un temperamento fuerte.

○ Muy bien. Es perfecto.

■ Sí, es una persona inteligente, abierta, y sincera.

○ ¿Puede ser un buen jefe?

■ Sí, estoy seguro.

○ Bueno. Muchas gracias.

VOCABULARY

la personalidad	personality
creer (que)	to believe (that)
adecuado	suitable
trabajador	hardworking
honrado	honest
el compañero/la compañera	colleague
simpático	friendly
tranquilo	calm
el temperamento	temperament
fuerte	strong
inteligente	intelligent
abierto	open, frank
sincero	sincere
seguro	sure

✅ Expressing an opinion using *creer que*

The verb **creer** followed by **que** is used to ask for or express an opinion:

¿Usted **cree que** tiene la personalidad adecuada? Do you think he has the right personality?
Creo que Celia es floja. I think Celia is lazy.
Creo que sí. **Creo que** no. I think so. I don't think so.

✅ Agreement of adjectives ending in -e or a consonant

With the exception of nationalities (see page 49), most adjectives ending in **-e** or a consonant have the same form in the singular. In the plural, an **-s** is added to those ending in **-e**, and **-es** to those ending in a consonant.

María es **inteligente** y sus hermanas son **inteligentes**. María is intelligent and her sisters are intelligent.
Manuel es **hábil** y sus hermanos son **hábiles**. Manuel is skillful and his brothers are skillful.

There are also some adjectives which vary slightly from the regular -o pattern, e.g. **trabajador** ('hard-working'):

Juan es **trabajador** y María es **trabajadora**. Juan y Pablo son **trabajadores**. María y Josefina son **trabajadoras**.

Note that in Spanish the noun **persona** is feminine, and any adjectives used with it must be feminine:

Juan es **simpático**. Es **una persona abierta**.
Juan is friendly. He is an open person.

ACTIVITY 8

Choose three adjectives from the list below to describe the person in each sentence. Remember to make the adjectives agree. You may use the same adjective more than once.

Example: Él estudia mucho. Es **inteligente, serio, trabajador**.

nervioso / tranquilo / inteligente / generoso / serio / sincero / antipático / flojo / honrado / feliz / trabajador / simpático / abierto

1 Raúl tiene muchos amigos.
2 Alicia tiene un trabajo muy difícil.
3 Él y su mujer son felices.
4 Él tiene problemas en su trabajo.

🔊 Now do activities 9 and 10 on the recording.

Tengo que comprar …

(🎧) **ACTIVITY 11** is on the recording.

ACTIVITY 12

There are 6 mistakes. Correct them.

Hoy es el cumpleaños de la mamá de (1) Beatriz y tiene que comprarle un regalo. Beatriz recomienda (2) un vestido pero Antonio prefiere una pulsera. Beatriz necesita (3) una blusa y Antonio tiene que comprar (4) una camisa. (5) Antonio tiene una buena idea. Él va a la sección de ropa de caballeros y Beatriz busca (6) una pulsera.

DIALOGUE 3

○ Tengo que comprar un pantalón.

■ ¡Y yo un vestido para la fiesta de cumpleaños de tu mamá!

○ ¡Ah sí! ¿Qué puedo comprar para mi mamá?

■ Mira. Esta blusa blanca. Es preciosa.

○ Sí, es bonita. Pero ésta es más bonita. Mira.

■ Sí, también. ¡Ah, ésta! Es la más bonita de todas.

○ Sí. Es muy bonita. Pero creo que una pulsera es mejor.

■ Mira. Tengo una idea. Tengo que comprar un vestido. ¿Por qué no vas a la sección de ropa de caballeros, compras el pantalón y después un regalo para tu mamá?

○ Está bien. Nos vemos en la cafetería a las seis.

VOCABULARY

el pantalón/los pantalones	pants
el cumpleaños	birthday
el vestido	dress
la pulsera	bracelet
la blusa	blouse
la camisa	shirt
buscar	to look for
el regalo	gift
la fiesta	party
precioso	beautiful
éste	this one
mejor	better
la sección	department
la ropa (de caballeros)	(men's) clothing

✅ Demonstrative pronouns

There are three forms of the demonstrative pronoun: **éste** ('this one'), **ése** ('that one'), and **aquél** ('that one'). Their endings vary depending on gender and number:

sing.		pl.	
masc.	*fem.*	*masc.*	*fem.*
éste	ésta	éstos	éstas
ése	ésa	ésos	ésas
aquél	aquélla	aquéllos	aquéllas

The demonstrative pronoun is the same as the demonstrative adjective, except that the pronouns take an accent:

Quiero **este suéter**. Me gusta **éste**. I want this sweater. I like this one.
Quiero **esa camisa**. Me gusta **ésa**. I want that shirt. I like that one (just over there).
Quiero **aquellos aretes**. Me gustan **aquéllos**. I want those earrings. I like those ones (right over there, far away).

✅ Comparatives and superlatives

To form the *comparative*, **más** ('more') or **menos** ('less') is added before the adjective. To make an explicit comparison, **que** is used:

La casa es **más grande** que la mía. The house is bigger than mine.
Esta película es **menos interesante que** la otra. This movie is less interesting than the other one.
Estas pulseras son **más caras que** las otras. These bracelets are more expensive than the others.

A number of adjectives have irregular comparative forms:

bueno – mejor	good – better	**grande – mayor**	big – bigger
malo – peor	bad – worse	**pequeño – menor**	small – smaller

For the *superlative*, the appropriate definite article is added to the comparative form. **de** ('of') is used for 'in':

Estos anillos son **los más caros de** la tienda. These rings are the most expensive in the store.

ACTIVITY 13

Using the correct form of the comparative, describe a house in 4 sentences:
It's [bigger / smaller / better / worse] than this house.

Describe the house again, this time using the superlative:
It's the [biggest / smallest / best / worst] house in the street.

 Now do activities 14 and 15 on the recording.

127

At the shopping mall
En el centro comercial

CULTURE

ACTIVITY 16

Study Juan's shopping list and decide which department he has to go to for each item. You may not have seen these items in Spanish before, but you can probably guess most of them.

1 compact disc	7 anillo
2 perfume	8 video
3 raqueta de tenis	9 rollo de fotos
4 blusa	10 sobres
5 chamarra	11 disquete
6 collar	12 tenis

Write sentences to consolidate your answers, for example:

Compra un compact disc en la sección de sonido.

DIRECTORIO

Piso

6ª   CAFETERÍA, Ofertas

5ª   ELECTRÓNICA. T.V. Video, Aparatos de sonido, Computación

4ª   DEPORTES, Camping

3ª   Moda Joven ÉL Y ELLA

2ª   Moda Sport, Zapatería

1ª   LIBROS, DISCOS, Películas de video, REGALOS

Bª   ACCESORIOS: Cinturones, Bolsas, Medias, Pañuelos, Sombreros

FOTOGRAFÍA, RELOJERÍA, JOYERÍA, BISUTERÍA, PAPELERÍA, PERFUMERÍA, COSMÉTICA, TURISMO

Sº 3   ESTACIONAMIENTO

Sº 4   ESTACIONAMIENTO

ACTIVITY 17

Read the article about Mexican shopping malls and answer the following questions.

Los centros comerciales no sólo son un centro de compras sino también un centro de reunión para los mexicanos. Allí se encuentran los amigos para ver chamarras, faldas, trajes, vestidos y zapatos, y también para tomar un café en su moderna cafetería o comer en el restaurante.

Los centros comerciales ofrecen gran variedad de artículos, objetos para acampar, videos, computadoras, teléfonos, discos, libros y muchas cosas más.

Los horarios de los centros comerciales son diferentes de los horarios de las tiendas en general. La gran diferencia es que no cierran a mediodía.

---

1 Look at the following words from the article. They are similar to English words. What do they mean?

el centro / la reunión / moderno / la variedad / el artículo / el objeto / diferente / en general / la diferencia / el aire acondicionado

2 ¿Los mexicanos van a los centros comerciales sólo a comprar?

3 ¿Se puede comer en los centros comerciales?

4 En el directorio, ¿qué pisos visitas si quieres comprar las cosas mencionadas en el texto?

5 ¿Cuál es la gran diferencia entre los centros comerciales y las tiendas normales?

sino	but
la chamarra	jacket
la falda	skirt
el traje	suit
el zapato	shoe
la computadora	computer

Un extraño en la ciudad

MARÍA Y SU MAMÁ
MARÍA AND HER MOTHER

María está en casa de su mamá en el pueblo. Pregunta por la familia y por los amigos de la familia. También habla del Sr. Jimeno.

preguntar por	to ask about
regular	OK
el vecino/la vecina	neighbor
el primo/la prima	cousin
perezoso	lazy
preocupado	worried
extraño	strange
¡qué susto!	what a shock!

ACTIVITY 18

The people mentioned in the dialogue are listed below. Underneath are words used to describe each person.

1 Sort the words into physical descriptions and descriptions of personality.

2 Write down who is being described by each word. Don't forget to make the adjectives agree.

	1	delgado
	2	extraño
	3	fuerte
	4	generoso
la vecina	5	gordito
la tía Leticia	6	guapo
Julia	7	inteligente
Tomás	8	mayor
la mamá de Julia y Tomás	9	misterioso
Jorge	10	perezoso
	11	preocupado
	12	simpático
	13	trabajador

ACTIVITY 19

Who ...

1 helps María's mother?
2 goes out every night?
3 has a shock?
4 has no husband?
5 knows a man in Mexico City?
6 talks with the neigbor?
7 lives in the house on the corner?
8 studies a lot?

STORY TRANSCRIPT

María	Mamá, ¿cómo estás?
Mamá	Regular. Una vecina me ayuda mucho. Trae la leche y las compras.
María	¿La vecina?
Mamá	Sí, Rosa. ¿No la conoces?
María	No. ¿Es la vecina nueva? No está casada ¿verdad?
Mamá	No. Hablamos mucho juntas. Es muy simpática y generosa.
María	¿Dónde vive?
Mamá	En aquella casa de la esquina.
María	¡Ah sí! ¿Y cómo está la tía Leticia?
Mamá	Muy bien. Está bastante gorda y ahora más vieja. Pero es fuerte.
María	¿Y los primos, Tomás y Julia? ¿Cómo están?
Mamá	Julia está muy bien. Es muy inteligente y trabajadora. Estudia mucho y ayuda a su mamá.
María	Pero Tomás no, ¿verdad?
Mamá	No, Tomás es perezoso. Sale todas las noches con los amigos, bebe, no quiere trabajar. No sé. Su mamá está muy preocupada.
María	Tengo que ir a su casa y hablar con él. Me quiere mucho.
Mamá	Sí, es buena idea.
María	Bueno, mamá. Quiero hablarte de una cosa. Conozco a un hombre que es de Chihuahua y ahora está en la Ciudad de México. Creo que tú lo conoces.
Mamá	¿Cómo se llama?
María	No sé su nombre completo, pero se llama Jorge.
Mamá	¡Jorge! ¿Y cómo es?
María	Bueno, es bastante mayor, de tu edad, más o menos, alto, bastante guapo, delgado, tiene pelo negro.
Mamá	¿Y dice que me conoce?
María	Sí. Es un poco extraño ... es muy misterioso. Y tiene fotos ...
Mamá	Pues, no sé ... no sé. No lo conozco. Es imposible. ¡Ay!
María	Mamá, ¿qué te pasa? ¿Estás bien? ¿Quieres agua?
Mamá	Sí, hija. Estoy bien. ¡Qué susto!

Test

Now it's time to test your progress in Unit 9.

1 Give the Spanish for these sentences. (Score 3 points for a correct answer, and deduct 1 point for each mistake.)

    1 He is tall, slim, and very good-looking.
    2 She is short with blond hair.
    3 The brothers are strong, short, and a bit fat.
    4 The sisters are slim and blond.
    5 The man is older; he's tall and has black hair.

15

2 Complete the sentences using an appropriate adjective from the list below, making sure you make the adjective agree.

simpático / inteligente / nervioso / trabajador / sincero

    1 Él trabaja mucho. Es muy _____ .
    2 Son buenos amigos. Son _____ .
    3 Ella estudia en la universidad. Es muy _____ .
    4 Él dice la verdad. Es muy _____ .
    5 Hoy Juan hace los exámenes. Está muy _____ .

5

3 Your friend tells you what she thinks about another friend. You think the opposite. Complete the responses with the appropriate adjective.

Example: A: Jorge es flojo. B: No. Es trabajador.

    1 A: Gloria es tranquila.   B: No. Es _____
    2 A: Carlos es malo.   B: No. _____
    3 A: Javier no es inteligente.   B: Sí. _____
    4 A: Luis no tiene la personalidad
          adecuada.   B: Sí. _____
    5 A: Manuel es antipático.   B: No. _____

5

4 Complete the following items of clothing.

1 c _ _ _ _ _ _ _   5 v _ _ _ _ _ _
2 c _ _ _ _ _   6 f _ _ _ _
3 p _ _ _ _ _ _ _   7 z _ _ _ _ _ _
4 b _ _ _ _   8 s _ _ _ _ _

| | 8 |

5 Write a sentence in Spanish saying who each gift is for.

Example: necklace – mother: **El collar es para mi mamá**.

1 bracelet – mother   5 blouse – friend
2 necklace – sister   6 compact disk – father
3 ring – grandmother   7 video – male friend
4 book – brother   8 sweater – aunt

| | 16 |

6 You want some things from a store. Choose the appropriate demonstrative pronouns.

Example: You don't want this book. You want that one.
No quiero este libro. Quiero **ése**.

1 You don't want that skirt. You want that one a bit further away.
2 You don't want this bracelet. You want this one.
3 You don't want this dress. You want this one.
4 You don't want that sweater over there. You want that one on the other side of the store.
5 You don't want that ring over there. You want that one.
6 You don't want these earrings. You want these.

| | 6 |

7 Make comparative sentences following the example.

Example: Este anillo es bonito. **Ése es más bonito**.

1 Esta casa es grande.   4 Esta película es mala.
2 Este carro es nuevo.   5 Este programa es interesante.
3 Este libro es bueno.

| | 5 |

TOTAL SCORE | 60 |

If you scored less than 50, look at the Language Building sections again before completing the Summary on page 134.

Now try this final test, summarizing the main points covered in this unit.

How would you:
1 say he is very tall?
2 say you think Juan is sincere?
3 say you have to buy a gift for your father?
4 (looking at rings) say you don't want this one, you want that one?
5 say your house is bigger than theirs?
6 say your house is the biggest in the street?
7 say that this movie is better than the other?

REVIEW

Write a list of people you know – friends, work colleagues, other acquaintances – and write down words to describe their physical appearance and their personality.

Use every opportunity to compare things: prices in a supermarket – **más barato**, **más caro** – buildings on a street – **grande**, **más grande**, **(el/la) más bonito/a**, and so on.

When you're at home, practice demonstrative adjectives and pronouns by saying what items are next to you, a little further away, and further away still. Build your vocabulary at the same time by learning the names for everyday household objects, together with their gender.

Free time
El tiempo libre

OBJECTIVES

In this unit you'll learn how to:

- ✓ talk about your likes and dislikes
- ✓ talk about your hobbies and interests
- ✓ say what you do in your free time
- ✓ say what you did last weekend
- ✓ talk about parties and other celebrations

And cover the following grammar and language:

- ✓ the past tense of regular verbs
- ✓ the past tense of **hacer** and **ir**
- ✓ the construction **gustar** + noun for describing likes and dislikes
- ✓ the construction **gustar** + infinitive for describing what you like doing
- ✓ the preposition **a** to express frequency

LEARNING SPANISH 10

Try to get hold of any Spanish-language material such as newspapers and magazines. If you live in a big city this shouldn't be too difficult. The Internet can also be a useful resource. Begin by reading some of the shorter articles and see how much you can understand without resorting to the dictionary. Try to work out the meaning of the words you don't know. Don't worry about the meaning of every word, but concentrate on the main point of the story and only look up key words for comprehension. You will soon find that your reading speed and vocabulary acquisition increase considerably.

Now start the recording for Unit 10.

What do you do in your free time?
¿Qué haces en tu tiempo libre?

ACTIVITY 1 is on the recording.

ACTIVITY 2

Who might say the following: Pepe, Margarita, or Margarita's husband?

1 Mi esposa siempre quiere ir al teatro. Yo prefiero descansar.
2 Quiero ir al concierto, pero tengo mucho trabajo.
3 ¿No quieres ir al teatro conmigo? No quiero ir sola.
4 ¡Niños! ¿Quieren ir al cine? Vamos todos.
5 Podemos ver películas en la televisión.

DIALOGUE 1

○ ¿Le gusta la música clásica?
■ Sí, me gusta mucho.
○ Hay un concierto de Mozart esta noche. ¿Quiere ir?
■ No puedo. Tengo que preparar unos documentos para la conferencia. Es una lástima. Me gusta mucho la música.
○ A mí me gusta mucho el teatro. Pero a mi esposo no le gusta. Trabaja mucho y quiere descansar en casa.
■ ¿Le gusta el cine?
○ No, no me gusta mucho. Pero veo muchas películas en la televisión.
■ A mí me gustan las películas buenas. Pero a mis hijos les gustan las caricaturas. Vamos al cine a ver películas para niños.

VOCABULARY	
gustar	to please, to be pleasing
la música clásica	classical music
el concierto	concert
esta noche	tonight
preparar	to prepare
el documento	document
la conferencia	conference
es una lástima	it's a pity
varios	several
el teatro	theater
las caricaturas	cartoons

✅ Expressing likes and dislikes

To say that you like something, you use the verb **gustar** with an indirect object pronoun:

Me gusta el teatro. I like the theater. [*literally* The theater pleases me.]

The thing that is liked – **el teatro** – is the subject of the sentence and determines the ending of the verb **gustar**, in this case the third person singular. The pronoun refers to the person(s) doing the liking:

¿**Te gusta** el teatro? Do you like the theater?
Le gusta la tele. He/she likes television.
Les gusta el carro nuevo. They like their new car.

When you're referring to more than one thing, the verb is plural (**gustan**):

Me gustan las películas buenas. I like good movies.

To say that you don't like something, you use the simple negative form:

No me gusta el cine. I don't like the movies.
No me gustan las películas. I don't like movies.

To emphasize or qualify the negative, you can use **nada** [*literally* 'nothing'] or **mucho**:

No me gusta nada/mucho. I don't like it at all/much.

a + noun/disjunctive pronoun is used to identify or emphasize the person expressing the like or dislike. The pronoun is still included:

A mi esposo no le gusta la música clásica. My husband doesn't like classical music. [*literally* To my husband classical music is not pleasing.]
A mí me gusta el cine, pero **a mis hijos les gusta** la televisión. I like the movies, but my children like television.

The verb **encantar** ('to love') is used in the same way as **gustar**: **me encanta** el cine ('I love the movies').

ACTIVITY 3

Complete the dialogue with the correct form of **gustar**.

Juan: ¿_____ _____ el cine?
Ana: ¡Ah sí! _____ encanta el cine. A mis papás también _____ _____ el cine.
Juan: Tengo una hermana. _____ _____ el cine también.
Ana: A mis hermanos no _____ _____ el cine.
Juan: ¿A ellos _____ _____ las discotecas?
Ana: Sí mucho. A mí también.

🎧 Now do activities 4 and 5 on the recording.

(◄») **ACTIVITY 6** is on the recording.

ACTIVITY 7

Rewrite correcting the mistakes.

Bernardo went dancing until midnight and didn't get to bed until about half past one in the morning. His sister woke him up at seven to go shopping. Bernardo helped her with her shopping and then went to a bar to meet some friends. After playing soccer he went to a friend's house to study. Elena feels sorry for Bernardo. She understands that he is tired because he went out dancing and played soccer. She'll call him tomorrow.

DIALOGUE 2

○ ¿Por qué no quieres salir? ¿Estás enfermo?

■ No estoy enfermo. Estoy cansado.

○ ¿Por qué? ¿Qué hiciste anoche?

■ Fui a bailar. Bailé hasta la una de la mañana.

○ ¡Qué tarde!

■ A las ocho de la mañana mi mamá tocó a la puerta.

○ ¿Te levantaste?

■ Claro. Me levanté y fuimos al centro de compras. La ayudé con las compras y después fui a jugar futbol con mis amigos. Después del partido, fuimos a una cafetería a tomar algo y un amigo me llevó a casa. Luego me hablaste tú.

○ Bueno. Te gusta salir por la noche, ¿verdad? Te gusta bailar. Te gusta jugar futbol. Vamos a tomar algo ahora.

VOCABULARY	
anoche	last night
enfermo	ill
cansado	tired
bailar	to dance
claro	that's right, of course
ayudar	to help
jugar	to play
el futbol	soccer
el partido	game
llevar	to take, to give someone a lift

✓ The simple past of regular verbs

The simple past is used to describe a specific event in the past: **bailé anoche** ('I danced last night'). To form the past tense of regular -ar, -er, and -ir verbs, the following endings are added to the stem:

bail**é**	com**í**	sal**í**
bail**aste**	com**iste**	sal**iste**
bail**ó**	com**ió**	sal**ió**
bail**amos**	com**imos**	sal**imos**
bail**aron**	com**ieron**	sal**ieron**

-er and -ir verbs are conjugated in exactly the same way. Note that the first person plural in -ar and -ir verbs is the same in the present and simple past tense:

Cenamos en aquel restaurante. We have dinner/had dinner in that restaurant.
Salimos a la una. We leave/left at one.

✓ The past tense of *hacer* and *ir*

hacer and **ir** are irregular in the past tense:

hacer: hice, hiciste, hizo, hicimos, hicieron
ir: fui, fuiste, fue, fuimos, fueron

Note that the past tense of **ir** is exactly the same as **ser** (see page 141).

¿Qué **hiciste** (tú) anoche? What did you [*informal*] do last night?
¿Adónde **fuiste** (tú) ayer? Where did you [*informal*] go yesterday?
Fui al cine. I went to the movies.

To say you went dancing/skiing, etc., you use the past of the verb **ir** followed by the preposition **a** + infinitive:

Fuimos a bailar. We went dancing.

ACTIVITY 8

Put the verb in brackets in the simple past.

1 Anoche Juan y Ana (**cenar**) en aquel restaurante.
2 Ayer yo (**salir**) con mis amigos.
3 Nosotros (**bailar**) hasta la una.
4 Juan, ¿dónde (**ir**) anoche?
5 Mi mamá (**comprar**) un anillo para su hermana.
6 Carmen, ¿qué (**hacer**) anoche?

🎧 Now do activities 9 and 10 on the recording.

10.3 Yesterday was my birthday
Ayer fue mi cumpleaños

🎧 **ACTIVITY 11** is on the recording.

ACTIVITY 12

¿Bernardo o Elena? ¿Quién …

1 hace deporte?
2 prefiere estar en casa?
3 viajó a Estados Unidos?
4 festejó su cumpleaños ayer?
5 escucha música?
6 celebra su compleaños en julio?

DIALOGUE 3

○ Ayer fue mi cumpleaños.
■ ¿Ah sí? ¡Felicidades! ¿Qué hiciste?
○ Por la noche salí con unos amigos. ¿Cuándo es tu cumpleaños?
■ En el verano, en julio. El mes que viene. El año pasado viajé a Estados Unidos el día de mi cumpleaños.
○ ¿Adónde fuiste?
■ Fui a Miami. Nadé, comí muy bien, bailé.
○ Yo bailo. Tomo clases de baile tres veces a la semana. El mes pasado gané un premio en el concurso de baile.
■ A mí me gustan los deportes. En el invierno juego futbol.
○ Yo prefiero estar en casa. Me gusta ver la tele, escuchar música.

VOCABULARY

¡felicidades!	congratulations!
¿cuándo?	when?
el verano	summer
el mes que viene	next month
el año pasado	last year
¿adónde?	where (to)?
nadar	to swim
los deportes	sports
el invierno	winter
las clases de baile	dance classes
tres veces a la semana	three times a week
el mes pasado	last month
ganar	to win [a prize or competition]
el premio	prize
el concurso	competition

✓ The past tense of *ser*

The past tense of **ser** is exactly the same as the past tense of **ir**:

fui, fuiste, fue, fuimos, fueron

Ayer **fue** mi cumpleaños. Yesterday was my birthday.
La semana pasada Juan **fue** a Estados Unidos. Last week Juan went to the United States.

✓ *gustar* and *encantar* + infinitive

You've already seen how to talk about *things* you like: **me gusta el cine**. To describe *activities* you like doing, you use **gustar** or **encantar** followed by the infinitive:

Me **gusta** escuchar música. I like listening to music.
¿Te **gusta** viajar? Do you like traveling?
Nos **encanta** bailar. We love dancing.

Note that **encantar** is not generally used in the question form.

✓ Saying how often you do something

To say you do an activity a number of times a week, month, or year, use the following expressions:

Bailo **tres veces a la semana**. I dance three times a week.
Viajo **dos** veces **al año**. I travel twice a year.

To say you do something every day, week, or month, use either of the following expressions:

Voy a la alberca **cada semana**. I go to the pool every week.
Voy a la alberca **todas las semanas**. I go to the pool every week.

ACTIVITY 13

Translate these sentences using the past tense of **ser** or **ir**.

1 We went to the movies yesterday.
2 The movie was good.
3 Yesterday was my father's birthday.
4 They went to Peru for their holidays.
5 Did you [*plural*] go to the party?
6 Was it you who called?

Now do activities 14 and 15 on the recording.

10.4 Mexican national holidays
Las fiestas nacionales de México

ACTIVITY 16

Below is a list of dates and Mexican national holidays. Can you work out which fiestas have an English equivalent and match them with the appropriate date? Then translate the remaining fiestas into English and try to work out the dates for each of them.

1	1 de enero	a	Año Nuevo
2	6 de enero	b	Noche Vieja
3	marzo / abril	c	Todos los Santos / Día de Muertos
4	12 de diciembre	d	Semana Santa
5	2 de noviembre	e	Fiesta Nacional: Día de la Independencia
6	20 de noviembre	f	Día de Reyes
7	25 de diciembre	g	Día del Trabajo
8	31 de diciembre	h	Día de la Virgen de Guadalupe
9	1 de mayo	i	Día de Navidad
10	15/16 de septiembre	j	Día de la Revolución

ACTIVITY 17

The following phrases describe the fiestas (a–j). Match each description with the correct fiesta.

1 En algunas ciudades hay procesiones religiosas por las calles. La gente sale a las calles para ver las procesiones.
2 Trabajamos mucho. Esta fiesta es para nosotros.
3 Esta fiesta se celebra por todo el mundo a las doce de la noche. La gente cena en casa o sale con los amigos para celebrar el nuevo año.
4 El día que se celebra el nacimiento del Niño Jesús.
5 El día para celebrar la Revolución Mexicana.
6 En esta fiesta tres señores muy importantes traen regalos a los niños.
7 Durante este día todo el mundo duerme después de la fiesta de la noche anterior.
8 Esta fiesta es para recordar a las personas muertas de la familia. La gente visita los cementerios y cena con amigos y parientes. Es un día alegre.
9 Esta fiesta religiosa se celebra en honor de la Virgen María.
10 El día que celebra la independencia de España.

la procesión	procession
celebrar	to celebrate
la revolución	revolution
el nacimiento	birth
recordar	remember
muerto	dead
la gente	people
los parientes	relatives
alegre	happy, joyous
el cementerio	cemetery
la independencia	independence

ACTIVITY 18

Using the sentences from Activity 17, describe what you did during some of the fiestas.

Example: ¿Qué hiciste en la Noche Vieja?
Cené con mis padres en casa y salí con mis amigos.

1 ¿Qué hiciste en Semana Santa?
2 ¿Qué hicieron el Día del Trabajador?
3 ¿Qué hiciste el día del Año Nuevo?
4 ¿Qué hiciste el Día de Muertos?
5 ¿Qué hicieron el Día de Reyes?

ACTIVITY 19

In this word search find nine of the fiestas from the list above.

R	A	A	V	A	M	F	V	D	F	M	R	M
E	F	S	T	Ñ	N	O	X	J	C	Q	F	N
V	H	D	R	O	K	P	C	K	M	W	D	S
O	T	E	A	N	O	U	X	W	U	E	Q	D
L	N	W	B	U	P	W	L	Q	E	D	A	A
U	Y	J	A	E	T	Q	A	Y	R	F	D	Q
C	P	K	J	V	Y	S	A	N	T	O	S	W
I	J	G	O	O	W	Q	C	T	O	V	H	C
O	K	F	E	B	R	E	Y	E	S	K	P	V
N	O	C	H	E	V	I	E	J	A	J	J	U
S	E	M	A	N	A	S	A	N	T	A	U	I
I	N	D	E	P	E	N	D	E	N	C	I	A

10.5 Un extraño en la ciudad

 ¿QUIÉN ES JORGE?
WHO IS JORGE?

La mamá de María está preocupada por su hija. Le pregunta sobre su trabajo, su casa y sus amigos.

preocuparse (por)	to worry (about)
demasiado	too much, too many
enseñar	to show
explicar	to explain
recibir	to receive
decir	to say
prometer	to promise

ACTIVITY 20

Listen to the story again: **¿verdadero o falso?**

1 A María le gusta su trabajo.	V/F
2 No tiene mucho trabajo.	V/F
3 Vive sola y no tiene amigos.	V/F
4 Sale mucho al cine y al teatro y le gusta bailar.	V/F
5 La mamá se preocupa por María.	V/F
6 La foto es del año pasado.	V/F
7 Es una foto de María y su mamá.	V/F
8 Jorge mandó una tarjeta a María a casa de su mamá.	V/F
9 La mamá de María le explica todo.	V/F

ACTIVITY 21

Imagine you are a friend of María in Mexico City and her mother is telling you she is worried about María. Respond to each statement using the information given in the conversation. Use extra phrases where necessary to reassure her.

Example: María trabaja mucho. **Sí, trabaja mucho pero le gusta trabajar.**

1 Vive sola.
2 No tiene amigos.
3 No come bien, está muy delgada.
4 Está cansada.
5 Hace demasiadas cosas.

STORY TRANSCRIPT

Mamá	¿Qué tal tu trabajo?
María	Bien. Me gusta bastante.
Mamá	Trabajas mucho, ¿verdad?
María	Sí, hay mucho trabajo pero me gusta trabajar.
Mamá	¿Y, qué haces en tu tiempo libre? ¿Estás sola en el departamento? ¿Tienes amigos?
María	Sí, mamá. No te preocupes. Prefiero vivir sola pero tengo muchos amigos y salgo mucho al teatro y al cine. También me gusta bailar. Estoy bien.
Mamá	No comes bien. Estás muy delgada, hija.
María	Mamá, no te preocupes. Estoy bien. Vivo muy bien.
Mamá	Pero, estás cansada, ¿verdad? Haces demasiadas cosas. Me preocupo por ti.
María	Pues no te preocupes. Hago muchas cosas pero no demasiadas.
Mamá	Es que ya no eres mi hija pequeña. Eres una mujer. Es difícil para mí.
María	Ya lo sé.
Mamá	Tengo que enseñarte una cosa. Mira lo que tengo aquí. Unas fotos tuyas. En ésta, tienes tres años.
María	¡Ah, sí! ¡Qué bonita! ¡Pero, mamá! ¿Quién es el señor que está en la foto a tu lado?
Mamá	¿Lo conoces, verdad? Es el señor de Chihuahua. Se llama Jorge. Mira. Te mandó esta tarjeta de cumpleaños el año pasado.
María	A ver. "De Jorge, desde Chihuahua. Tengo que explicarte muchas cosas." Mamá, no la recibí.
Mamá	Porque Jorge mandó la tarjeta a esta casa, no a la Ciudad de México y no te la mandé. No sé por qué. Es que Jorge es … es …
María	Es mi papá, ¿verdad? ¡Jorge es mi papá!
Mamá	Sí, hija, sí. Lo siento. No puedo explicarte más ahora. Y no puedes decirle nada a Jorge. Por favor. ¿Me lo prometes? Necesito tiempo.
María	Te lo prometo.

Test

Now it's time to test your progress in Unit 10.

1 Choose something you like and something you don't like from each of the three lists and write a sentence about them using **gustar**.

el cine	la fruta	los periódicos
el teatro	la verdura	los libros
la televisión	la carne	las caricaturas
la música (pop/clásica)	el chocolate	
las películas de Hollywood		

_____ **6**

2 Now write down two activities you like doing and two activities you don't like doing from the following:

1 dance   2 read   3 work   4 listen to music

_____ **8**

3 Insert the appropriate indirect and direct pronouns and the correct form of **gustar**.

Example: Mi mamá. **A ella le gusta** el cine.

1 Mi papá. _____ los restaurantes italianos.
2 Mi hermano y yo. _____ la música rock.
3 Mis amigos. _____ el futbol.
4 Tú y tu hermana. _____ las discotecas.
5 Yo. _____ el teatro.
6 Tú. _____ la ciudad.
7 Las hermanas. _____ su trabajo.

_____ **14**

4 Complete your side of this conversation.

A: ¿Quieres ir a un concierto de música clásica?
B: (You're very sorry. You don't like classical music at all.)
A: No importa. ¿Te gusta la música popular?
B: (You don't like it much. You don't like music. You prefer the movies. Ask if she likes the movies.)
A: Sí, a mí también me gusta. ¿Te gusta bailar?
B: (No you don't.)
A: A mí me gusta mucho salir.

B: (You like going to the movies once a month, but you prefer to be at home reading a book or watching television.)

| | 10 |

5 Read the following commentary on what Raúl did yesterday. Put the verbs into the correct form of the simple past tense.

Ayer, sábado, (**levantarse**) temprano, a las ocho. Mi amiga Elisa y yo (**ir**) al centro de la ciudad a comprar ropa y regalos para mis hermanos. Yo (**comprar**) dos camisas y Elisa (**comprar**) una falda muy bonita. (**Comer**) en un restaurante y después (**ir**) a buscar a las amigas de Elisa. Ellas (**ir**) al cine. Yo (**visitar**) a un amigo que está en el hospital. Después de la visita (**ir**) a mi casa. (**Salir**) a las ocho de la noche y (**encontrarse**) a un amigo, Enrique, en una cafetería cerca de mi casa. Enrique y yo (**tomar**) una cerveza.

| | 12 |

6 Ask these questions in Spanish.

1 Ask a colleague formally what he did yesterday.
2 Ask the same colleague where he went the day before yesterday.
3 Ask your friend what she did last week.
4 Ask your friend where she went last month.
5 Ask two colleagues formally where they went yesterday.

| | 10 |

7 Complete these sentences, using the appropriate time expression.

1 Juego futbol _____ . (twice a week)
2 Tomo clases de baile _____ . (three times a week)
3 Visito a mis papás _____ . (once a month)
4 Viajo a Querétaro _____ . (three times a year)
5 Tomo café _____ . (twice a day)
6 Voy a la alberca _____ . (every week)

| | 12 |

TOTAL SCORE | | 72 |

If you scored less than 62, look at the Language Building sections again before completing the Summary on page 148.

Summary 10

 Now try this final test, summarizing the main points covered in this unit.

How would you:
1 say you like classical music?
2 ask someone you don't know well if he likes the movies?
3 ask your friend if she likes dancing?
4 say you don't like it at all?
5 ask your brother what he did last night?
6 ask your sister where she went last week?
7 say your parents visited you last week?
8 say you swim three times a week?

REVIEW

First make a list of *things* you like, for example, which cars, books, movies, or newspapers do you like, and which do you not like at all? Practice saying them in Spanish. You may need to use your dictionary to look up any words you don't know. Build up your list of likes and dislikes and practice using the constructions **me gusta** and **me gustan**.

Now think about *activities* you like, for example skiing (**esquiar**), skating (**patinar**), or walking (**caminar**), and practice using **gustar** + infinitive. Again, use your dictionary to find new verbs.

Note down the things you do regularly – every day, every week, every month, every year – and make sentences, for example: **voy al cine dos veces al mes/una vez a la semana**. Then think about the last time you did a particular thing practice the past tense of **ir: fui al cine la semana pasada**.

Review 3

VOCABULARY

1 Complete the gaps with the appropriate word from the list below.

retrasado / boletos / reservación / autobús / ida / ida y vuelta / andén / está

El 1 _____ sale a las diez del 2 _____
número tres, pero 3 _____ 4 _____veinte
minutos. Aquí tengo dos 5 _____ para ti, uno de
6 _____ para ti, porque no regresas, y otro de
7 _____ para mí. Yo regreso el miércoles. Tengo
8 _____ .

2 Roberto is tall and thin. He has black hair. His sister is the opposite. They both have blue eyes. Describe them in Spanish.

1 Roberto es _____ y _____. Tiene el pelo
_____.
2 La hermana de Roberto es _____
y _____. Es _____
3 Tienen ___ _____ _____.

3 Describe each of these people using the correct form of the adjectives given.

1 sincero: Roberto
2 honrado: Juana
3 inteligente: los hermanos
4 tranquilo: mi papá
5 nervioso: mi mamá
6 serio: las hermanas
7 simpático: Javier
8 antipático: Carmen
9 feliz: los niños
10 generoso: mi abuelito

4 Choose the correct preposition: **para** or **a**?

   1 Un boleto _____ Guadalajara, por favor.
   2 ¿A qué hora llegamos _____ Chihuahua?
   3 Tomamos un autobús _____ Querétaro.
   4 Este autobús va _____ la Ciudad de México.

5 Translate these sentences into Spanish, using the verbs below.

querer / viajar / cambiar / poder / necesitar / tomar / desear / tener que / comprar

   1 I want to buy a roundtrip ticket.
   2 Can you have coffee in the hotel?
   3 They need to buy a ticket.
   4 We wish to change our room.
   5 I have to travel to Chihuahua.

6 Ask your friend the following questions.

   1 How long does it take to get to work?
   2 How long do you take to go to work on the bus?
   3 How far away is your work (in kilometers)?

7 Complete the sentences with the correct form of the demonstrative pronouns **éste**, **ése**, or **aquél**.

   1 El anillo: _____ (this one) es más caro que _____ (that one nearby) y mucho más caro que _____ (the one over there).
   2 Las pulseras: _____ (the ones over there) son mejores que _____ (these), pero _____ (those nearby) son las mejores.
   3 La camisa: _____ (the one nearby) es bonita, pero _____ (the one over there) es más bonita. No me gusta _____ (this one).
   4 Los zapatos: Me gustan _____ (these) pero son muy caros. _____ (those nearby) son buenos pero prefiero _____ (those over there).

8 Write the Spanish for the following:

   1 These shoes are better than those.
   2 My job is worse than yours.
   3 His car is bigger than my car.
   4 His car is better than my car.
   5 The movie isn't as interesting as the book.

9   Write the following in Spanish using the appropriate form
    of **gustar**.

    1   I like the movies.
    2   I like playing soccer.
    3   They like fast cars.
    4   We like cartoons.
    5   Do you [*informal*] like listening to music?
    6   I don't like the theater at all.

10 Javier talks about his terrible day. Put the verbs in brackets
    into the simple past tense.

    Ayer 1_____(**ser**) un día terrible. 2_____(**levantarse**)
    tarde. 3_____(**desayunar**) rápidamente y
    4_____(**salir**) de casa. El camión 5_____(**llegar**) tarde
    y yo 6_____(**llegar**) muy tarde a mi trabajo. A mi jefe no
    le 7_____ (**gustar**), es muy antipático. 8_____
    (**terminar**) mi trabajo y 9_____ (**ir**) a mi casa. Cuando
    10_____ (**entrar**) tú me 11_____ (**hablar**).

ⓐ LISTENING

11 Listen to these conversations and decide which of the
    people below is being described. Listen as many times as
    you like for each description.

    1   This person is rather plump and quite short.
    2   This person is tall and thin and always wears white
        pants.
    3   This person is tall and a bit fat, and wears big sweaters
        all the time.
    4   This person has blue eyes and blond hair, and is quite
        tall.
    5   This person is dark-haired, short, and thin.
    6   This person is blond and is neither short nor tall.

    Now listen again and fill in the extra information for each
    person.

12 Josefina is talking to María and Gustavo about what to do tonight. They all want to go out, but can't decide where. Listen once and indicate who likes what by ticking the appropriate column.

	música clásica	música rock	baile	cine	café	restaurante
Josefina	☐	☐	☐	☐	☐	☐
María	☐	☐	☐	☐	☐	☐
Gustavo	☐	☐	☐	☐	☐	☐

Now listen again. Say which two things they all like doing but can't do. Give the reason they can't do them.

SPEAKING

13 You're buying a bus ticket. Prepare your side of the conversation and then check it against the recording.

A: ¿Qué desea?
You: (Say you'd like a ticket to Querétaro.)
A: ¿De ida y vuelta?
You: (Yes.)
A: ¿Para cuándo?
You: (You want to go tomorrow and come back on the seventeenth.)
A: Hay un autobús a las nueve de la mañana.
You: (Ask how long it takes.)
A: Cuatro horas y media. ¿De primera o segunda clase?
You: (You want second class.)
     (Say thank you and ask how much the ticket is.)

14 Tell a friend about what you did yesterday. Prepare your answers and then check the recording to see if you got them right.

Example: You got up at eight. **Me levanté a las ocho**.

You went to town with your friend.
You bought some shoes.
You ate at a restaurant.
You went home.
You studied.
Your friends called you.
You all went to a bar.
You all went to the movies.
You went home by bus at eleven.

Talking about the past
Hablamos del pasado

OBJECTIVES

In this unit you'll learn how to:

- ✓ describe vacations, visits, and events
- ✓ say what you did in the past
- ✓ talk about what you used to do
- ✓ describe important events in your life

And cover the following grammar and language:

- ✓ the past tense of more regular verbs
- ✓ the past tense of irregular verbs: **estar**, **tener**
- ✓ the imperfect tense

LEARNING SPANISH 11

You should now be expanding your stock of common expressions to include everyday things that do not appear in this book. Make a mental note of subjects you discuss at work, at home, and with your friends. Be alert to phrases that come up again and again in conversation, and think to yourself: 'how do you say that in Spanish?' If you're lucky enough to know someone who speaks Spanish, ask them to help you with the Spanish versions of what you want to say. Otherwise, make use of a good dictionary, which will not only give translations of single words, but provide examples of context and common expressions.

🎧 Now start the recording for Unit 11.

¿Adónde fuiste de vacaciones?

ACTIVITY 1 is on the recording.

ACTIVITY 2

1 ¿Por qué está bronceada Beatriz?
2 ¿Estuvieron en hoteles Beatriz y Antonio?
3 ¿Cuándo estuvo Beatriz en Londres?
4 ¿Con quién fue Antonio a Londres?
5 ¿Cómo se llama el castillo que visitó Antonio?

DIALOGUE 1

○ ¡Qué bronceada estás!
■ Sí. Ayer regresé de mis vacaciones.
○ Yo fui a Londres con mis papás. ¿Adónde fuiste de vacaciones tú?
■ Fui a la playa, a un hotel con dos amigas.
○ Yo también estuve en un hotel con mis papás. Vimos el Parlamento y el Big Ben. Fuimos en un barco por todo el Támesis.
■ Yo estuve en Londres hace dos años. Fue muy interesante pero llovió constantemente. Prefiero descansar, nadar en la playa y no hacer nada.
○ ¿Nadaste todos los días?
■ Sí, nadé mucho en el mar porque hizo muy buen tiempo y mucho sol.
○ Nosotros visitamos el castillo de Windsor.
■ Pues yo un día fui a unas pirámides.

VOCABULARY

ir de vacaciones	to go on vacation
¡qué bronceada estás!	how tanned you are!
el barco	boat
el Támesis	Thames
hace dos años	two years ago [*literally* it makes two years]
llover	to rain
constantemente	constantly
nadar	to swim
hacer buen tiempo	to be fine (weather)
hacer sol	to be sunny
el castillo	castle
la pirámide	pyramid

✓ The simple past of *estar* and *tener*

In the simple past tense, **estar** changes its stem:

est<u>uve</u>   est<u>uvimos</u>
est<u>uviste</u>   est<u>uvieron</u>
est<u>uvo</u>

tener and verbs related to it also change in this way: **tener (tuve)**,
obtener (obtuve), 'to obtain', **detener (detuve)**, 'to detain', **sostener**
(sostuve), 'to sustain'.

✓ Describing the weather

The verb **hacer** ('to do', 'to make') is used in many expressions describing
the weather:

Hace buen/mal tiempo. The weather is good/bad.
Hace un buen día. It's a fine day.
Hace sol/calor/frío. It's sunny/hot/cold.

✓ Expressing time in the past using *hace*

To say how long ago something happened, use **hace** [*literally* 'it makes'] +
the period of time:

Fui a Londres **hace dos años**. I went to London two years ago.
La vi **hace cinco minutos**. I saw her five minutes ago.
Comí **hace poco**. I ate a short while ago.
Fui a Australia **hace mucho**. I went to Australia a long time ago.

ACTIVITY 3

Write these sentences in Spanish.

1 I was in a good hotel.
2 I went to the beach on vacation.
3 They came back yesterday.
4 We came back three days ago.
5 It rained a lot.
6 The weather was bad.
7 They saw the Thames.
8 I saw Juan an hour ago.

🎧 Now do activities 4 and 5 on the recording.

11.2 I like the beach
Me gusta la playa

🔊 **ACTIVITY 6** is on the recording.

ACTIVITY 7

¿Antonio o Beatriz? ¿(A) quién …

1 fue a la playa y a quién le gusta el sol?
2 no le gusta el sol?
3 fue a las montañas?
4 le gusta acampar?
5 le gustan las vacaciones organizadas?

DIALOGUE 2

○ ¿No te gusta la playa? ¿No te gusta nadar en el mar?
■ Sí, me gusta un poco, pero prefiero ver monumentos.
○ A mí también me interesa. Cuando era pequeña, mi papá me llevaba por muchas ciudades de México.
■ A mí me gustan las montañas. Cuando era pequeño mis papás me llevaban a acampar. Visitábamos pueblos pequeños.
○ Una vez yo fui a las montañas, pero no me gustó. No me gustan las montañas y no me gusta acampar.
■ Sí, pero si vas a acampar, puedes hacer lo que quieres.
○ Estoy de acuerdo. Pero yo prefiero las vacaciones organizadas por una agencia. No tienes que preocuparte de nada. Te diviertes más.
■ Yo creo que no. Yo odio las vacaciones 'turísticas'.

VOCABULARY	
el mar	sea
interesar	to interest
acordarse	to remember
la montaña	mountain
acampar	to camp
la agencia	agency
divertirse	to enjoy oneself
odiar	to hate

✓ The imperfect tense of *-ar* verbs and *ser*

The imperfect tense is used to describe events or states in the past which continued for some time or which occurred repeatedly. It is often translated in English by 'used to' or 'was -ing'. The following endings are added to the stem:

llevar	llev**aba**	llev**ábamos**
	llev**abas**	llev**aban**
	llev**aba**	

Note that in the singular the first and third person are the same, and in the plural the first person is stressed on the first syllable after the stem.

Mi papá me **llevaba** a visitar las ciudades de México. My father used to take me to Mexican cities.

Visitábamos pueblos pequeños. We used to visit small villages.

ser is irregular:

era	éramos
eras	eran
era	

It is used to describe a state persisting over a long period:

Cuando **era** niña … When I was young …

ACTIVITY 8

Write the imperfect form of the verb in brackets for this account of Carmen's memories.

Cuando yo (1 **ser**) niña mi mamá (2 **trabajar**) para una empresa muy importante. Mi papá y yo (3 **comprar**) toda la comida para la semana en el supermercado. Cada año nosotros (4 **visitar**) a mis abuelitos. Durante aquellos años nosotros (5 **estar**) en Colima.

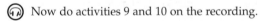 Now do activities 9 and 10 on the recording.

Cuando era joven

(🎧) **ACTIVITY 11** is on the recording.

ACTIVITY 12

1 Margarita lived in a big house.	V/F
2 Her family was quite rich.	V/F
3 Pepe lived in a big apartment.	V/F
4 Margarita didn't see much of her father.	V/F
5 Pepe used to go to the coast in the summer.	V/F

DIALOGUE 3

○ Tengo recuerdos muy buenos de mi juventud. Cuando era joven vivíamos en una casa muy grande en las afueras de la Ciudad de México. Éramos muy ricos.

■ Nosotros vivíamos en un departmento pequeño en Cuernavaca. Éramos cinco hermanos. Mi papá perdió su trabajo. Éramos muy pobres.

○ ¿Ah sí? Mi vida era muy diferente. Mi papá viajaba mucho. Nosotros íbamos a la playa durante el verano.

■ Pues yo pasaba el verano en Cuernavaca. No teníamos dinero, pero mis papás estaban siempre con nosotros. Nunca podíamos ir de vacaciones.

○ ¡Qué triste!

■ No, no, éramos una familia muy feliz.

○ Yo era feliz también, pero extrañaba a mi papá.

VOCABULARY	
el recuerdo	memory
la juventud	youth, childhood
las afueras	outskirts [of a city]
rico	rich
perder	to lose
pobre	poor
la vida	life
pasar	to spend [time]
nunca	never
triste	sad
extrañar	to miss

✓ The imperfect tense of *-er* and *-ir* verbs

The imperfect tense of **-er** and **-ir** verbs is formed as follows:

tener		**vivir**	
tenía	teníamos	vivía	vivíamos
tenías	tenían	vivías	vivían
tenía		vivía	

ir is irregular: **ir: iba, ibas, iba, íbamos, iban**

✓ Use of the imperfect and simple past

The imperfect is used to describe things that either went on for a long time, or to describe things that happened regularly in the past:

Vivíamos en Acapulco. We lived in Acapulco.
Íbamos a la playa durante el verano. We used to go to the beach in the summer.

In contrast the simple past is used to describe one specific action that occurred once in the past:

Fuimos a la playa el año pasado. We went to the beach last year.
Mi papá **perdió** su trabajo. My father lost his job.

✓ Describing numbers of people

The verb **ser** is used to describe how many there are in a group:

Éramos cinco hermanos. There were five brothers and sisters.
Somos tres. There are three of us.

ACTIVITY 13

Rewrite the following acount in Spanish, using the imperfect or the simple past for each verb as appropriate.

When I was young I used to live in the city, but every summer I used to go to my grandparents' house with my two brothers. My grandparents had a big old car and I remember that once, my grandfather took us to the mountains. My father worked a lot and he didn't have long vacations, but every weekend he came to see us and gave us presents.

ACTIVITY 14

Now write a few sentences about your childhood, including one or two things that only happened once. Use your dictionary for words you haven't yet seen.

 Now do activities 15 and 16 on the recording.

CULTURE

11.4 Mexican fiestas
México en fiestas

ACTIVITY 17

Read the passage below about Mexican fiestas and answer these questions.

1 Name five things that you get in a Mexican fiesta.
2 Name one thing you can't do in a Mexican fiesta.
3 Where are many people during fiesta nights ?
4 What is the name of the most important Mexican fiesta?
5 What do most Mexicans do during this fiesta?
6 What is the name of the ceremony that takes place during this fiesta?
7 Where does it take place?
8 How do people celebrate this moment?

México es un país de fiestas: fiestas regionales, fiestas de las ciudades, fiestas de los pueblos, fiestas del campo; fiestas grandes y fiestas pequeñas. Todas tienen las mismas características: la música, el baile, los fuegos artificiales, los juegos infantiles, el ruido y el no dormir. Si vives en un pueblo pequeño durante las fiestas, olvídate de dormir. La gente está por la calle durante toda la noche.

Una de las fiestas más importantes de México ocurre en el Día de la Independencia que se celebra el día 15 y el día 16 de septiembre por todo México. Es una fiesta nacional y muchos mexicanos van a la playa durante unos días de descanso. Lo más importante de esta fiesta es 'El Grito'. Es una ceremonia muy tradicional para los mexicanos. A las once de la noche, desde el Balcón Presidencial en el Palacio Nacional, el Presidente toca la campana de la Independencia y grita: '¡Viva México! ¡Vivan los héroes que nos dieron patria y libertad!' La gente en la playa y en la ciudad observa la ceremonia por la televisión y corea los 'vivas' del Presidente. En cada playa del país y en cada pueblo sucede un acto igual hecho por los Gobernadores o delegados. Depués del 'Grito' la gente celebra la fiesta con fuegos artificiales. Hay puestos de comida, juegos y mucha música y baile.

el campo	the countryside
los fuegos artificiales	fireworks
el ruido	noise
olvidar	to forget
el descanso	rest, relaxation
el balcón	balcony
tocar la campana	to toll the bell
gritar	to shout
el grito	shout
los héroes	heroes
la patria	homeland, fatherland
la libertad	freedom
observar	to observe
corear	to chant
suceder	to happen

ACTIVITY 18

Write the following sentences in Spanish. Use the passage to help you with the vocabulary.

1 You celebrated the 'national fiesta'.
2 You went to the beach on 15 September.
3 You watched the ceremony on television.
4 You saw the fireworks.
5 You didn't sleep all night.

Now write two or three more sentences in the simple past using information from the passage.

Un extraño en la ciudad

MARÍA Y JORGE HABLAN POR TELÉFONO
MARÍA AND JORGE TALK ON THE PHONE

María quiere hablar más con Jorge. Le invita a cenar.

¡hola!	hello
saber	to know
comportarse	to behave
amable	kind, friendly
quizás	perhaps
entonces	then
por casualidad	by coincidence
estupendo	great! terrific!

ACTIVITY 19

¿Verdadero o falso?

1 María invita a Jorge a cenar en un restaurante.
2 Lo invita porque la otra cena fue muy buena.
3 María dice que fue a visitar a unos amigos.
4 Lo invita porque quiere hablar.
5 Jorge no puede aceptar la invitación.
6 Jorge no quiere decir cómo se llama la persona a quien visita.
7 Jorge y María fueron a Temixco por casualidad.
8 Pueden cenar juntos el sábado.

ACTIVITY 20

Answer the questions using the appropriate information from this episode of the story. Your answer doesn't have to be exactly the same as in the recording.

Jorge: ¿Adónde fuiste?
María: _____
María: ¿Quiere venir a mi casa a cenar?
Jorge: _____
María: ¿El pueblo está lejos?
Jorge: _____
María: ¿Cómo se llama el pueblo?
Jorge: _____
Jorge: ¿Podemos cenar el viernes por la noche?
María: _____

ACTIVITY 21

Complete this part of the story by filling in the gaps. All the words which are missing consist of one or two letters only.

Fui 1_____ ver 2_____ unos amigos. Mire usted,
3_____ hablo para invitar 4 _____ 5 _____ cenar
6_____ 7_____ casa. Es que, 8_____ otra noche,
9_____ comporté muy mal. ¿Quiere venir? Quiero hablar
con usted 10_____ algunas cosas.

STORY TRANSCRIPT

Jorge	¿Bueno?
María	Señor Jorge, ¡Hola!, soy yo, María.
Jorge	¡Ah! ¡Hola! ¿Cómo estás? ¿Cómo conseguiste mi número de teléfono?
María	Por el señor Herrera.
Jorge	¡Ah sí! ¿Qué tal el viaje? ¿Adónde fuiste?
María	Oh, fui a ver a unos amigos. Mire usted, lo llamo para invitarlo a cenar a mi casa. Es que, la otra noche, me comporté muy mal. ¿Quiere venir? Quiero hablar con usted de algunas cosas.
Jorge	Oh, no te preocupes, no fue nada. Eres muy amable y gracias por la invitación, pero lo siento – no puedo ir.
María	Ah … bueno, no importa. Quizás otro día.
Jorge	Tengo que ir a un pueblo a visitar a una vieja amiga.
María	Ah. ¿Está lejos?
Jorge	No, está bastante cerca de Cuernavaca, a unos ciento cincuenta kilómetros de aquí.
María	¿Cómo se llama el pueblo?
Jorge	Se llama Temixco – es muy pequeño.
María	¡Temixco! ¿El pueblo se llama Temixco?
Jorge	Sí, sí, Temixco. … María – ¿estás bien?
María	Sí, sí, no pasa nada. Conozco el pueblo, muy bien. ¡Y usted va allí!
Jorge	¡Qué casualidad! Es muy pequeño.
María	Dice que va a visitar a una amiga. ¿Cómo se llama? Quizás la conozco.
Jorge	Oh, es una amiga que conocí hace muchos años. Regreso el viernes. ¿Podemos cenar el viernes por la noche?
María	Sí, sí. Podemos cenar en mi casa.
Jorge	Estupendo. Podemos hablar entonces.
María	Está bien. Hasta el viernes.
Jorge	Adiós.

Test

Now it's time to test your progress in Unit 11.

1 Complete this postcard using the correct form of the verb in the simple past.

¡Hola Pepe! ¿Cómo estás? Ayer (yo) (1 **regresar**) de mis vacaciones. ¿Dónde (2 **ir**) (tú?) Mis papás y yo (3 **ir**) a Taxco. (Nosotros) (4 **hacer**) muchas cosas en Taxco. (Nosotros) (5 **estar**) en un hotel. (Nosotros) (6 **ver**) la iglesia de Santa Prisca. (Yo) (7 **nadar**) en el mar. Nosotros (8 **visitar**) muchos monumentos. ¡Adiós! Ana.

8

2 Write the correct form of these reflexive verbs.

1 Mis papás (**levantarse**) tarde ayer.
2 Me gusta (**divertirse**) en el baile.
3 No (**acordarse**) de como termina la película.
4 Ellos (**aburrirse**) los domingos.

8

3 Give the Spanish for these sentences using the simple past of **ser**, **estar**, or **ir**, as appropriate.

1 Yesterday I went to the village.
2 They were in Taxco.
3 He was a big man.
4 We went to a church.
5 She was a good actor.

8

4 How would you describe the weather in Spanish?

1 It's raining.   4 It's hot.
2 It's sunny.   5 The weather is good.
3 It's cold.

10

5 Supply the Spanish for each response below.

1 A: ¿Cuándo fuiste a Monterrey?
  (You went two years ago.)
2 A: ¿Dónde está Pablo?
  (You saw him five minutes ago.)
3 A: ¿Quieres un café?
  (You had coffee a short while ago.)
4 A: ¿Cuándo fuiste a Acapulco?
  (You went to Acapulco a long time ago.)
5 A: ¿Tu carro es nuevo?
  (You bought it two years ago.)

10

6 Translate these sentences into English.

1 Vivieron en la costa durante muchos años.
2 Yo trabajaba antes en una fábrica de muebles.
3 Fuimos a ver el partido de futbol el domingo.
4 Íbamos a ver el futbol los domingos.
5 Mi papá manejaba muy mal.
6 Estuvo en la discoteca.
7 Siempre estabas en el cine.
8 Ayer compré un regalo para mi amiga.

16

7 Here is an advertisement for the Oaxaca region. Read the
  information, then write a short letter to a friend telling him
  what you did there. Use the simple past tense.

Querido Juan,
Fui a Oaxaca …

> **Visitar Oaxaca**
> • Pasear por el centro
> • Visitar el centro arqueológico
> • Comprar en los mercados
> • Comer en buenos restaurantes
> • Bailar en las discotecas
> • Ver la arquitectura colonial

6

TOTAL SCORE **66**

If you scored less than 56, look at the Language Building
sections again before completing the Summary on page 166.

Summary 11

 Now try this final test, summarizing the main points covered in this unit.

How would you:
1 ask someone where he went for his vacation?
2 say you went to England?
3 say you and your parents were in a hotel?
4 say you went to Argentina three years ago?
5 say you lived in a big house when you were young?
6 say you used to visit your grandparents?

REVIEW

Think of the things you used to do or things you did lots of times when you were younger. Practice using the imperfect tense to say or write down these things in Spanish. For example, if you used to go to the movies every Sunday, practice saying **iba al cine los domingos**. Then find an example of something you did once only on a specific occasion and say it using the simple past, for example: **Vi una película muy buena.**

Making plans
Haciendo planes

OBJECTIVES

In this unit you will learn how to:

✓ talk about your future plans and activities

✓ invite someone to do something

✓ accept and refuse invitations

✓ apologize for not being able to accept an invitation

And cover the following grammar and language:

✓ the future tense

✓ the verb **ir** + **a** + infinitive for describing plans

✓ the conditional tense used for invitations

✓ the verb **querer** + infinitive for invitations

LEARNING SPANISH 12

Practice improvising ways of getting your meaning across when speaking spontaneously, even if you don't know the exact words or phrases in Spanish. If you know a Spanish speaker, he or she will probably help you when you get into difficulties. If not, think of things you might want to say whenever you have spare time – while you're traveling, for example. A basic example is the use of tenses. If you don't know the past tense but want to talk about yesterday, use the verb in the present tense and use the word 'yesterday'. With practice, you'll find that you will improve your ability to approximate and to describe things, even if you are aware that you do not have the exact vocabulary or specific phrases. Use facial expressions, hand movements, anything to get your meaning across. The important thing is to build up confidence so you're not afraid of getting involved in a conversation.

🎧 Now start the recording for Unit 12.

12.1 | Would you like to come?

¿Te gustaría venir?

ACTIVITY 1 is on the recording.

ACTIVITY 2

Complete the sentences.

Example: **No voy a hacer nada** porque estoy cansado.

1 _____ porque tengo que trabajar en mi casa.
2 _____ porque es una casa bonita.
3 _____ porque va a hacer buen tiempo.
4 _____ porque mi hijo va a jugar futbol.
5 _____ porque su esposa tiene que estudiar.

DIALOGUE 1

○ ¿Qué vas a hacer este fin de semana?

■ No voy a hacer nada. ¡Estoy tan cansado! Voy a dormir y a descansar.

○ ¡Qué suerte! Yo voy a ir a Cuernavaca con la familia. Vamos a preparar la casa para las vacaciones. Es mucho trabajo.

■ Pero vale la pena, ¿verdad? Es una casa muy bonita.

○ ¿Te gustaría venir, con la familia? Podemos hacer una carne asada en el jardín.

■ A mí me gustaría ir pero no podemos. Mi hijo va a jugar futbol el sábado.

○ ¡Qué lástima! Pero ¿por qué no vienen el domingo?

■ No sé. Mi esposa tiene un examen el lunes. Va a estudiar todo el domingo.

○ ¿Quieres venir tú solo con los niños? Tu esposa puede estudiar tranquilamente.

■ Sí, es una buena idea. Voy a preguntarle a mi esposa si está de acuerdo.

VOCABULARY	
la esposa	wife
¡qué suerte!	you lucky thing! [*literally* what luck!]
vale la pena	it's worth it
¿te gustaría venir?	would you like to come?
la carne asada	barbecue
el examen	exam
tranquilamente	quietly

✓ Talking about the future with *ir* + a + infinitive

ir + a followed by the infinitive is used to talk about plans for the future. It is very similar to the English construction 'going to (do)':

¿Qué vas **a hacer** este fin de semana? What are you going to do this weekend?
Voy a visitar a mis papás. I'm going to visit my parents.
Vamos a preparar la casa. We're going to prepare the house.
No voy **a hacer** nada. I'm not going to do anything.

✓ Giving invitations and expressing wishes

The verb **gustar** is used in the conditional to give invitations and to express what you would like to do:

¿Te gustaría venir? Would you like to come?
Me gustaría ir al campo. I'd like to go to the countryside.

✓ Using *¡qué!* in exclamations

The structure **¡qué!** (meaning 'what (a)' or 'how') + an appropriate noun/adjective is often used for exclamations:

¡Qué suerte! What luck!	**¡Qué inteligente es!** He's so intelligent.
¡Qué lástima! What a pity!	**¡Qué bronceado estás!** You're so tanned.

ACTIVITY 3

Change the subjects of these sentences as indicated.

Example: Voy a estudiar esta noche. (**nosotros**)
Nosotros vamos a estudiar esta noche.

1 No voy a salir con mis amigos mañana. (**ellos**)
2 No vamos a salir el sábado. (**ustedes**)
3 Vamos a estar en casa todo el fin de semana. (**tú**)
4 ¿Vas a venir a mi fiesta de cumpleaños? (**ella**)
5 Van a comprar un carro nuevo. (**yo**)
6 No va a visitar a sus papás. (**tú**)
7 ¿Van a ir al teatro? (**él**)

🎧 Now do activities 4 and 5 on the recording.

Vamos por la mañana

🎧 **ACTIVITY 6** is on the recording.

ACTIVITY 7

See page 171 for the future tense. ¿Quién(es) …

1 … irá(n) por la mañana?
2 … hará(n) una carne asada?
3 … jugará(n)?
4 … no podrá(n) ir?
5 … prepará(n) la comida?
6 … hablará(n) a Alfonso?

DIALOGUE 2

○ Alfonso nos invita a su casa de Cuernavaca el fin de semana.
■ Este fin de semana yo no puedo ir. Voy a estudiar.
○ Ya lo sé pero podemos ir los niños y yo.
■ Es una buena idea. ¿A qué hora van?
○ Vamos temprano por la mañana. Es una casa preciosa, con jardín. Vamos a hacer una carne asada en el jardín. Los niños van a jugar. ¿No puedes venir? ¡Qué lástima!
■ Sí, pero puedo estudiar mejor sola, sin los niños.
○ Además, tienen una alberca. Podremos nadar y tomar algo en el patio.
■ ¡Qué envidia!
○ ¿Porque no vamos todos otro día?
■ Pues no sé. Creo que iré con ustedes. Llevo mis libros y estudio en el jardín mientras tú y Alfonso preparan la comida. ¿Qué te parece?
○ ¡Estupendo! Le voy a hablar a Alfonso ahora mismo.

VOCABULARY	
temprano	early
precioso	beautiful, wonderful
sin	without
el patio	patio
¡qué envidia!	I'm so envious, jealous! [*literally* what envy!]
mientras	while
¿qué te parece?	what do you think?
¡estupendo!	great!
ahora mismo	right now

✓ The future tense

In Spanish there are two ways of talking about the future: **ir** + **a** + infinitive and the future tense. They are roughly equivalent to the English 'going to' and 'will'.

For regular **-ar**, **-ir**, and **-er** verbs, the future is formed by adding the following endings to the infinitive:

trabajar	trabajar**é**	trabajar**emos**
	trabajar**ás**	trabajar**án**
	trabajar**á**	

Trabajaran mañana. They will work tomorrow.
Iremos el fin de semana. We'll go at the weekend.

The following verbs change stems in the future, but the endings are regular: **venir** (**vendr-**), **tener** (**tendr-**), **hacer** (**har-**), **poder** (**podr-**), **salir** (**saldr-**).

Tendrá problemas. He/She will have problems.

✓ More about the future

You will seldom be wrong if you use **ir** + **a** + infinitive for the future, but you will often read and hear the future tense. It is very common in news reports and it often shows that the writer or speaker is being slightly formal. It can also be used for carefully thought out plans, as in the exercise below.

ACTIVITY 8

Translate the following into Spanish.
We'll go early next Saturday morning. We'll arrive at the house at ten o'clock. The children will play in the garden and swim in the pool while I prepare lunch. We'll be able to go for a walk in the afternoon and we'll visit the village. You'll come in the evening and we'll all have supper together. We'll have to go to bed early because we're going to leave early in the morning for Cuernavaca. We'll arrive in Cuernavaca at about midday and I'll call my mother. In the evening we'll relax and watch television.

🎧 Now do activities 9 and 10 on the recording.

We're going to the movies
Vamos al cine

🎧 **ACTIVITY 11** is on the recording.

ACTIVITY 12

Translate the phrases which are true into Spanish.

1 Elisa won't be able go to the movies tonight.
2 She's busy.
3 She'll stay at home tonight.
4 She can go on Sunday.
5 The boys can't go on Sunday.
6 They'll do something else tonight.
7 Elisa will call at 5.30.
8 They'll go and see a comedy movie.
9 They'll decide later.

DIALOGUE 3

○ ¡Hola Elisa! Federico y yo vamos a ir al cine esta noche. ¿Quieres venir?

■ Me gustaría pero no puedo. Lo siento.

○ ¿Qué te pasa? ¿Estás enferma?

■ No, estoy ocupada. Voy a una boda mañana y tengo que preparar las cosas. Me voy a quedar en la casa esta noche.

○ ¿Y el domingo? ¿Te gustaría venir el domingo? Esta noche podemos hacer otra cosa.

■ Está bien. ¿Dónde nos vemos y a qué hora?

○ Yo voy a estar en la casa el domingo a partir de las cinco de la tarde. ¿Me puedes hablar?

■ Está bien. Te hablo a las cinco y media. ¿Está bien?

○ ¿Y qué película vamos a ver?

■ No sé. Hay una película cómica muy buena.

○ Bueno, ya decidiremos el domingo.

VOCABULARY	
ocupado	busy
la boda	wedding
quedarse	to stay
otra cosa	something else
la (película) cómica	comedy (movie)
decidir	to decide

⊘ Making excuses

Estoy enfermo/a.	I'm not well/I'm ill.
Estoy cansado/a.	I'm tired.
Estoy ocupado/a.	I'm busy.
Tengo gripa.	I have the flu.
Mi mamá está enferma.	My mother is ill.
Voy a una boda mañana.	I'm going to a wedding tomorrow.
Tengo que preparar las cosas.	I have to prepare things.

ACTIVITY 13

Make excuses for these invitations using the constructions **estar** or **tener que**.

1 ¿Quieres venir al cine? (You're tired.)
2 ¿Te gustaría salir con nosotros esta noche? (You aren't well.)
3 ¿Por qué no vamos a bailar? (You're busy.)
4 ¿Quieres salir mañana? Podemos ir a tomar algo.
   (You have to visit your mother.)
5 ¿Quieres venir de compras con nosotros?
   (You have to prepare lunch.)
6 ¿Te gustaría salir mañana? Es mi cumpleaños.
   (Tomorrow you're going to Oaxaca.)

ACTIVITY 14

In the sentences below, you will see one form of the future. Complete your response using the other form: for example if you see **voy a comer** you respond using **comeré**.

1 Voy a comer en el restaurante Las Delicias. ¿Y tú?
   Yo_____ (restaurante Bella Vista).
2 Visitaré a mis tíos en Argentina.
   Yo _____ (Venezuela).
3 Vamos a trabajar todo el fin de semana.
   Nosotros _____ (toda la semana).
4 ¿Saldrán a las siete?
   No. Ellos _____ (a las ocho).
5 Vamos a llegar a las diez, ¿verdad?
   No, ustedes _____ (a las once).

◎ Now do activities 15 and 16 on the recording.

12.4 Entertainments and listings

La cartelera

Mexicans go to the movies a lot. Read the passage below and answer the questions which follow:

> El cine es muy popular en México. En las ciudades hay muchos cines que pasan todo tipo de películas, nuevas y antiguas, desde las cuatro de la tarde hasta la medianoche. Todas las películas (normalmente de Estados Unidos) se pasan subtituladas en versión original. Sólo las que son para niños, de caricaturas, se doblan.
>
> Las películas están recomendadas para distintas edades, por ejemplo: 'Toda la familia', '13 años', '18 años'.
>
> El teatro es menos popular que el cine pero en muchas ciudades hay por lo menos un teatro que pone obras populares o clásicas. Y también hay espectáculos, a veces con cena incluida y también con canciones y baile.

pasar (una película)	to show (a movie)
todo tipo	all kinds
doblarse	to be dubbed
subtitulado/a	subtitled
el subtítulo	subtitle
versión original	original version
la edad	age
la obra	play, work
el espectáculo	show
la canción	song

ACTIVITY 17

¿Verdadero o falso?

1 El cine es más popular que el teatro.
2 Hay más películas norteamericanas que mexicanas.
3 Todas las películas se pasan subtituladas.
4 Un niño de diez años puede ver una película recomendada para 'Toda la familia'.
5 Hay dos o tres teatros en todas las ciudades.
6 Puedes cenar y ver un espectáculo.

ACTIVITY 18

Study 'la cartelera' and answer the questions

1 ¿Cuántas salas hay en el cine Prado?
2 ¿En qué película actúa Nicolas Cage?
3 ¿Por qué calle entras al cine Dorado 70?
4 ¿Tienes que tener dieciocho años o más para ver 'El chico ideal'?
5 Quieres reservar un boleto para el teatro. ¿A qué número llamas?
6 ¿Cómo se llama el restaurante que tiene espectáculo?

CARTELERA

TEATROS

TEATRO DE LA ESTACION
Teniente Coronel Pueyo presenta *Mas o menos Shakespeare* de Rafael Campos. Hoy, 22,30 h; sábado, 22,30 h; domingo 20,00 h. ¡Local climatizado! Reservaciones: 521 8689

CINES

PRADO. 3 salas – Cádiz, 13. 5666452. Dolby SR.
PRADO – *Hampones*. 5–7,30, 10,30. 18 años.
PRADO – *El Coyote*. 5–7–9–11. Todos públicos.
PRADO – *Misión imposible*. 24 semanas. ¡Ultimo días! 5–7,30–10,30. Todos públicos.
HIPÓDROMO – DDS. 5–7–9–11. *City of Angels*. Nicolas Cage, Meg Ryan. Apta.

CINE FORUM. – Digital SDDS. Paseo Independencia, 19. *Asesinos de reemplazo*. 5–7–9–11. 18 años.
CINE PLAZA HOLLYWOOD. – DDS. 5–8–11. *Armageddon*. Bruce Willis. Apta.
CINE DORADO 70. – entrada por avenida Juárez. *El chico ideal*. 5–7–9–11. Todos públicos.

RESTAURANTES ESPECTACULO

CLUB NAUTICO. – Magníficas cenas, copas, música y karaoke. Teléfonos 5813416 400 y 5813045.
GARDEN. – Restaurante espectáculo. Viernes y sábados, cenas con espectáculo y baile con orquesta, con menús desde 220 pesos. Jueves, domingos y festivos, comidas con menú del día. San Juan Bosco, 3. Teléfono no. 5272829.

12.5 Un extraño en la ciudad

¿QUÉ TAL EL VIAJE?
HOW WAS THE TRIP?

Jorge regresa de su viaje. María sabe quien es 'la amiga' de Jorge. Jorge se lo explica todo.

enterarse	to find out
sospechar	to suspect
explicar	to explain
pasar	to happen
pelear(se)	to quarrel, to fight
contigo	with you
entender	to understand
querer	to love
dejar	to give up, leave

ACTIVITY 19

Choose the correct answer for each question:

1 María tiene
  a la tarjeta y la foto.
  b la tarjeta.
  c la foto.
2 María se enteró del secreto
  a cuando vio a Jorge la primera vez.
  b cuando fue a visitar a su mamá.
  c durante la cena.
3 Jorge y la mamá de María
  a no tenían problemas pero no tenían dinero.
  b tenían dinero pero tenían problemas.
  c tenían problemas y no tenían dinero.
4 Jorge
  a no encontró trabajo y no llamó a su esposa.
  b encontró trabajo y llamó a su esposa.
  c encontró trabajo pero no llamó a su esposa.
5
  a Jorge dejó a su esposa.
  b La esposa dejó a Jorge.
  c Se separaron por mutuo acuerdo.

176

6 Jorge regresó porque quería ver
   a a su mujer y a María.
   b a su mujer.
   c a María.

ACTIVITY 20

Here are the answers to some questions from the dialogue. What are the questions? Check your answers against the transcript.

María	¿_____?
Jorge	Muy bien, gracias. Mi amiga está muy bien.
María	¿_____?
Jorge	Sí, soy yo. Soy tu papá.
Jorge	¿_____?
María	Cuando fui a visitar a mi mamá.
María	¿_____?
Jorge	Encontré un trabajo bueno en Chihuahua.
María	¿_____?
Jorge	Porque tengo que verla y tenía que verte a ti también.

STORY TRANSCRIPT

María	¿Cómo te fue de viaje?
Jorge	Muy bien, gracias. Mi amiga está muy bien.
María	Mira … tengo unas fotos. Mira esta foto. Y esta tarjeta. Ya sé quién es tu amiga. Es mi mamá, ¿verdad? Y este señor de la foto eres tú, ¿verdad?
Jorge	Sí, soy yo. Soy tu papá. ¿Cuándo te enteraste?
María	Cuando fui a visitar a mi mamá. Ya lo sospechaba. ¿Me vas a explicar lo que pasó? Le prometí no decir nada pero tenemos que hablar.
Jorge	Sí, pero es difícil. Tuvimos muchos problemas durante mucho tiempo. No teníamos dinero. Siempre nos peleábamos. Fui a buscar trabajo en Chihuahua.
María	¿Pero por qué no fuimos contigo?
Jorge	¿No lo entiendes? Tuve que irme.
María	Pero, ¿no querías a mi mamá?
Jorge	Sí, mucho, y ella me quería a mí. Pero no podíamos vivir juntos.
María	Entonces, ¿por qué no regresaste?
Jorge	Encontré un trabajo bueno en Chihuahua y llamé a tu mamá. No quería venir a Chihuahua conmigo.
María	Y tú no querías regresar.
Jorge	No, porque no podía dejar mi trabajo. Me quedé allí. Cada año pensaba regresar, pero no podía. Al final decidí no regresar.
María	Y olvidaste a mi mamá.
Jorge	¡No, no! Nunca la olvidé. Pero, no podíamos vivir juntos.
María	Y ahora. ¿Por qué regresas?
Jorge	Porque tengo que verla y tenía que verte a ti también. ¡Eres mi hija!

Test

Now it's time to test your progress in Unit 12.

1 ¿Qué van a hacer? Write out the sentences in full.

    1 Roberto / ir / cine
    2 Elisa / ir / boda
    3 Nosotros / ir / bailar
    4 Ellos / visitar / unos amigos
    5 Tú / estudiar
    6 Ustedes / preparar / cena
    7 Yo / comprar / carro nuevo
    8 Mis hermanos / jugar / futbol
    9 Tú y yo / ver / película
  10 Yo / terminar / libro

20

2 Write down three ways of inviting someone to the movies.

  1 ¿____ _____ venir al cine?
  2 ¿ ____ venir al cine?
  3 ¿ ____ al cine?

6

3 Write the correct form of the future tense in this letter.

Querida Sara

Mañana (1 **ir**) a mi nuevo trabajo. (2 **Empezar**) a las nueve.
(3 **Estar**) nervioso porque no conozco a mis nuevos
compañeros. (4 **Salir**) de casa a las ocho porque quiero
llegar temprano. Mi amiga (5 **venir**) conmigo porque
trabaja cerca de mi nueva oficina. El primer día (6 **hacer**)
una visita a varios departamentos. Mis nuevos compañeros
(7 **comer**) conmigo el primer día. Mis compañeros y yo
(8 **tener**) mucho trabajo porque es una compañía nueva.
Mi jefe (9 **tener**) que ayudarme los primeros días. Ahora
(10 **preparar**) mis cosas.

Saludos.

10

4 Someone asks you if you want to go out. Make five different excuses.

1 ____ ocupado/a.   4 ____ cansado/a.
2 ____ ____ trabajar. 5 ____ ____ visitar a un amigo.
3 ____ ____ examen.

| 5 |

5 Give the Spanish for the following expressions.

1 You lucky thing!
2 It's worth it.
3 What a pity!
4 What do you think about that?
5 Great!
6 Next week.
7 I'm sorry.
8 It doesn't matter.
9 OK, agreed.
10 What's the matter?

| 10 |

6 In this word search, there are ten verbs in the future tense. Find each verb, and write it down adding the accent in the appropriate place where necessary.

E	S	T	A	R	E	P	N	Y	D
S	X	Q	O	H	X	C	P	U	E
T	J	U	G	A	R	E	M	O	S
A	Y	F	Z	R	W	N	A	E	C
R	W	I	R	A	B	A	M	D	A
A	J	G	H	N	V	R	T	U	N
N	I	P	O	D	R	E	L	J	S
C	K	H	L	L	A	M	A	R	A
S	L	R	F	G	K	O	A	E	R
B	C	I	R	E	I	S	D	I	A

| 10 |

TOTAL SCORE | 61 |

If you scored less than 51, look at the Language Building sections again before completing the Summary on page 180.

Summary 12

 Now try this final test, summarizing the main points covered in this unit.

How would you:
1 say you're going to study tonight?
2 say they're going to see a movie tomorrow?
3 ask your friend if she would like to go out?
4 say you're sorry but you can't?
5 say you're tired?
6 say that he's going to the US next week?
7 say that you're going to stay at home?
8 ask your friend what she thinks about something?

REVIEW

Go over the exclamations in this unit and remember them when you use the English equivalent, for example **¡qué lástima!**, **¡qué suerte!**, **¡qué envidia!**, etc.

Finally, practice inviting people to different outings and events, and also practice turning down invitations. Perhaps you're not feeling well, or you're tired, or you have a lot of work to do, or you have to study your Spanish, for example!

The world of work
El mundo del trabajo

OBJECTIVES

In this unit you'll learn how to:

- ✓ make professional telephone calls
- ✓ give instructions
- ✓ make an appointment
- ✓ introduce yourself and your company

And cover the following grammar and language:

- ✓ the formal imperative in polite instructions – **pase por aquí**, **tenga usted**, **perdone**
- ✓ the use of **poder** in formal exchanges
- ✓ **quisiera** ('I'd like')
- ✓ the present continuous tense: **estoy trabajando** ('I am working')
- ✓ the relative pronoun **que** (which, that, who)
- ✓ **sin** ('without') + infinitive

LEARNING SPANISH 13

Previous units have stressed the importance of a wide vocabulary as the key to effective language learning. There is a great deal of vocabulary in this book, but you'll also find it useful to develop your own personalized vocabulary lists. Perhaps areas of your job or study require specialized vocabulary which it would be useful to learn. This will enable you to talk about these subjects confidently in Spanish. If you have a hobby, do a sport, or are interested in a particular subject, look up some of the relevant vocabulary and start to build it into your speaking and writing practice.

🎧 Now start the recording for Unit 13.

ACTIVITY 1 is on the recording.

ACTIVITY 2

1 Why can't Bernardo: a talk to Sr. García?
                              b phone later?
                              c attend the interview?
2 How can the receptionist help?

DIALOGUE 1

○ ¿Bueno?
■ ¿Puedo hablar con el señor García, por favor?
○ Sí. ¿De parte de quién?
■ De Bernardo Díaz.
○ Un momentito. Ahora lo llamo … Perdón, señor Díaz. El
  señor García está ocupado en estos momentos. Está en una
  reunión. ¿Podría hablarle usted más tarde?
■ No; voy a estar fuera. ¿Puedo dejarle un recado?
○ Sí, espere un momentito … dígame.
■ Dígale que no voy a poder asistir a la entrevista. Tengo que
  viajar. Quisiera cambiarla.
○ ¿Podría pasar por la oficina el miércoles próximo a las tres
  de la tarde?
■ Perfecto.
○ Gracias. Hasta el miércoles.

VOCABULARY	
¿de parte de quién?	who's calling?
un momentito	one moment, please
ahora lo llamo	he's just coming
en estos momentos	at the moment
la reunión	meeting
fuera	away
un recado	a message
esperar	to wait
asistir	to attend
dígale …	could you tell him …
la entrevista	interview
quisiera …	I'd like to …
pasar por la oficina	to come to the office

✓ Formal imperatives 2

Formal imperatives – certain expressions used in everyday formal situations such as offices, receptions, or stores, where politeness and formality are expected – are given in Spanish in the subjunctive:

Dígale ... Could you tell him ...?
Tenga usted. Here you are. [*literally* have]
Pase por aquí. Please come through. [*escorting someone into a room*]
Perdone. I'm sorry.

See 3.1 for more examples and the Grammar Summary, page 235, for more details.

✓ The use of *poder* in formal exchanges

The verb **poder** is often used in the conditional to make an inquiry or a request in a formal situation, for example:

¿**Podría** hablar usted más tarde? Could you call later?
¿**Podría** pasar por la oficina a las tres? Could you come to the office at three?

✓ *quisiera* ... ('I'd like ...')

quisiera is used to say 'I'd like' in formal situations:

Quisiera cambiar la hora. I'd like to change the time.
Quisiéramos hablar con el Sr. García. We'd like to talk to Sr. García.

quisiera is in fact the past subjunctive form of **querer** ('to want'). As with the formal imperatives above, this form does come up a lot in everyday conversation and is worth practicing.

ACTIVITY 3

Using Dialogue 1 create a similar dialogue for the following exchange:

Call and ask the receptionist if you can speak to Sra. Blasco. The receptionist asks who is calling and then tells you that Sra. Blasco is in a meeting. Tell her you're calling about the interview on Monday. Say you can't attend the interview and would like to change the time. The receptionist says she can change it. The receptionist asks if you can come on Wednesday afternoon. That's perfect for you. She asks if you can go to the office at 2 p.m. You agree.

🎧 Now do activities 4 and 5 on the recording.

13.2 An interview

Una entrevista

 ACTIVITY 6 is on the recording.

ACTIVITY 7

What does Sr. García **not** ask Bernardo Díaz in the interview?

1 his reasons for wanting the job
2 his current activities and responsibilities
3 his reasons for leaving his current job
4 when he can start
5 proof of experience
6 necessary qualities for the new job

DIALOGUE 2

○ ¿Por qué está usted interesado en este puesto?

■ Estoy haciendo un trabajo parecido en mi empresa actual, pero la empresa es pequeña. Creo que hay más posibilidades en una empresa más grande como ésta.

○ Explíqueme qué funciones tiene en su trabajo actual.

■ Soy el encargado de servicio al cliente. Trabajo con un equipo de quince personas. El trabajo que estoy haciendo es parecido al trabajo que ustedes ofrecen. Yo creo que tengo la experiencia adecuada.

○ ¿Cuáles son las cualidades que se necesitan para este puesto?

■ Creo que tengo motivación y experiencia. Estoy bien calificado y tengo iniciativa.

VOCABULARY

interesado (en)	interested (in)
el puesto	position, post
actual	current
la posibilidad	possibility
el encargado/la encargada	person responsible
el servicio al cliente	client service
el equipo	team
ofrecer	to offer
la cualidad	quality
la motivación	motivation
calificado	qualified
la iniciativa	initiative

✅ Present continuous tense

The present continuous describes an action taking place at the moment of speaking. It is formed with the present tense of the verb **estar** + a verb in the gerund. The gerund is made up of the stem of the verb + the endings **-ando** for **-ar** verbs, and **-iendo** for **-er** and **-ir** verbs.

Estoy cen<u>ando</u>/com<u>iendo</u>/viv<u>iendo</u>. I'm having supper/eating/living.
Estoy estudiando en la universidad. I'm studying at the university.

The following verbs do not normally appear in the present continuous:
ser, estar, ir, venir, regresar.

✅ The relative pronoun *que*

This is used in much the same way as the English 'which' or 'that'; unlike English, it must always be included.

El trabajo **que** estoy haciendo es parecido al trabajo **que** ustedes ofrecen. The job (that) I am doing is similar to the job (that) you are offering.

When it refers to a person, **que** is sometimes replaced by **quien**.

El equipo tiene un jugador **que / quien** es muy bueno. The team has a player who is very good.

ACTIVITY 8

Read the following text and write the numbered verbs in the simple present or present continuous form. Which of the verbs are describing a continuing action? Write these in the present continuous. Note that one of the verbs is in the future.

¡Hola! me llamo Alejandro. (1 **Vivir**) en la Ciudad de México pero no tengo casa. Estos días (2 **vivir**) en la casa de unos amigos mientras están de vacaciones. No (3 **tener**) trabajo. Cada día (4 **ir**) a la oficina de empleo, (5 **comprar**) periódicos y (6 **leer**) los anuncios pero no hay nada. (7 **buscar**) trabajo. Si no (8 **encontrar**) nada (9 **regresar**) a mi pueblo. Al mismo tiempo (10 **estudiar**) por las noches. (11 **Querer**) hacer unos exámenes importantes.

🎧 Now do activities 9 and 10 on the recording.

13.3 I'm head of personnel
Soy jefe de personal

ACTIVITY 11 is on the recording.

ACTIVITY 12

1 List three things that information technology allows us to do which we couldn't do in the past.
2 What three questions does Jorge ask at the end?

DIALOGUE 3

○ Me llamo Jorge García. Trabajo para Nexus. Soy jefe de personal del departamento de computación. Hoy voy a hablar de la influencia que tiene la informática en nuestras vidas. En la actualidad podemos comunicarnos con más rapidez y con más información que nunca. Dentro de unos años la capacidad de nuestros sistemas de informática crecerá mucho. Cuando yo empecé con esta compañía hace veinticinco años, mandábamos la información por correo. Hoy podemos ver la última información sin esperar y mandar mensajes a nuestros compañeros en un segundo. Podemos asistir a reuniones sin salir de la oficina. Estoy llevando a cabo un estudio sobre los efectos de la computación en nuestra vida profesional y hoy quisiera enseñarles los resultados. La cuestión es … ¿Cómo podemos manejar esta explosión de información? ¿La necesitamos? ¿La queremos?

VOCABULARY	
el departamento	department
la computación	information technology
la informática	information technology
hablar (de)	to talk (about)
la influencia	influence
con más rapidez que nunca	more rapidly than ever
crecer	to grow
llevar a cabo	to carry out
el efecto	effect
enseñar	to show, teach
el resultado	result
la cuestión	question
manejar	to manage, cope with
la explosión	explosion

✓ *sin* + infinitive

The preposition **sin** followed by the infinitive is used for the English construction 'without -ing':

> Vemos la información **sin esperar**. We see the information without waiting.
> He trabajado dieciocho horas **sin parar**. I worked 18 hours without stopping.

✓ Ways of expressing what you do

To say what you do, use **ser** with the name of your job:

> **Soy profesor**. I'm a teacher.

Other ways of describing what you do are:

> **Trabajo por mi cuenta**. I'm freelance/self-employed [*literally* I work for myself].
> **Estoy desempleado/a**. I'm unemployed.
> **Tengo mi propio negocio**. I have my own business.
> **Trabajo medio tiempo**. I work part-time.

ACTIVITY 13

Write about yourself in the same way Jorge presents himself. Introduce yourself, give your position, and say what you do and are going to do in the future.

ACTIVITY 14

1 Select the appropriate form of **de, de la, del, de los, de las** in the following sentences.

   1 Voy a hablar _____ efecto de la computación en nuestras vidas.
   2 El profesor habló _____ estudiantes _____ su clase.
   3 Hablaremos _____ vacaciones.
   4 Vamos a hablar _____ contaminación atmosférica.

2 Now complete these sentences using **sin** + an appropriate verb in the infinitive.

   1 I visited my family without seeing my sister.
   2 I worked all day without eating.
   3 I did my exams without studying.
   4 I'm in the office all day and never go out.

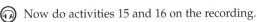 Now do activities 15 and 16 on the recording.

13.4 Job advertisements
Anuncios de trabajo

ACTIVITY 17

Study the job advertisements from a Mexican newspaper and then answer the questions below.

1 Which post is in a hotel?
2 Which post is in the construction industry?
3 Which post is for a company which has been in the market for more than 10 years?
4 Which post has duties that involve covering all of Mexico?
5 What three jobs require experience and knowledge of English?
6 Which job requires a knowledge of information technology?
7 Which jobs require a team leader?
8 Which job insists on a knowledge of written English?

1	Somos la filial mexicana de una de las empresas líderes de Latinoamérica en la producción de baterías. Para nuestra expansión, buscamos: **JEFE DE VENTAS PARA MÉXICO** Se requiere formación de técnico electrónico o ingeniero, y experiencia en dirección de un equipo de ventas.
2	Importante Grupo Empresarial necesita **DIRECTOR HOTEL** para Hotel de Cuatro Estrellas en Oaxaca Se requiere: amplia experiencia; capacidad en dirección de equipos; inglés hablado y escrito.
3	Empresa Multinacional de Ingeniería, Construcción y Mantenimiento necesita **INGENIERO MECÁNICO** Se requiere 10 años de experiencia; dominio del idioma inglés.

4 | Organización Independiente de Control de
Calidad en Construcción
para su área de instalaciones
necesita

INGENIERO TÉCNICO INDUSTRIAL

Se requiere
• experiencia mínima de dos años en control de
calidad de instalaciones de edificación
• conocimientos de inglés

5 | Compañía líder en el sector de la información y
gestión de Comercio Exterior con más de 10
años en el mercado, requiere

PROGRAMADORES

requisitos: licenciado (computación, física,
matemáticas, o ingeniería)

ACTIVITY 18

1 On the left is a list of new words taken from the job
advertisements. On the right are their English equivalents.
First find the Spanish words in the advertisements, then
match each one to the appropriate English translation.

filial	graduate
estrellas	fluency
amplia	leader
dominio	requirements
edificación	subsidiary
líder	stars
licenciado	wide
se requiere/requisitos	building

2 Now rewrite the advertisements in English for the
companies who wish to recruit English speakers. It may be
a bit of a challenge!

13.5 Un extraño en la ciudad

VOY A QUEDARME AQUÍ
I'M GOING TO STAY HERE

Jorge explica más detalles de su negocio y de sus planes. Está buscando empleados.

el motivo	reason, motive
ponerse en contacto	to make contact
ir bien	to go well
la sucursal	branch [*of a company*]
la fábrica	factory
las conservas	canned food products
dirigir	to direct, to manage
con más frecuencia	more frequently
alguien	someone
pronto	soon

ACTIVITY 19

1 Give two reasons why Jorge will stay in Mexico City.
2 What most surprises María?
3 Who owns the company in Chihuahua and what position does Jorge hold?
4 Who will take over the work in Chihuahua?
5 What qualities is Jorge looking for in the person he wishes to employ?
6 What does María want to do before anything else?

ACTIVITY 20

Five of the questions below come from the conversation. Which are they? Indicate who asks each question and give the relevant answer.

1 ¿Vas a regresar a Chihuahua?
2 ¿Vas a llevar a mi mamá?
3 ¿Qué haces en Chihuahua?
4 ¿Qué vas a hacer aquí?
5 ¿Quién va a dirigir la empresa de Chihuahua?
6 ¿Quieres trabajar en mi empresa?
7 ¿Cuándo puedes empezar?
8 ¿Quieres llamar a tu mamá?

ACTIVITY 21

Below are some of the things Jorge tells María. Rewrite the text below as if you were María on the telephone to her mother, telling her the news.

Jorge   Voy a quedarme aquí. Quiero estar cerca de mi familia. En Chihuahua, tengo mi propia empresa. Tengo bastante dinero. Estoy buscando un sitio para abrir una sucursal. Tengo un jefe muy bueno allí. Yo me quedo aquí. Necesito un jefe de personal para la compañía aquí en la Ciudad de México. Tú eres la persona adecuada.

María   Mamá, Jorge va a quedarse aquí. Quiere estar cerca de su familia …

STORY TRANSCRIPT

María	¿Qué vas a hacer? ¿Vas a regresar a Chihuahua? ¿Vas a llevar a mi mamá?
Jorge	Voy a quedarme aquí. Quiero estar cerca de mi familia.
María	¿Y tu trabajo?
Jorge	Estoy en la Ciudad de México por dos motivos. El primero es ponerme en contacto con ustedes. Pero hay otro motivo.
María	¿Qué es?
Jorge	En Chihuahua, tengo mi propia empresa. Me va muy bien. Tengo bastante dinero. Estoy buscando un sitio para abrir una sucursal. Tengo el dinero. Y la empresa necesita crecer.
María	¿Qué tipo de empresa es?
Jorge	Es una fábrica de conservas.
María	¿Y la de Chihuahua? ¿Quién va a dirigir la empresa de Chihuahua?
Jorge	Tengo un jefe muy bueno allí. Yo me quedo aquí.
María	¡Qué buena idea! Estoy muy contenta, después de tanto tiempo. Estoy contenta por mi mamá. Podrás visitarla con más frecuencia.
Jorge	Además … otra cosa. Necesito un jefe de personal para la compañía aquí en la Ciudad de México. Alguien que conoce la Ciudad de México. Alguien con experiencia.
María	Yo puedo ayudarte a buscar a alguien.
Jorge	Estoy buscando a una persona bien calificada, con iniciativa y motivación.
María	Bueno.
Jorge	No tengo que buscarla más. Tú eres la persona adecuada. ¿Quieres trabajar en mi empresa?
María	¡Yo! Pues sí, me gustaría mucho.
Jorge	Estupendo. ¿Cuándo puedes empezar?
María	Pronto. Pero primero quiero hablarle a mi mamá.

Test

Now it's time to test your progress in Unit 13.

1 Put this jumbled telephone conversation in the correct order.

¿De parte de quién?
Gracias.
¿Bueno?
Un momentito, por favor, ahorita lo llamo.
¿Puedo hablar con la señora Gil por favor?
De nada.
Daniel Jiménez.

7

2 Make the following requests on the telephone in Spanish.

1 Ask if you can speak to Sr. García.
2 Ask someone if they can call back later.
3 Ask if you can leave a message.
4 Say you would like to change the time of an interview.
5 Ask someone if they can come to the office tomorrow.

10

3 Using formal imperatives, what do you say when:

1 you want someone to wait for a moment?
2 you want to attract someone's attention?
3 you want someone to look at something?
4 you give something to someone?
5 you are escorting someone into another office?
6 you want to apologize?

6

4 Complete each sentence with the appropriate word or phrase from the list below.

una entrevista   **el encargado/la encargada**   **un recado**
puesto   **una empresa**
las cualidades   **una reunión**

1 Soy _____ de la sección de control de calidad.
2 Trabajo para _____ de electrodomésticos.
3 ¿Por qué está usted interesado en este _____?

4 Para este trabajo se necesitan _____ de motivación y creatividad.
5 Tengo _____ el lunes. No puedo asistir.
6 El Sr. Gil está en _____ . Termina a las doce.
7 ¿Puede dejar _____ ?

7

5 Write the verb in brackets in the simple present or present continuous tense.

1 No puedo salir ahora porque (**trabajar**).
2 (**Terminar**) mi trabajo muy tarde todos los días.
3 ¿Qué (**hacer**) tú ahora?
4 Mi papá me (**hablar**) por la noche.
5 Normalmente yo (**descansar**) después de comer.
6 ¿Dónde está Juan? – (**Jugar**) futbol.
7 Todos los días Juan (**llegar**) al trabajo a las ocho.

7

6 Translate these sentences into Spanish using **sin** + infinitive.

1 I work all day without stopping.
2 I'm going to do the exams without studying.
3 I went shopping yesterday and didn't eat.
4 I was at home on the weekend and didn't go out.

8

TOTAL SCORE **45**

If you scored less than 35, look at the Language Building sections again before completing the Summary on page 194.

Summary 13

 Now try this final test, summarizing the main points covered in this unit.

How would you:
1 answer the phone?
2 ask if you can speak to Sr. García?
3 ask if you can call him later?
4 ask if you can leave a message?
5 ask someone if they'd like to come this way?
6 ask your friend what he is doing?
7 introduce yourself and say who you work for?

REVIEW

Review and extend the language of this unit by using your own personal details to practice talking about your job, your position, your responsibilities, what you do every day, and what you are doing at the moment. Also, work out how much of the professional vocabulary in this unit is relevant to your own job, and what you can add to it to create a set of useful vocabulary. Then practice talking about your own professional circumstances.

Health and fitness
La salud

OBJECTIVES

In this unit you'll learn how to:

- ✓ describe different kinds of sport and other activities
- ✓ describe illnesses and injuries
- ✓ give instructions

And cover the following grammar and language:

- ✓ the perfect tense
- ✓ the verbs **tener** and **doler** to describe how you feel
- ✓ irregular past participles
- ✓ reflexive verbs in the perfect tense
- ✓ the informal imperative
- ✓ the verb **deber** to express obligation

LEARNING SPANISH 14

Now you've completed the course, the most important thing is to consolidate what you have learned by practicing as much as you can. You'll find several useful suggestions throughout the Learning Spanish sections at the beginning of each unit and the Introduction contains a summary of learning strategies. There are two key elements in learning a language; one is your knowledge (vocabulary, tense, and verb forms) and the other is your ability to communicate fluently. There is no substitute for trying out your Spanish whenever you can. As you grow more comfortable with the language, the more you'll enjoy speaking Spanish and the more fluent you'll become.

🔊 Now start the recording for Unit 14.

I've got a temperature

Tengo fiebre

ACTIVITY 1 is on the recording.

ACTIVITY 2

Tick Carmen's symptoms. She says when 2 of them started.
Write this down, beginning **Empezó ...**

la fiebre ☐   dolor de garganta ☐
la tos ☐   dolor de pecho ☐
la gripa ☐   inflamación de la garganta ☐

DIALOGUE 1

- ■ Tengo fiebre y me duele la garganta.
- ○ ¿Cuántos días ha estado así?
- ■ Desde el lunes con la fiebre, y la garganta desde el miércoles.
- ○ A ver ... abra la boca, por favor ... Sí, sí, está inflamada. ¿Tiene tos? ¿Le duele el pecho?
- ■ No, pero me siento muy mal.
- ○ Tiene gripa. Tiene que quedarse en cama y tomar unas pastillas cada cuatro horas.
- ■ De acuerdo. ¿Puedo tomar algo para la garganta?
- ○ Sí, le voy a recetar un jarabe para el dolor de garganta. Pero lo importante es quedarse en cama unos días.

VOCABULARY	
la fiebre	temperature, fever
doler (duele)	to hurt
la garganta	throat
la boca	mouth
inflamado	swollen, inflamed
la tos	cough
el pecho	chest
sentirse	to feel
la gripa	flu
la cama	bed
la pastilla	pill, tablet
recetar	to prescribe
el jarabe	syrup [*e.g., cough syrup*]
el dolor	pain

✓ The perfect tense

The perfect tense is only used to describe events in the recent past, which continue into the present. It is formed using the present of **haber** ('to have') + the past participle of the verb. The past participle is made up of the stem of the verb + the endings **-ado** for **-ar** verbs, and **-ido** for **-er** and **-ir** verbs. It does not vary in gender or number:

Has estado enfermo mucho tiempo. You've been ill for a long time.
Ha vivido allí siempre. He/she has always lived there.

In many Latin American countries, the simple past is used instead.

The following verbs have irregular past participles:

hacer	**hecho** ('done')	romper	**roto** ('broken')
ver	**visto** ('seen')	decir	**dicho** ('said')
poner	**puesto** ('put')	escribir	**escrito** ('written')

✓ Using *tener* and *doler* to describe how you feel

The verb **tener** is often used with a noun to describe how you feel. The definite article (**el, la, los, las**) is not normally used:

Tengo fiebre/tos. I've got a temperature/a cough.
Tengo dolor de cabeza/espalda. I've got a headache/backache.
Tengo frío. I'm cold.

The verb **doler** is used with an indirect object pronoun in the following way to describe symptoms:

Me duele la garganta. My throat hurts.
Te duelen los ojos. Your eyes hurt.

Note that **doler** behaves like **gustar** (see Unit 10). The ending is governed by the thing that hurts rather than the person(s) affected.

ACTIVITY 3

Put the verb in each sentence into the perfect tense.

1 Mis abuelitos siempre (vivir) en esta casa.
2 Este año mi abuelito (venir) a nuestra casa para pasar las vacaciones.
3 Pedro (hacer) el mismo trabajo durante años y le gusta.
4 Yo siempre (comprar) la fruta en este mercado.
5 Juan y yo (ser) amigos desde niños.

Now do activities 4 and 5 on the recording.

14.2 I have a broken leg

Tengo la pierna rota

ACTIVITY 6 is on the recording.

ACTIVITY 7

1 Both Juan and the other player hurt themselves.   V/F
2 Juan has been in hospital.   V/F
3 The other player is in hospital.   V/F
4 Juan has twisted his knee.   V/F
5 Carmen tells Juan to lie on the bed to ease his ankle.   V/F

DIALOGUE 2

○ ¿Qué te pasó?

■ Me torcí el tobillo jugando futbol. Un choque con otro jugador. Él está en el hospital. Tiene la pierna rota. Tengo que ponerme esta pomada.

○ ¿De verdad? El futbol puede ser muy peligroso.

■ También puedes hacerte daño en otros deportes.

○ Sí, tienes razón. ¡Pero el futbol es peligroso para las piernas! Mi papá jugó durante muchos años y tuvo varias lesiones en las rodillas.

■ Pues me dijo el médico que no puedo jugar más en toda la temporada. ¡Ah! Me duele mucho el tobillo.

○ Levanta la pierna y ponla encima de esta silla.

VOCABULARY	
torcer	to twist
el tobillo	ankle
roto	broken
la pomada	ointment
el choque	collision, crash
el jugador/la jugadora	player
romper	to break
la pierna	leg
peligroso	dangerous
hacerse daño	to hurt oneself
la lesión	injury
la rodilla	knee
el médico	doctor
la temporada	(sports) season
encima de	on top of
la silla	chair

✅ Describing injuries using reflexive verbs

To describe an injury, the relevant reflexive verb is used in the preterite. The pronoun comes before the verb:

¿Qué te pasó? What has happened to you?
Me rompí la pierna. I've broken my leg.
Se ha hecho daño. He has hurt himself.

To say you've hurt a specific part of your body, use the preposition **en**:

Me he hecho daño **en** la espalda/**en** las piernas. I've hurt my back/legs. [*literally* I've hurt myself in the back/legs.]

✅ Informal imperative

For regular verbs the singular informal imperative has the same form as the third person singular. The plural form **ustedes** is used in both formal and informal situations.

[sing.]	*[pl.]*	
Levanta los brazos.	**Levanten los brazos.**	Raise your arms.
Come.	**Coman.**	Eat (your dinner).
Abre la puerta.	**Abran las puertas.**	Open the door(s).

The most common irregular verbs used in the imperative form are: **ven, vengan** ('come'); **haz, hagan** ('do'); **pon, pongan** ('put').

ACTIVITY 8

What a day! Write a postcard to your best friend from your vacation apartment:

Last Sunday was terrible. You twisted your ankle playing soccer on the beach. You also have a temperature and a sore throat and the doctor ordered you to stay at home in bed for the rest of the vacation. You have been in bed for four days and your ankle aches a lot. You want to return home.

🎧 Now do activities 9 and 10 on the recording.

You have to lose weight

Tienes que adelgazar

ACTIVITY 11 is on the recording.

ACTIVITY 12

Which of these apply to Antonio and which don't?

1 tiene energía   5 come mal
2 quiere descansar   6 fuma
3 trabaja demasiado   7 adelgaza
4 hace ejercicio

DIALOGUE 3

○ No sé qué me pasa. No tengo energía. Sólo quiero
 descansar.
■ Tu problema es que trabajas demasiado, no haces ejercicio,
 comes mal.
○ Sí, tienes razón. Pero dejé de fumar y me siento mejor.
■ Muy bien, pero debes comer menos carne y más verduras.
○ Y beber más jugos y menos cerveza.
■ Exactamente. Y debes hacer ejercicio. Tienes que adelgazar
 un poco.
○ Sí, tengo que perder peso. Pero juego tenis.
■ Juegas tenis una vez a la semana con tu hermano. Eso no es
 deporte. Tienes que entrenar, dos o tres veces a la semana.
 Ven conmigo al club.
○ No sé si tengo tiempo.
■ No quiero excusas. Tienes que hacer ejercicio.
○ Bueno. ¿Quieres salir a comer una pizza?

VOCABULARY

adelgazar	to lose weight
la energía	energy
demasiado	too much
mal	badly
fumar	to smoke
dejar de fumar	to give up smoking
deber	to have to
hacer ejercicio	to exercise/to play a sport
perder peso	to lose weight
entrenar	to train

✓ demasiado

The adjective **demasiado** agrees in gender and number with the noun it describes. It generally comes in front of the noun:

Como **demasiada carne**. I eat too much meat.
Bebe **demasiado alcohol**. He drinks too much alcohol.
Hay **demasiados carros**. There are too many cars.
Están construyendo **demasiadas casas** en esta zona. They're building too many houses in this area.

Used as an adverb, **demasiado** means 'too much' or 'too hard' and its form doesn't change: **trabajas demasiado** ('you work too hard').

✓ deber

To express an obligation or to offer advice, the verb **deber**, followed by the infinitive, is used:

Debes comer menos carne. You should eat less meat.
No **debes fumar**. You shouldn't smoke.
Debe adelgazar. He should lose weight.

✓ dejar de + infinitive

dejar de followed by the infinitive is used to say you have stopped or given up doing something:

Dejé de fumar. I've given up smoking.
Voy a dejar de jugar tenis. I'm going to give up playing tennis.

ACTIVITY 13

Form sentences by matching up the verbs 1–5 with the correct phrase from a–e.

1	Trabajas	a	demasiada cerveza
2	Como	b	más fruta
3	Bebe	c	demasiado
4	Debes comer	d	demasiadas papas
5	Debe	e	adelgazar

ACTIVITY 14

Make sentences to describe three things that you do, but which you shouldn't; three things you don't do which you should; and three things you have given up doing over the last few years. Use your dictionary if necessary, and invent if you have to!

🎧 Now do activities 15 and 16 on the recording.

14.4 Holiday sports
Deportes de vacaciones

ACTIVITY 17

Below is some information on six of the most popular holiday and beach sports in Spain.

1 Find the Spanish equivalent for each sport in this list.

kite flying   hiking   beach volleyball

2 What do you think the following words mean in English? Try to work them out from the context, and then use your dictionary to check.

a beneficios   e el brazo   i la mano
b la ampolla   f las lesiones   j el estrés
c los reflejos   g el codo   k la torcedura
d fortalecer   h la muñeca

3 Which of the following sport(s) …
1 strengthens your arms?
2 could get you lost and give you blisters?
3 improves your reflexes?
4 could hurt your fingers?
5 is a great antidote to stress?

El cometa

Esta divertida manera de jugar con las posibilidades del viento te permite fortalecer los músculos de las manos y de los pies.
Beneficios: coordinación y equilibrio. Excelente antídoto contra el estrés. Ejercita los músculos de las manos y de los brazos.
Peligros: lesiones en manos y codos.

Frisbee

El disco volador se ha convertido en una imagen habitual en todas las playas del país. Un sencillo disco de plástico volando por las playas.
Beneficios: actividad relajante, mejora los reflejos, fortalece piernas y brazos.
Peligros: se pueden producir lesiones en los codos y las muñecas.

Voleiplaya

Uno de los deportes que más se practica en las costas. Uno de los juegos que forman parte del programa de las Olimpiadas de verano.
Beneficios: mejora la forma física general, los reflejos y la flexibilidad. Fortalece los músculos de las piernas y la capacidad cardiovascular.
Peligros: lesiones de dedos de las manos y muñecas.

Excursionismo

Pasear por el campo, hacer excursiones es algo que todos hemos practicado alguna vez. Es muy popular.
Beneficios: mejora la capacidad cardiovascular y la forma física en general. Es bueno para el estrés y fortalece las piernas.
Peligros: torceduras de tobillos y ampollas en los pies; la posibilidad de perderse.

mejorar	to improve
el equilibrio	balance
los dedos de las manos	fingers
algo que ...	something that ...
la actividad deportiva	sporting activity

LA FAMILIA
THE FAMILY

María invita a Jorge a cenar con ella y su mamá. Por fin la familia está reunida.

la champaña	champagne
la ayuda	help
el sitio	room, space
ganar	to earn
el edificio	building

ACTIVITY 18

1 ¿Por qué están contentos?

2 ¿Dónde están?

3 ¿Por qué vivirá la mamá en el departamento de María?

4 ¿Cuántas recámaras tiene María en el departamento?

5 Podrán cambiarse a otro departamento si no hay sitio. ¿Por qué?

6 Jorge encontró dos cosas ayer. ¿Cuáles son?

7 ¿Cuándo abrirá la empresa?

8 ¿Por qué estaba triste Jorge?

ACTIVITY 19

Supply the appropriate response from the dialogue, without looking at the transcript.

María   Mamá, te vas a quedar aquí conmigo. ¿De acuerdo?

Mamá   Sí, hija. Quiero _____. ¿Pero tienes sitio?

María   Sí, mamá. Tengo _____. ¿Dónde vivirás?

Jorge   Encontré _____.

María   ¿Cuándo vamos a empezar?

Jorge   _____.

ACTIVITY 20

These phrases are in the order they appear in the story. Rearrange them into chronological order from the past to the future.

1 Aquí estamos los tres.
2 Vamos a abrir la champaña.
3 He decidido que no debes vivir sola.
4 Te vas a quedar aquí conmigo.
5 Ganaré más dinero en mi nuevo puesto.
6 Encontré un edificio.
7 Podremos empezar dentro de seis meses.
8 Tendré que hablar con mi jefe pronto.
9 Las dejé hace muchos años.

ACTIVITY 21

Listen to the story again and, without reading the transcript, write sentences about what happened in this episode using the following time expressions:

ayer / dentro de seis meses / pronto / hace muchos años / ahora / hoy

Example: Ayer Jorge encontró un edificio muy bueno para la empresa.

STORY TRANSCRIPT

María	Bueno. Aquí estamos los tres. No sé qué decir. Estoy muy contenta.
Jorge	Yo también. Vamos a abrir la champaña.
María	Mamá, he decidido que no debes vivir sola en el pueblo. Estás enferma y necesitas ayuda. Te vas a quedar aquí conmigo. ¿De acuerdo?
Mamá	Sí, hija. Quiero estar con mi familia. ¿Pero tienes sitio aquí?
María	Sí, Mamá. Tengo dos recámaras. Si queremos un departamento más grande podemos cambiarnos. Ganaré más dinero en mi nuevo puesto. Papá, ¿has encontrado un sitio para la empresa?
Jorge	Sí, ayer encontré un edificio muy bueno para la empresa.
María	¿Dónde vivirás?
Jorge	He encontrado un departamento muy cerca de aquí. Lo encontré ayer.
María	¡Qué bien! ¿Cuándo vamos a empezar?
Jorge	Yo creo que podremos empezar dentro de seis meses. ¿Qué te parece?
María	Me parece muy bien. Tendré que hablar con mi jefe pronto.
Jorge	Tengo que decirles una cosa. Las dejé hace muchos años. Estuve muy triste durante muchos años. Las echaba de menos pero no podía regresar. Pero ahora estoy aquí y voy a quedarme.
María	Hoy ha sido un día muy especial.

Test

Now it's time to test your progress in Unit 14.

1 Describe how you feel using **me duele(n)** or **tengo**.

1 You have a headache.
2 You have a temperature.
3 Your eyes hurt.
4 You have a pain in your chest.
5 Your throat hurts.
6 You have a cough.
7 Your arms ache.
8 You have a pain in your back.

16

2 Now say that you feel:

1 well   4 ill
2 bad   5 terrible
3 very well

5

3 Say you have to take the following remedies, beginning each sentence with **tengo que tomar/ponerme**.

1 some ointment   3 some aspirin
2 some pills   4 cough syrup

4

4 Choose the correct form of **doler** for each sentence.

1 A mí ___ _____ los pies y también ___ _____ la espalda.
2 ¿Qué ___ _____ a usted? A mí ___ _____ la cabeza.
3 ¿Qué ___ _____ a ustedes? A nosotros ___ _____ los oídos.
4 A ti ___ _____ algo? No, a mí no ___ _____ nada.

8

5 ¿Qué te pasó? Translate these sentences using the perfect of the appropriate reflexive verb.

1 I've twisted my ankle.   4 He's hurt his head.
2 I've hurt my knee.   5 She's burnt herself.
3 He's broken his leg.

10

6 Insert the correct form of the informal imperative.

1 ¡Hola! ¿Qué tal? (**pasar**)
2 (**Abrir**) la puerta, por favor.
3 (**Hacer**) la tarea ahora mismo.
4 Vamos a comer; (**poner**) la mesa.

Now insert the correct form of the formal imperative.

1 (**Pasar**) por aquí.
2 (**Levantar**) los pies.
3 (**Venir**) aquí.
4 (**Seguir**) esta calle.

8

7 ¿**Demasiado/a/os/as?** Complete the sentences with the appropriate form of the word.

1 Trabajo _____.
2 Bebe _____ alcohol.
3 Veo la televisión _____.
4 Siempre está en el sofá. Descansa _____.
5 Fumas _____ cigarros.
6 No come verdura. Come _____ carne.
7 Estás muy gordo. Comes _____.
8 Comes _____ papas.

8

8 Now give appropriate advice for each sentence in Activity 7, using the correct form of **deber**. For 1 and 8 use the informal form; for 2–7, use the formal.

8

TOTAL SCORE **67**

If you scored less than 57, look at the Language Building sections again before completing the Summary on page 208.

Summary 14

Now try this final test, summarizing the main points covered in this unit.

How would you:
1 ask someone you don't know well what the matter is?
2 say you have a temperature?
3 say you have a headache?
4 say you feel terrible?
5 tell a friend to open the door?
6 tell your friend she shouldn't smoke?
7 tell her you've given up smoking?

REVIEW

Now that you've completed this course, go back over all the units and read through the review notes for each one. In this way you will remind yourself of things you may have forgotten. Practice structures and vocabulary you are less confident about. Develop the subject matter of the earlier units in the light of what you now know.

Constantly practice verb forms and recycle vocabulary every day. Develop your vocabulary by actively adding to your word store. Use a dictionary and make sure you learn the words by using them appropriately. Get hold of articles, newspapers, and books in Spanish and build your vocabulary in this way too. Most important, try to gain the opportunity to speak to Spanish people. The sooner you use your Spanish in real situations the faster it will develop.

Review 4

1 Write the Spanish for the following reflexive verbs.

1 to get tired   6 to worry
2 to bathe   7 to enjoy oneself
3 to get bored   8 to stay
4 to get burnt   9 to feel
5 to remember   10 to hurt oneself

2 Complete the story using the following items of vocabulary, giving the correct forms as necessary.

campamento / barco / costa / carne asada / jardín / estupenda

Estuve en un 1_____ durante el verano. Estuvimos en la 2_____. Un día fui de excursión en un 3_____ . Otro día me quedé en el campamento y preparé carne para una 4_____ en el 5_____ de un amigo. ¡Fue una comida 6_____!

3 Match the complaints on the left with the appropriate remedy on the right.

1 la espalda quemada   a pastillas
2 dolor de cabeza   b una pomada
3 una tos   c un jarabe

4 What is the Spanish for the following phrases?

1 You're right. [*informal sing.*]
2 To miss someone.
3 It's worth it.
4 To begin with.

5 Give the Spanish for the following.

1 I returned.
2 He was in Oaxaca.
3 What did they do?
4 We went to the beach.
5 They bought a house by the sea.

6 Write three sentences describing good weather and three sentences describing bad weather.

7 Answer the following questions about yourself using **hace** + time period. **¿Cuánto hace que ...**

1 viste la televisión?
2 fuiste de vacaciones?
3 te cambiaste de casa?
4 comiste?
5 estuviste de vacaciones?

8 Choose the imperfect or simple past to complete these sentences.

1 (**Jugar**) futbol cada domingo. (Yo)
2 (**Comprar**) la camisa ayer. (Yo)
3 Cuando yo (**ser**) pequeño mi papá (**viajar**) mucho.
4 Nosotros (**vivir**) en esta casa hace muchos años.
5 (**Tener**) fiebre la semana pasada. (Yo)

9 Put the verbs in brackets into the imperative.

1 (**Pasar**) por aquí. (usted)
2 (**Abrir**) la puerta. (tú)
3 (**Poner**) la mesa. (ustedes)
4 (**Levantar**) el pie. (tú)

10 Say what these people are doing, using the present continuous.

1 Yo (**estudiar**).
2 Ellos (**comer**).
3 Nosotros (**viajar**) a la Ciudad de México.
4 Ustedes (**terminar**) el trabajo.
5 Tú (**vivir**) con un amigo.

11 **¿Qué te pasó?** Say what happened to you using the preterite.

1 (**Torcer**) el tobillo.
2 (**Hacer daño**) en el pie.
3 (**Romper**) el brazo.
4 (**Quemar**) la espalda.

12 Listen to the conversation. What are Antonio and Beatriz doing?

    1 Esta tarde   3 Esta noche
    2 A las siete   4 El mes que viene

13 Listen to these phone conversations and answer the questions. Who …

    1 is coming to the phone?
    2 will call later?
    3 is on vacation?
    4 can't come to the phone?

SPEAKING

🔊 14 Complete your side of the conversation and then check against the recording.

    A: ¡Qué bronceado estás!
    You: (Say you've been on vacation.)
    A: ¿Adónde fuiste?
    You: (You went to Alicante.)
    A: ¿Estuviste en un campamento?
    You: (You were in your parents' apartment.)
    A: ¿Con quién fuiste?
    You: (You went with some friends.)
    A: ¿Te gusta nadar?
    You: (Yes, you do, but you also like to visit towns and villages.)
    A: ¿Cómo estuvo el clima?
    You: (It was sunny every day except Saturday, when it rained all day.)
    A: ¿Qué hiciste por las noches?
    You: (You danced and enjoyed yourself.)

15 Now answer these questions about yourself using **voy** + **a** + infinitive.

   1 ¿Qué vas a hacer esta noche?
   2 ¿A qué hora te vas a acostar esta noche?
   3 ¿Qué vas a hacer este fin de semana?
   4 ¿Tienes planes para el año que entra?
   5 ¿Qué vas a hacer la semana que entra?

16 Complete your side of the telephone conversation and then check your answers on the recording.

A: ¿Bueno?
You: (You want to speak to Sr. Solano.)
A: No está. Está de viaje.
You: (Ask when he will be back.)
A: El jueves.
You: (Ask if you can leave a message.)
A: Sí. Un momentito. Dígame.
You: (The message is that you called and that you cannot attend a meeting on Friday. Can you change it?)
A: Yo lo puedo cambiar. ¿Qué día le acomoda?
You: (Suggest next Tuesday.)
A: ¿A qué hora?
You: (Suggest 10 o'clock.)
A: Muy bien.
You: (Say see you on Tuesday.)

Answers

Unit 1

2 1 c; 2 a; 3 b

3 1 usted; 2 tú; 3 usted; 4 tú; 5 usted

7 1 F: they take place in the morning; 2 F; 3 T; 4 F: he asks her what her name is

8 1 c; 2 a; 3 b

12 *María*: jugo de naranja; *Juan*: café, torta de jamón

13 1 Una torta de jamón y una torta de queso, 2 Un jugo de papaya y un café.

14 1 d; 2 a; 3 e; 4 f; 5 b; 6 c

17 *Drinks*: café, té solo, té limón, jugo de naranja, jugo de jitomate, Coca cola, limonada; *Food*: ensalada, torta de jamón y queso, hamburguesas, ensalada de fruta, pastel de chocolate
María: Quiero el pastel de chocolate y un café. *Juan*: Yo quiero una Coca cola y una ensalada. *Miguel*: Un jugo de naranja/jitomate y una torta de jamón y queso, por favor.

18 3, 2, 6, 1, 4, 5

19 1 M; 2 H; 3 S; 4 H; 5 S

Test

1 1 i; 2 f; 3 h; 4 b; 5 a; 6 d; 7 e; 8 c; 9 g

2 1 Un café con leche y un helado. 2 Una torta de queso y una cerveza. 3 Un jugo de jitomate y una ensalada. 4 Un té y una torta de jamón.

3 1 ¿Es usted; 2 soy; 3 ¡Encantado! 4 ¡Mucho gusto! 5¿Cómo está (usted)? 6 Bien

4 1 ¿Es usted la Sra. Martín? 2 ¿Cómo está usted? 3 ¡Buenos días! 4 Le presento a la Sra. Martín. 5 Quiero un café con leche.

5 1 Quiero un café. 2 Sí. Quiero una torta de jamón y queso y una ensalada. 3 Nada más, gracias.

6 1 la señora; 2 la señorita; 3 el mesero; 4 la mesera; 5 el amigo

Summary 1

1 Buenos días, Buenas tardes, Buenas noches. *2* ¿Cómo está usted? *3* ¿Cómo estás? *4* Muy bien, gracias. *5* Le presento a la Sra. Martín. *6* Encantado/Encantada/Mucho gusto. *7* Quiero un café y un jugo de naranja, por favor. *8* Gracias.

Unit 2

2 *the cathedral*: in a square; 5 minutes away
Frida Kahlo's house: in a suburb; 15

minutes away

6 1 T; 2 F: it's at the end of avenida Canal de Miramontes on the left; 3 F: it's the third house on the left; 4 T

7 1 d; 2 c; 3 a; 4 b

11 1 A supermarket; B bank; C restaurant; D hospital

12 1 e; 2 a; 3 d; 4 g; 5 f; 6 c; 7 h; 8 b

13 1 a ¿Hay un banco por aquí? b ¿Hay un hotel por aquí? c ¿Hay un supermercado por aquí? 2 ¿Dónde está la estación? ¿Dónde está el restaurante?

16 A Teatro Blanquita; B Torre Latino Americana; C Palacio de Bellas Artes; D Museo Nacional de la Estampa; E Monumento Juárez; F Museo Nacional de Arte Popular

17 1 Siga derecho al final de la calle. Está enfrente. 2 Siga a la derecha. Tome la primera a la izquierda. Siga derecho. Tome la segunda a la derecha. Está a la derecha. 3 Siga a la derecha. Tome la primera a la derecha. Siga derecho. Está a la izquierda.

18 1 Teatro Blanquita; 2 Museo Nacional de Arte Popular; 3 Torre Latino Americana

19 3, 1, 4, 6, 2, 5

20 1 F: el hotel está cerca; 2 F: está enfrente de la terminal de la autobuses; 3 V; 4 F: la biblioteca está cerca de la casa de María; 5 V

21 1 ¿Hay periódicos antiguos? Sí. 2 ¿Cómo se llama? Se llama Hotel Oriente. 3 ¿Hay una sección de periódicos? Sí, hay. 4 ¿Hay un hotel por aquí? Sí, hay un hotel muy cerca. 5 ¿Dónde está la biblioteca municipal? Está cerca de la casa de María. 6 Usted conoce a María, ¿no? No. 7 ¿Dónde está? Está aquí. A la derecha. 8 ¿Aquí? Sí, aquí, enfrente de la oficina.

Test

1 1 g; 2 h; 3 e; 4 b; 5 c; 6 f; 7 d; 8 a

2 1 La segunda a la derecha y todo derecho al final de la calle. 2 La tercera (calle) a la izquierda y está a la derecha. 3 Todo derecho al final de la calle, a la izquierda y está a la izquierda. 4 La primera a la derecha, la segunda a la izquierda y está a la derecha.

3 1 disculpe; 2 ¿Hay; 3 aquí; 4 final; 5 primera/segunda/tercera; 6 ¿dónde; 7 lado; 8 Está; 9 a

4 1 dieciséis; 2 diecisiete; 3 siete; 4 veinte;

5 trece; 6 tres; 7 once; 8 doce; 9 cinco;
10 ocho
5 Está en la plaza del Virrey.
Está a cinco minutos en el camión.
Catorce./El número catorce.
La primera (calle) a la izquierda.
6 1 las casas; 2 los melones; 3 los pasteles;
4 los jitomates; 5 las plazas

Summary 2

1 ¿Hay un museo por aquí? *2* ¿Dónde está
el banco? *3* ¿Dónde está la avenida Canal
de Miramontes? *4* La catedral está a diez
minutos. *5* Es la segunda (calle) a la
izquierda. 6 Todo derecho al final de la
calle. 7 El hotel está enfrente de la
estación.

Unit 3

2 potatoes – a kilo; onions – two kilos; tomatoes – half a kilo; oil – a bottle; milk – two
liters
3 jitomates – lata; cebollas – kilo; queso –
cien gramos; jugo de naranja – botella;
aceite – litro
7 1 T; 2 T; 3 F: he buys a large envelope; 4 F:
it costs 30 pesos; 5 T
8 1 grande; 2 más; 3 cuesta; 4 para; 5 Deme;
6 cuánto; 7 Son; 8 mandar
12 1 un melón grande; 2 una piña; 3 dos
piñas; 4 la sandía
13 1 **Las papas fritas. Las** quiero; *or* **Un
paquete de papas fritas. Lo** quiero.
2 **Una lata de sardinas. La** quiero. 3 **Un
litro de aceite. Lo** quiero. 4 **Dos botellas de
cerveza. Las** quiero. 5 **Jamón. Lo** quiero.
6 **Timbres. Los** quiero.
16 tortillería – tortilla; carnicería – meat;
frutería – fruit; verdulería – vegetables;
pastelería – cakes; panadería – bread;
pescadería – fish; florería – flowers; salchichonería – ham
fruta; pasteles; pescado; pan; jamón; flores; tortilla; verdura; carne
17 **Across:** PESCADERIA, AZUCAR, TORTILLA,
DURAZNO, PAPA
Down: MERCADO, RES, PAN, PASTEL,
MANGO, PANADERIA
18 1 María; 2 María; 3 the stranger; 4 the
stranger; 5 the stranger knows María;
6 the stranger
19 1 M; 2 B; 3 M; 4 B; 5 S; 6 P
20 1 ¿Qué desea? 2 ¿Desea algo más? 3 ¿Me
conoce? 4 ¿Cuánto cuesta?

Test

1 1 g; 2 c; 3 f; 4 a; 5 b; 6 h; 7 e; 8 d; 9 f; 10 a
2 1 Quiero dos kilos de papas y medio kilo
de cebollas. 2 Quiero un litro de vino y

una lata de aceite. 3 Quiero cien gramos
de jamón y doscientos gramos de queso.
4 Quiero dos paquetes de papas fritas y
dos botellas de cerveza. 5 Quiero cuatro
tarjetas y cinco timbres para los Estados
Unidos.
3 1 dieciocho; 2 veintisiete; 3 treinta y cinco;
4 cincuenta y nueve; 5 cien; 6 doscientos
cincuenta; 7 quinientos; 8 trescientos
setenta; 9 cuatrocientos cuarenta; 10
noventa y nueve
4 1 la salchichonería, delicatessen; 2 la
salchichonería, delicatessen; 3 la carnicería,
butcher's; 4 la frutería, fruit store; 5 la
verdulería, grocery store; 6 la pescadería,
fish store; 7 el puesto de abarrotes,
grocery stand, 8 la frutería, fruit stand; 9
la pastelería, cake store; 10 la panadería,
baker's
5 ¿Cuánto cuestan las sandías?
Quiero dos.
No. Las quiero pequeñas.
Nada más. ¿Cuánto es?

Summary 3

1 Quiero medio kilo de jitomates. 2 Quiero
una botella de aceite. *3* Quiero un litro de
leche. *4* Nada más. *5* Quiero cien gramos
de queso. *6* Cuánto cuesta un timbre para
los Estados Unidos. *7* Son cuarenta y cinco
pesos. *8* Tenga.

Review 1

1 a: 2, 6; b: 5, 8; c: 1, 3; d: 4, 7
2 un café con leche; un té limón; un jugo de
naranja; una torta de queso; un pastel de
chocolate
3 1 c; 2 e; 3 a; 4 b; 5 d
4 1 ✓ 2 ✗ 3 ✓ 4 ✓ 5 ✗
5 1 A; 2 B; 3 A; 4 A; 5 B
6 1 está; 2 Deme; 3 a, de, al; 4 Hay; 5 cuesta;
6 Las
7 1 para; 2 del; 3 Es; 4 soy; 5 es
8 1 10 minutes; 2 left; 3 55; 4 a market; 5 a
bank
9 B: ¿Tiene latas de <u>sardinas</u> [**jitomates**]?
B: Sí. Quiero <u>cinco</u> [**cuatro**].
B: Sí. Deme <u>dos kilos</u> [**un kilo**] de <u>naranjas</u>
[**papas**].
B: <u>Deme dos.</u> [**Sí.**]
11 Mucho gusto. Soy …
Muy bien. ¿Y usted?
Sí, gracias. ¿Hay un café por aquí?

Unit 4

<table>
<tr><td>**2**</td><td></td><td>¿De dónde es?</td><td>¿Dónde vive?</td></tr>
<tr><td></td><td>Paco</td><td>México</td><td>México (Guadalajara)</td></tr>
<tr><td></td><td>Margarita</td><td>España</td><td>España</td></tr>
<tr><td></td><td>Jorge</td><td>Argentina</td><td>México (Guadalajara)</td></tr>
<tr><td></td><td>El hermano de Paco</td><td>México</td><td>España</td></tr>
</table>

3 1 estamos; 2 está; 3 trabajo; 4 estudia; 5 viajamos; 6 están; 7 cenamos; 8 Hablamos

7 1 bilingual secretary; 2 Carmen Soto; 3 Javier Montero; 4 next to Javier Montero; 5 Ana Vázquez; 6 two

8 1 escribimos; 2 llaman; 3 Hablamos; 4 manejo; 5 salgo; 6 sale; 7 viven; 8 salimos

12 1 A; 2 1975; 3 329 5568; 4 12; 5 17

13 dos, cuarenta y seis, ochenta y cinco, ochenta y tres; 2 Calle Central, veintiséis; 3 dos, treinta y ocho, noventa y nueve, sesenta y tres; 4 Avenida de la Independencia, treinta y cinco; 5 dos, cuarenta y cinco, cincuenta y cuatro, veintiocho; 6 Paseo de La Reforma, ciento cincuenta y tres

16 1 la norteña; 2 la música ranchera; 3 por todo el país; 4 los Estados Unidos; 5 cambian la letra y el ritmo; 6 la telenovela; 7 los Estados Unidos

17 1 popular; 2 país; 3 radio; 4 discos; 5 famosas

18 1 d; 2 e; 3 a; 4 b; 5 c

19 1 V; 2 V; 3 F; 4 V; 5 F; 6 F; 7 V; 8 V

20 1 ¿Cómo **está**? (d); 2 Usted conoce a María, ¿**verdad**? (e); 3 ¿De **dónde** es usted? (b); 4 ¿**En qué** trabaja? (c); 5 ¿Vive **cerca**? (a)

21 1 Sr. Herrera; 2 Jorge Jimeno; 3 María; 4 María; 5 Jorge Jimeno; 6 Jorge Jimeno; 7 María; 8 María

Test

1 1 **Le presento a la** señora Campos. Es **española**.
2 **Le presento a** Jorge Ballesteros. Es **mexicano**.
3 **Le presento a la** señorita Tomás. Es **argentina**.
4 **Le presento a la** señora Deschamps. Es **francesa**.
5 **Le presento a** Dieter Müller. Es **alemán**.
6 **Le presento a** Peter Jones y **él es** Barry Wright. **Son estadounidenses**.

2 1 llamo; 2 soy; 3 Vivo; 4 Trabajamos; 5

trabajo; 6 soy; 7 es; 8 estamos; 9 comemos; 10 vivimos

3 1 El señor Rodríguez **es profesor**.
2 La señorita Martín **es estudiante**.
3 El señor Ortega y la señora Sánchez **son ingenieros**. 4 La señora Serrano y la señorita Moreno **son secretarias**.
5 El señor Carrasco **es recepcionista**.

4 1 La calle Barlovento, veinticinco. Teléfono: cinco, treinta y tres, doce, treinta y siete. 2 Avenida Los Insurgentes, ciento, cuarenta y tres. Teléfono: cuatro, dieciocho, noventa y cinco, cincuenta y ocho. 3 Paseo de Acapulco, setenta y seis. Teléfono: tres, cuarenta y ocho, sesenta y ocho, noventa y cuatro. 4 Calle Seguro Social, noventa y siete. Teléfono: nueve, setenta y seis, veintinueve, noventa y dos. 5 Plaza Hidalgo, quince. Teléfono: cuatro, cincuenta y seis, treinta y dos, ochenta y cuatro.

5 Buenos días. Soy (add your name).
Soy gerente de ventas.
No. Soy (add your nationality), pero vivo y trabajo en la Ciudad de México.
Vivo en la calle Rivera.
Número diecisiete.

6 1 Traba**jamos** en un banco. 2 ¿Co**men** en un restaurante? 3 Vi**vo** en una plaza. 4 Mis papás habl**an** por teléfono. 5 Él no cono**ce** a María.

Summary 4

1 Le presento a la señora Martínez. *2* ¿Es usted argentino? *3* Vivo en Guadalajara. *4* ¿Trabajan en Colombia? *5* Soy profesor/a. *6* Conozco a María.

Unit 5

2 Óscar es **el esposo** de Margarita. Margarita es **la esposa** de Óscar. Pablo es **el hijo** de Margarita. **El papá** de Pepe es **el abuelito** de Carmen. Carmen es **la hermana** de José.

3 a cuántos; b cuántos; c cuántas; d Mi; e Su; f tu

7 1 P; 2 M; 3 M; 4 P; 5 P

8 1 pequeño; 2 moderno; 3 bonitas; 4 ancha; 5 antiguos

12 1 V; 2 F: es para tres noches; 3 V; 4 V; 5 F: está en el segundo piso

13 a el treinta y uno de marzo. b el tres de junio. c el diez de noviembre. d el doce de diciembre. e el veintitrés de mayo. f el cinco de septiembre

16 a 5; b 8; c 4; d 1; e 2; f 3; g 7; h 6

17 1 He's looking for an article about María. 2 He asks her for a photocopy of the article. 3 5 minutes on foot. 4 Because it is

quiet. 5 Because he wants to see the
street. 6 He can see María's house.
18 5, 4, 3, 1, 2
19 1 V; 2 F: dos o tres noches; 3 V; 4 F; 5 V; 6 F

Test

1 1 Tengo tres hermanos y una hermana.
2 Tengo dos hijos, un niño de ocho años y
una niña de seis años. 3 Mi papá tiene
sesenta años y mi mamá tiene cincuenta y
ocho años. 4 Estoy casado y mi esposa se
llama Josefina./Estoy casada y mi esposo se
llama José.

2 1 e; 2 d; 3 a; 4 b; 5 c

3 1 el abuelito; 2 el tío; 3 el hermano; 4 el
hijo; 5 la hermana; 6 el papá; 7 la mamá; 8
la abuelita

4 1 para; 2 por; 3 por; 4 por; 5 para; 6 por

5 1 Una habitación doble para tres noches. 2
Quiero una habitación para el catorce de
febrero. 3 ¿Cuánto es? 4 ¿Está en el tercer
piso? 5 Tengo equipaje.

6 1 el veintitrés de junio; 2 el trece de
febrero; 3 el diecinueve de septiembre; 4
el treinta de julio; 5 el primero de mayo

Summary 5

1 ¿Está usted casada? *2* Tengo tres hijos. *3*
María es mi hermana. *4* Tiene tres años. *5*
Cuántos años tiene José? *6* ¿Cómo es su
departamento? *7* Quiero una habitación
doble para tres noches.

Unit 6

2 1 accountant; 2 furniture store; 3 5 p.m.; 4
2 hours

3 1 a Son las diez. b Son las once y media.
c Son las tres. d Son las seis y media. 2 a
Soy gerente de ventas. b Trabajo en una
empresa de muebles. c Soy jefe de
personal. d Trabajo en una tienda de
comestibles. 3 a de diez a una y de cuatro
a siete; b de nueve a cinco; c de nueve a
una y de cuatro a ocho; d de dos a diez

7 1 a las siete de la mañana; 2 a las ocho de
la mañana; 3 a las ocho y media 4 ; a las
ocho de la tarde; 5 a las nueve y media;
6 a las once y media o a las doce

8 Pepe se levanta a las siete y trabaja de las
nueve y cuarto a la una y cuarto. Come a
las dos y vuelve a trabajar a las cuatro.
Trabaja hasta cuarto para las ocho. Se
acuesta a las once y media.

12 a La película empieza a las seis y cuarto.
b La película termina a las ocho. c El
museo abre a las diez de la mañana.

13 *Suggested answers:* 1 La Máscara del Zorro
216 empieza a las cuatro/las seis/las ocho/las
diez. 2 La Máscara del Zorro termina a las

seis/las ocho/las diez/las doce. 3 La Máscara
del Zorro dura dos horas. 4 La pastelería
abre a las nueve y media. 5 La pastelería
cierra a la una y media. 6 La pastelería
abre a las cuatro y media de la tarde. 7 La
pastelería cierra a las ocho de la tarde. 8 El
museo está cerrado los lunes. 9 El museo
abre a las diez. 10 El museo cierra a las
siete. 11 El museo abre a las once los
domingos. 12 El museo cierra a las cinco
los domingos.

14 A: ¿Quieres ir al cine esta tarde?
B: ¿A qué hora empieza la película?
A: Empieza a las siete y termina a las
    nueve.
B: Cenamos después.

17 1 Se levanta a las seis y media. 2 Toma un
café. 3 Come en casa. 4 Cena a las nueve y
media. 5 Da un paseo. Come con la
familia.

19 *Horizontal:* PANDULCE, DESAYUNO,
SOBREMESA, PAN TOSTADO
Vertical: ALMUERZO, CENA, CAFÉ, TORTA

20 1 Jorge offers María a drink; 2 Jorge;
3 María; 4 María; 5 María; 6 Jorge invites
María to dinner; 7 María; 8 María

21 1 c; 2 a; 3 b; 4 e; 5 d

Test

1 1 Son las siete y cuarto de la mañana. 2 Es
la una y media de la tarde. 3 Son las seis y
media de la tarde. 4 Son las once de la
noche. 5 Son cuarto para las cinco de la
tarde.

2 1 Jaime trabaja desde las nueve hasta la
una (por la mañana) y desde las cuatro
hasta las ocho (por la tarde). 2 Carmen
trabaja desde las ocho y media hasta la
una y media y desde las cuatro y media
hasta las siete y media. 3 Jorge trabaja
desde las ocho de la tarde hasta las seis de
la mañana. 4 Puri trabaja desde las ocho
hasta las once. 5 Alfonso trabaja desde
cuarto para las tres hasta las ocho y media.

3 Me levanto a las … Desayuno a las …
Salgo de casa a las … Llego a mi trabajo a
las …Como a las … Termino mi (trabajo) a
las … Regreso a mi casa a las … Ceno a las
…
Y me acuesto a las …

4 1 cierra; 2 dura; 3 cierra; 4 empieza,
termina; 5 abre

5 No, no quiero ir al cine.
Quiero cenar en un restaurante.
Nos vemos a las siete y media en el
restaurante.

6 1 salgo; 2 regresa; 3 tengo; 4 quieren; 5
conozco

7 1 Quiero **cenar**. 2 Quiero **salir**. 3 Quiero

visitar a mis papás. 4 Quiero **ir a casa**.
*Note that **querer** is followed by the*
infinitive.

8 1 Me levanto a las siete; 2 Ceno a las
nueve de la noche. 3 Me acuesto a las
once. 4 Me baño por la mañana. 5
Descanso después de comer. 6 Salgo a las
ocho.

Summary 6

1 ¿Qué hora es? *2* Son cuarto para las
nueve de la mañana. *3* Trabajo de nueve a
cinco. *4* La película empieza a las seis y
termina a las ocho. *5* La tienda abre a las
diez y cierra a las seis. *6* Nos vemos en el
restaurante a las ocho.

Unit 7

2 *Appetizer*: sopa, ensalada; *Entrée*: pescado, pollo, mojarra; *Dessert*: flan, fruta;
Drinks: agua, cerveza

3 1 empezar; 2 Cómo; 3 Qué; 4 Quiero; 5
beber

7 1 Carmen; 2 Alfonso; 3 Carmen; 4 Alfonso

8 1 ¿Qué hay de postre? 2 Falta un tenedor.
3 ¿Puede traer un café? 4 Ahorita traen la
cuenta. 5 No puedo terminar mi postre.
6 Se come frío.

12 1 The table is dirty. 2 The soup is cold.
3 The fish is burnt. 4 The bill is wrong.
5 The restaurant is very bad.

13 El restaurante Cuatro Estaciones **es** muy
bueno. **Está** enfrente del cine Alameda. La
comida **es buena** también. Pero hoy hay
un problema. Hay dos meseros **nuevos**.
Son malos. La sopa **está fría** y la carne **está
quemada**. Los clientes **están enojados**. La
señora Martínez **es muy importante**. Ella
está enojada. La comida **es mala** y su
cuenta **está equivocada**.

14 1 ¿Podría cambiar**la**? 2 ¿Podría cambiar**lo**?
3 ¿Podría cambiar**las**? 4 ¿Podría
cambiar**los**, por favor? 5 ¿Podría
cambiar**lo**? 6 ¿Podría mirar**la**? 7 ¿Podría
limpiar**la**?

17 1 los tacos; 2 el mole poblano; 3 los
tacos; 4 arroz a la mexicana; 5 arroz a la
mexicana; 6 arroz a la mexicana; 7 el
mole poblano; 8 los tacos

18 1 Tiene chiles, cacahuates, tortilla frita,
caldo de pollo y chocolate. 2 Se prepara
una salsa con los ingredientes y se hierven
piezas de pollo en la salsa. Se sirve
caliente. 3 El mole poblano; 4 Los tacos; 5
Arroz con chícharos, zanahoria, puré de
tomate

19 Se cortan las papas. Se calienta el aceite y
se fríen las papas en el aceite. Se fríen las

hamburguesas en un poco de aceite.

21 1 F: no termina el pollo porque no tiene
hambre; 2 F: 3 F: quiere pedir la cuenta;
4 V; 5 V; 6 F: María sale primero

22 d, f, e, h, b, a, c, i, g, j

23 1 están; 2 come; 3 tiene; 4 quiere;
5 Quiere; 6 tiene; 7 conoce; 8 puede;
9 entiende; 10 se va

Test

1 1 el primer plato; 2 la sopa, la ensalada; 3
el segundo plato; 4 pescado, pollo; 5 el
postre; 6 flan, fruta, helado; 7 la cuenta

2 1 ¿Qué hay? 2 ¿Cómo es? 3 ¿Qué es?

3 A: ¿Qué **vas** a tomar para empezar? B:
Para **empezar** quiero la sopa. A: Yo **quiero**
la ensalada. B: ¿Y **luego**? A: El pollo, por
favor. B: **Para** mí, el pescado. ¿Y para
beber? A: Agua mineral. A: ¿Qué **hay** de
postre? B: El helado es **bueno**. ¿Y para
usted? A: No quiero **nada**. **Estoy**
satisfecho.

4 1 Falta un cuchillo. 2 Falta una cuchara. 3
Falta una copa. 4 Faltan (los) vasos. 5
Faltan (los) platos. 6 Falta un tenedor.

5 ¿Puede traer la sopa?
El pollo está frío.
¿Puede cambiarlo?
¿Puede traer la cuenta?
La cuenta está equivocada.

6 1 es 2 es 3 está 4 está

7 1 cambiarlo; 2 calentarla; 3 cambiarlas; 4
limpiarla; 5 traerlos; 6 traerlo; 7 mirarla; 8
traerla/cambiarla

Summary 7

1 Para empezar, quiero ensalada. *2* El
pescado está quemado. ¿Podría cambiarlo?
3 Faltan dos cuchillos. *4* ¿Podría traerlos? *5*
El restaurante es malo. *6* ¿Puede traer la
cuenta, por favor?

Review 2

1 1 una francesa; 2 un estadounidense; 3 dos
escocesas; 4 dos mexicanos; 5 un canadiense

2 1 José es periodista. 2 María es profesora.
3 La señora Gil es contadora. 4 Gustavo y
Javier son ingenieros. 5 Alicia y Celia son
recepcionistas. 6 Alfonso es secretario.

3 el papá; el esposo; la mamá; la hermana;
el hermano

4 recibidor; cocina; recámara; sala; comedor

5 me levanto; me baño; desayuno; salgo de;
llego a; termino; regreso a; ceno; descanso;
me acuesto

6 1 éste; 2 éstos; 3 ésta; 4 éste; 5 éstas

7 1 trabajamos; 2 vive; 3 comen; 4 viajo; 5
escribes; 6 quiero; 7 tienes

8 1 Nos levantamos a las siete. 2 Se acuesta a
las once. 3 Se viste a las ocho. 4 ¿Te bañas
a las siete?

9 1 limpiar; 2 calentar; 3 traer; 4 traer
10 1 ¿Podría limpiarla? 2 ¿Podría limpiarlo? 3 ¿Podría limpiarlos? 4 ¿Podría limpiarlas?
11 1 es; 2 está; 3 es; 4 está; 5 es

12

	Message 1	Message 2	Message 3
Time	7.00, 7.45, 10.00	8.00, 8.30, 11.00	1.30, 6.00, 9.00
Information	have a drink before	have supper before	have supper after

13 1 V; 2 F: it comes with potatoes; 3 V; 4 F: they both want lemon water; 5 F: the knife is dirty; 6 V; 7 F: she asks for it to be changed
14 Tengo dos niños/chicos y una niña/chica. La niña tiene doce y los chicos tienen ocho y seis.
Soy ingeniero/a.
Soy inglés/inglesa. ¿De dónde es usted?
Tengo un tío en México. Vive en Guadalajara.
15 Para empezar quiero sopa y de plato fuerte pollo. De beber, un jugo de piña. De postre quiero un helado. Falta una cuchara. ¿Puede traer una? Quiero un café. Esto es té. Yo quiero café. ¿Puede cambiarlo? La cuenta, por favor. Por favor – la cuenta está mal.

Unit 8

2 1 F; 2 V; 3 F; 4 F: el autobús sale del andén dos
3 1 A; 2 a; 3 para; 4 a

7

	Advantages	Disadvantages
Car	It's quicker. They can use it in Mexico City. They can leave luggage in it.	He doesn't want to drive. It's a long way. You have to eat in cafeterías by the freeway.
Bus	They can read and relax. It's more comfortable. It's cheaper.	They can't take much luggage.

8 1 ¿A cuántos kilómetros está la Ciudad de México? 2 Tarda media hora en autobús. 3 Tardo quince minutos en llegar al trabajo. 4 Guadalajara está a trescientos kilómetros.
12 1 C; 2 J; 3 J; 4 C; 5 J
13 1 B: **Tienen que hacer** la tarea.
2 B: **Tengo que visitar** a mi abuelita.
3 B: No. **Tengo que comer** en casa.
4 A: **¿Tienen que ir?**
16 1 pesero, camión, micro, colectivo; 2 en

los años 60; 3 cinco millones; 4 Los trenes llegan con mucha frecuencia. Son baratos. 5 andar sin limite en los camiones y metro durante quince días; 6 Una para el metro y otra para los camiones. 7 Tomas un tren ligero.
17 1 hay que; 2 puedes; 3 hay que; 4 puedes/hay que; 5 hay que; 6 puedes
18 1 Sí, vive sola en un pueblo cerca de Cuernavaca. 2 Voy en tren hasta Cuautla. 3 Sí, bastante. 4 Voy desde el viernes hasta el lunes. 5 Sí, señor. Tengo un problema. Tengo que hablar urgentemente con mi mamá.
19 1 María; 2 María; 3 la mamá de María; 4 la mamá de María; 5 la mamá de María; 6 María; 7 Jorge; 8 María
20 1 V; 2 V; 3 F: there's a bus to a nearby village; 4 F; 5 V

Test

1 1 ¿A qué hora sale el próximo autobús para la Ciudad de México? 2 ¿Puedo comprar un boleto de ida y vuelta? 3 ¿A qué hora llega? 4 ¿Está retrasado? 5 ¿De qué andén sale?
2 El **próximo** autobús para la Ciudad de México sale del **andén** dos **dentro de** diez minutos. Está **retrasado** cinco minutos. ¿Usted quiere **comprar** un boleto de **ida y vuelta**? Es un viaje muy **rápido** y el autobús es muy **cómodo**. ¿Tiene mucho **equipaje**?
3 1 Córdoba está a setecientos y nueve km de Acapulco. 2 Guadalajara está a novecientos y siete km de Acapulco. 3 Córdoba está a tresceintos ochenta y cuatro km de Cuernavaca. 4 Guadalajara está a doscientos cincuenta y un km de Aguas Calientes. 5 Acapulco está a mil ochocientos cincuenta y tres km de Mérida.
4 1 Voy en motocicleta. A veces voy a pie. 2 Voy en tren y luego en camión. 3 Voy en carro pero a veces voy a pie. 4 Voy en metro y camión. 5 Voy a pie a la parada de camión y luego en camión.
5 No puedo porque tengo que trabajar en casa.
No puedo. Tengo que visitar a mi mamá.
No puedo. Tengo que llevar el carro al garaje.
Lo siento. Tengo que limpiar la casa.
No puedo. Tengo que ir a mi trabajo.
6 1 **Los míos** son mayores. 2 **El nuestro** es nuevo. 3 **Los suyos** son muy interesantes. 4 **Las mías** son buenas. ¿Cómo son **las tuyas**? 5 ¿Son **los suyos**? 6 **La suya** es bonita. 7 **Los tuyos** son pequeños. 8 **El nuestro** es muy bonito. 9 **Los tuyos** son

buenos. 10 **El tuyo** es nuevo.

Summary 8

1 A qué hora sale el próximo autobús para Querétaro? *2* Quiero regresar el viernes. *3* ¿A qué hora llegamos a Guadalajara? *4* Tengo que trabajar. *5* ¿A cuántos kilómetros está Guadalajara de la Ciudad de México? *6* Tardo media hora en llegar a mi trabajo en camión.

Unit 9

2 *Carmen*: tall, slim, blond; *José*: short, plump, dark; *Claudia*: dark; *Pablo*: tall, dark; *Patricia* dark

3 1 bajita; 2 gordito; 3 bajitos; 4 altas; 5 delgada; 6 son; 7 es; 8 somos; 9 soy, es

7 1 V; 2 V; 3 F; 4 V; 5 V

8 *Sample answers*: 1 Raúl es simpático, generoso, sincero. 2 Alicia es trabajadora, tranquila, seria. 3 Él y su esposa son honrados, abiertos, sinceros. 4 Él es nervioso, antipático, flojo.

12 1 Antonio; 2 una blusa; 3 un vestido; 4 unos pantalones; 5 Beatriz; 6 un vestido

13 1 Es más grande / más pequeña / mejor / peor que esta casa.
2 Es la más grande / la más pequeña / la mejor / la peor casa de la calle.

16 1 ELECTRÓNICA. T.V. Vídeo, etc.;
2 PERFUMERÍA; 3 DEPORTES; 4 Moda Joven EL Y ELLA; 5 Moda Joven EL Y ELLA; 6 JOYERÍA; 7 JOYERÍA; 8 ELECTRÓNICA. T.V. Vídeo, etc.; 9 FOTOGRAFÍA; 10 PAPELERÍA; 11 ELECTRÓNICA. T.V. Vídeo, etc.
12 Moda Sport, Zapatería

17 1 center/meeting/modern/variety/article/object/different/generally/difference/air conditioning. 2 No. Van a encontrar a sus amigos. 3 Sí. Hay restaurantes y cafeterías. 4 la 3ª planta (chamarras/vestidos, etc.); la 2ª planta (ropa sport); la 4ª planta (camping); la 5ª (vídeos, ordenadores, etc.); la 1ª (discos, libros). 5 Los centros comerciales no cierran a mediodía.

18 1 delgado – Jorge; 2 extraño – Jorge; 3 fuerte – la tía; 4 generosa – la vecina; 5 gorda – la tía; 6 guapo – Jorge; 7 inteligente – Julia; 8 mayor – Jorge; 9 misterioso – Jorge; 10 perezoso – Tomás; 11 preocupada – la mamá de Tomás y Julia; 12 simpática – la vecina; 13 trabajadora – Julia

19 1 the neighbor; 2 Tomás; 3 María's mother; 4 the neighbor; 5 María; 6 María's mother; 7 the neighbor; 8 Julia

Test

1 1 Es alto, delgado y muy guapo. 2 Es bajita y rubia. 3 Los hermanos son gorditos, fuertes y bajitos. 4 Las hermanas son delgadas y rubias. 5 El hombre es mayor; es alto y tiene el pelo negro.

2 1 trabajador; 2 simpáticos; 3 inteligente; 4 sincero; 5 nervioso

3 1 Es nerviosa. 2 Es bueno. 3 Es inteligente. 4 Tiene la personalidad adecuada. 5 Es simpático.

4 1 chamarra; 2 camisa; 3 pantalón; 4 blusa; 5 vestido; 6 falda; 7 zapatos; 8 suéter

5 1 La pulsera es para mi mamá. 2 El collar es para mi hermana. 3 El anillo es para mi abuelita. 4 El libro es para mi hermano. 5 La blusa es para mi amiga. 6 El disco compacto es para mi papá. 7 El vídeo es para mi amigo. 8 El suéter es para mi tía.

6 1 No quiero esa falda. Quiero aquélla. 2 No quiero esta pulsera. Quiero ésta. 3 No quiero este vestido. Quiero éste. 4 No quiero aquel suéter. Quiero aquél. 5 No quiero aquel anillo. Quiero ése. 6 No quiero estos aretes. Quiero éstos.

7 1 Ésa es más grande. 2 Ése es más nuevo. 3 Ése es mejor. 4 Ésa es peor. 5 Ése es más interesante.

Summary 9

1 Es muy alto. *2* Creo que Juan es sincero. *3* Tengo que comprar un regalo para mi papá. *4* No quiero éste, quiero ése. *5* Mi casa es más grande que la suya. *6* Mi casa es la más grande de la calle *7* Esta película es mejor que la otra.

Unit 10

2 1 Margarita's husband; 2 Pepe; 3 Margarita; 4 Pepe; 5 Margarita

3 Te gusta; me; les gusta; Le gusta; les gusta; les gustan

7 Bernardo went dancing until **one in the morning**; his **mother** woke him up at **eight; Bernardo went to play football with his friends. After the match, they went to a bar to have a drink. Elena is angry that he went out without her and that now he is too tired to go out. They go out together.**

8 1 cenaron; 2 salí; 3 bailamos; 4 fuiste; 5 compró; 6 hiciste

12 1 Bernardo; 2 Elena; 3 Bernardo; 4 Elena; 5 Elena; 6 Bernardo

13 1 Fuimos al cine ayer. 2 La película fue buena. 3 Ayer fue el cumpleaños de mi papá. 4 Fueron a Perú de vacaciones. 5 ¿Fueron a la fiesta? 6 ¿Fuiste tú quien llamó?

16 1 a, 2 f, 3 d, 4 h, 5 c, 6 j, 7 i, 8 b, 9 g, 10 e

17 1 d; 2 g; 3 b; 4 i; 5 j; 6 f; 7 a; 8 c; 9 h; 10 e

18 *Sample answers*: 1 Salí a la calle para ver las procesiones. 2 Descansamos en casa. Hice una cena especial. 3 Dormí. 4 Visité el cementerio. 5 Celebré con los niños.

19 *Across*: Santos, Reyes, Noche Vieja, Semana Santa, Independencia
Down: Revolución, Trabajo, Año Nuevo, Muertos

20 1 V; 2 F: tiene mucho trabajo; 3 F: vive sola y tiene amigos; 4 V; 5 V; 6 F: es de hace mucho tiempo; 7 F: es una foto de María, su mamá y un señor; 8 V; 9 F

21 1 Sí, pero prefiere vivir sola. 2 Tiene muchos amigos. 3 Come bien, no se preocupe. 4 Está muy bien, tiene una vida muy buena. 5 Hace muchas cosas, pero no demasiadas.

Test

1 *Sample answers*: Me gusta/No me gusta el cine/el teatro/la televisión/la música/la fruta/la verdura/la carne/el chocolate
Me gustan/No me gustan las películas de Hollywood/los periódicos/los libros/las caricaturas

2 Me gusta/No me gusta bailar/leer/trabajar/escuchar música

3 1 A él le gustan; 2 A nosotros nos gusta; 3 A ellos les gusta; 4 A ustedes les gustan; 5 A mí me gusta; 6 A ti te gusta; 7 A ellas les gusta

4 Lo siento mucho. No me gusta nada la música clásica.
No me gusta mucho. No me gusta la música. Prefiero el cine. ¿Te gusta el cine? No. No me gusta.
A mí me gusta ir al cine una vez al mes, pero prefiero estar en casa y leer un libro o ver la televisión.

5 me levanté; fuimos; compré; compró; Comimos; fuimos; fueron; visité; fui; Salí; me encontré; tomamos

6 1 ¿Qué hizo usted ayer? 2 ¿Dónde fue usted anteayer? 3 ¿Qué hiciste la semana pasada? 4 ¿Dónde fuiste el mes pasado? 5 ¿Dónde fueron ustedes ayer?

7 1 dos veces a la semana; 2 tres veces a la semana; 3 una vez al mes; 4 tres veces al año; 5 dos veces al día; 6 todas las semanas

Summary 10

1 Me gusta la música clásica. *2* ¿Le gusta el cine? *3* ¿Te gusta bailar? *4* No me gusta nada. *5* ¿Qué hiciste anoche? *6* ¿Adónde fuiste la semana pasada? *7* Mis papás me visitaron la semana pasada. *8* Nado tres veces a la semana.

Review 3

1 1 autobús; 2 andén; 3 está; 4 retrasado; 5 boletos; 6 ida; 7 ida y vuelta; 8 reservación

2 1 alto y delgado; negro; 2 bajita y gordita; rubia; 3 los ojos azules

3 1 Roberto es sincero. 2 Juana es honrada. 3 Los hermanos son inteligentes. 4 Mi papá es tranquilo. 5 Mi mamá es nerviosa. 6 Las hermanas son serias. 7 Javier es simpático. 8 Carmen es antipática. 9 Los niños son felices. 10 Mi abuelito es generoso.

4 1 para; 2 a; 3 para; 4 a

5 1 Quiero comprar un boleto de ida y vuelta. 2 ¿Se puede tomar un café en el hotel? 3 Necesitan comprar un boleto. 4 Deseamos cambiar de habitación. 5 Tengo que viajar a Chihuahua.

6 1 ¿Cuánto tardas en llegar al trabajo? 2 ¿Cuánto tardas en llegar al trabajo en camión? 3 ¿A cuántos kilómetros está tu trabajo?

7 1 Éste, ése, aquél; 2 Aquéllas, éstas, ésas; 3 Ésa, aquélla, ésta; 4 Éstos, Ésos, aquéllos

8 1 Estos zapatos son mejores que aquéllos/ésos. 2 Mi trabajo es peor que el tuyo. 3 Su carro es más grande que el mío/mi carro. 4 Su carro es mejor que el mío/mi carro. 5 La película es menos interesante que el libro.

9 1 Me gusta el cine. 2 Me gusta jugar futbol. 3 Les gustan los carros rápidos. 4 Nos gustan las caricaturas. 5 ¿Te gusta escuchar la música? 6 No me gusta el teatro nada.

10 1 fue; 2 me levanté; 3 Desayuné; 4 salí; 5 llegó; 6 llegué; 7 gustó; 8 Terminé; 9 fui; 10 entré; 11 hablaste

11 1 Jorge; 2 Juan; 3 Juana; 4 Javier; 5 Ana (la hermana de Juan); 6 Ana (la hermana de Javier)

12 *Josefina*: música clásica, baile, cine, bar, restaurante
María: música rock, baile, cine, bar, restaurante
Gustavo: música rock, cine, restaurante

13 Quiero un boleto para Querétaro. Sí. Quiero ir mañana. Quiero regresar el día dieciséis. ¿Cuánto tarda? De segunda clase. Gracias. ¿Cuánto cuesta el boleto?

14 Fui a la ciudad con mi amigo/a. Compré unos zapatos. Comimos en un restaurante. Fui a casa. Estudié. Me hablaron mis amigos. Fuimos a un café. Fuimos al cine. Fui a casa en un camión a las once.

Unit 11

2 1 porque ayer regresó de sus vacaciones;

2 sí; 3 hace dos años; 4 con sus papás. 5 Windsor

3 1 Estuve en un buen hotel. 2 Fui a la playa de vacaciones. 3 Regresaron ayer.
4 Regresamos hace tres días. 5 Llovió mucho. 6 Hizo mal tiempo. 7 Vieron el Támesis. 8 Vi a Juan hace una hora.

7 1 B; 2 A; 3 A; 4 A; 5 B

8 1 era; 2 trabajaba; 3 comprábamos; 4 visitábamos; 5 estábamos

12 1 V; 2 V; 3 F: en un departamento pequeño; 4 V; 5 F: pasaba el verano en Cuernavaca

13 Cuando era joven vivía en la ciudad pero cada verano iba a la casa de mis abuelitos con mis dos hermanos. Mis abuelitos tenían un carro viejo y grande y me acuerdo que una vez, mi abuelito nos llevó a las montañas. Mi papá trabajaba mucho y no tenía vacaciones largas, pero todos los fines de semana venía a vernos y nos daba regalos.

17 1 la música, el baile, los fuegos artificiales, los juegos infantiles, el ruido; 2 dormir; 3 por las calles; 4 El Día de la Independencia; 5 Descansan. Van a la playa. 6 'El Grito'; 7 El Palacio Nacional: el Balcón Presidencial; 8 Observan, corean y después bailan.

18 1 Celebré la Fiesta Nacional. 2 Fui a la playa el 15 de septiembre. 3 Observé la ceremonia en la televisión. 4 Vi los fuegos artificiales. 5 No dormí en toda la noche.

19 1 F: a su casa; 2 F: María se comportó mal; 3 V; 4 V; 5 V; 6 V; 7 F; 8 F: el viernes

20 Fui a ver a unos amigos.
Lo siento – no puedo ir.
Está bastante cerca de Cuernavaca.
Se llama Temixco.
Sí, sí. Podemos cenar en mi casa.

21 1 a; 2 a; 3 lo; 4 lo; 5 a; 6 a; 7 mi; 8 la; 9 me; 10 de

Test

1 1 regresé; 2 fuiste; 3 fuimos; 4 hicimos; 5 estuvimos; 6 Vimos; 7 nadé; 8 visitamos

2 1 se levantaron; 2 divertirme; 3 me acuerdo; 4 se aburren

3 1 Ayer fui al pueblo. 2 Estuvieron en Taxco. 3 Fue un hombre grande. 4 Fuimos a una iglesia. 5 Fue una buena actriz.

4 1 Llueve. 2 Hace sol. 3 Hace frío. 4 Hace calor. 5 Hace buen tiempo.

5 1 Fui hace dos años. 2 Le vi hace cinco minutos. 3 Tomé café hace poco. 4 Fui a Acapulco hace mucho. 5 Lo compré hace dos años.

6 1 They lived on the coast for many years. 2 I used to work for a furniture company.

3 We went to see the football match on Sunday. 4 We used to go to watch football on Sundays. 5 My father used to drive badly. 6 He/She was in the disco. 7 You always used to be in the movie theater. 8 Yesterday I bought a present for my friend.

7 *Sample answer*: Paseé por el centro. Visité el centro arqueológico. Compré cosas en los mercados. Comí en buenos restaurantes. Bailé en las discotecas. Vi la arquitectura colonial.

Summary 11

1 ¿Adónde fuiste de vacaciones? *2* Fui a Inglaterra. *3* Estuvimos en un hotel. *4* Fui a Argentina hace tres años. *5* Vivía en una casa grande cuando era joven. *6* Visitaba a mis abuelitos.

Unit 12

2 1 No voy al campo; 2 Vale la pena; 3 Podemos hacer una carne asada; 4 no podemos ir; 5 no puede ir el domingo

3 1 No van; 2 No van; 3 Vas; 4 Va; 5 Voy; 6 No vas; 7 Va

7 1 Bernardo y los niños; 2 Bernardo y Alfonso; 3 Los niños; 4 Clara; 5 Bernardo y Alfonso; 6 Bernardo

8 Iremos temprano por la mañana el sábado que viene. Llegaremos a la casa a las diez. Los niños jugarán en el jardín y nadarán en la alberca mientras preparo la comida. Podremos pasear por la tarde y visitaremos el pueblo. Vendrás por la tarde y cenaremos juntos. Tendremos que acostarnos temprano porque regresaremos a Cuernavaca temprano por la mañana. Llegaremos a Cuernavaca a mediodía y llamaré a mi mamá. Por la tarde descansaremos y veremos la televisión.

12 False statements are 5 and 8.
1 Elisa no podrá ir al cine esta noche.
2 Está ocupada. 3 Se quedará en casa.
4 Puede ir el domingo. 6 Harán otra cosa esta noche. 7 Elisa hablará a las cinco y media. 9 Decidirán más tarde.

13 1 Estoy cansado/a. 2 Estoy enfermo/a. 3 Estoy ocupado/a. 4 Tengo que visitar a mi mamá. 5 Tengo que preparar la comida. 6 Tengo que ir a Oaxaca mañana.

14 1 Yo comeré en el restaurante Bella Vista. 2 Yo voy a visitar a mis tíos en Venezuela. 3 Nosotros trabajaremos toda la semana. 4 No, van a salir a las ocho. 5 No, ustedes llegarán a las once.

17 1 V; 2 V; 3 F; 4 V; 5 F: en muchas ciudades hay por lo menos un teatro; 6 V

18 1 3; 2 City of Angels; 3 Avenida Juárez; 4 no; 5218689; 6 Club Náutico

19 1 a; 2 b; 3 c; 4 b; 5 a; 6 a

20 ¿Cómo te fue de viaje? Y este señor de la foto eres tú, ¿verdad? ¿Cuándo te enteraste? ¿Por qué no regresaste? ¿Por qué regresas?

Test

1 1 Roberto va (a ir) al cine. 2 Elisa va (a ir) a una boda. 3 Nosotros vamos a bailar. 4 Ellos van a visitar a unos amigos. 5 Tú vas a estudiar. 6 Ustedes van a preparar la cena. 7 Yo voy a comprar un carro nuevo. 8 Mis hermanos van a jugar futbol. 9 Tú y yo vamos a ver una película. 10 Yo voy a terminar el libro.

2 1 ¿Te gustaría ir al cine? 2 ¿Quieres venir al cine? 3 ¿Vamos al cine?

3 1 iré; 2 Empezaré; 3 Estaré; 4 Saldré; 5 vendrá; 6 haré; 7 comerán; 8 tendremos; 9 tendrá; 10 prepararé

4 1 Estoy ocupada. 2 Tengo que trabajar. 3 Tengo un examen. 4 Estoy cansado/a. 5 Tengo que visitar a un amigo.

5 1 ¡Qué suerte! 2 Vale la pena. 3 ¡Qué lástima! 4 ¿Qué te parece? 5 ¡Estupendo! 6 La semana que viene. 7 Lo siento. 8 No importa. 9 De acuerdo. 10 ¿Qué (te) pasa?

6 *Across*: estaré, jugaremos, irá, podré, llamará, iréis
Down: estarán, harán, cenaremos, descansará

Summary 12

1 Voy a estudiar esta noche. *2* Van a ver una película mañana. *3* ¿Te gustaría salir? *4* Lo siento pero no puedo. *5* Estoy cansada/Estoy cansado. *6* Va a ir a los Estados Unidos la semana que viene. *7* Me voy a quedar en la casa. *8* ¿Qué te parece?

Unit 13

2 1 a Sr. García is in a meeting; b Bernardo is going away; c he's travelling; 2 she can make a new appointment for him

3 Recepcionista: ¿Bueno?
You: ¿Puedo hablar con la señora Blasco, por favor?
Recepcionista: Sí. ¿De parte de quién? … Perdone. La señora Blasco está en una reunión.
You: No voy a poder asistir a la entrevista del lunes próximo. Quiero cambiarla.
Recepcionista: Yo puedo cambiarla. ¿Puede venir el miércoles por la tarde?
You: Perfecto.

Recepcionista: ¿Podría pasar por la oficina a las dos?
You: De acuerdo. Gracias.
Recepcionista: De nada. Hasta el miércoles.

7 3, 4, 5

8 1 Vivo; 2 estoy viviendo; 3 tengo; 4 voy; 5 compro; 6 leo; 7 estoy buscando; 8 encuentro; 9 regresaré; 10 estoy estudiando; 11 Quiero

12 1a We can communicate more rapidly and with more information than ever. b We can see the latest information without waiting and can send messages to our colleagues in a second. c We can attend meetings without leaving the office. 2a How can we manage this information explosion? b Do we need it? c Do we want it?

14 1 del; 2 de los; de; 3 de las; 4 de la
1 Visité a mi familia sin ver a mi hermana. 2 Trabajé todo el día sin comer. 3 Hice los exámenes sin estudiar. 4 Estoy en la oficina todo el día sin salir.

17 1 Director Hotel; 2 Ingeniero mecánico/ Ingeniero técnico industrial; 3 Programadores; 4 Jefe de ventas para México; 5 Director Hotel, Ingeniero mecánico, Ingeniero técnico industrial; 6 Programadores; 7 Jefe de ventas para México, Director Hotel; 8 Director Hotel

18 1 **filial**, subsidiary; **estrellas**, stars; **amplia**, wide; **dominio**, fluency; **edificación**, building; **líder**, leader; **licenciado**, graduate; **se requiere/requisitos**, requirements
2 Important Company Group requires: HOTEL MANAGER
for a four-star hotel in Oaxaca
Requirements: wide experience; ability to manage teams; written and spoken English.
3 Multinational Engineering , Building, and Maintenance Company requires: MECHANICAL ENGINEER
10 years' experience, fluency in English
4 Independent Organization for Quality Control in the Building Industry requires for its installation area: INDUSTRIAL TECHNICAL ENGINEER
• minimum of two years' experience in quality control of building installations
• knowledge of English

19 1 He wants to be with his family and he wants to open a new branch of his company. 2 Jorge wants to employ her in his company. 3 He is the boss of his own company. 4 He has a very good manager there who will take over. 5 Someone who knows Mexico City and who is well-qualified, with experience, initiative, and motivation. 6 Call her mother.

20 Questions from the conversation and responses:
1 María. Voy a quedarme aquí.
2 María. Quiero estar cerca de mi familia.
5 María. Tengo un jefe muy bueno allí.
6 Jorge. ¡Yo! Pues sí, me gustaría mucho.
7 Jorge. Pronto.

21 *María*: Jorge va a quedarse aquí. Quiere estar cerca de su familia. En Chihuahua tiene su propia empresa. Tiene bastante dinero. Está buscando un sitio para abrir una sucursal. Tiene un jefe muy bueno allí. Él se queda aquí. Necesita un jefe de personal para la compañía aquí en la Ciudad de México. Yo soy la persona adecuada.

Test

1 A: ¿Bueno? B: ¿Puedo hablar con la señora Gil por favor? A: ¿De parte de quién? B: Daniel Jiménez. A: Un momentito, por favor, ahorita lo llamo. B: Gracias. A: De nada.

2 1 ¿Puedo hablar con el Sr. García, por favor? 2 ¿Puede hablar más tarde? 3 ¿Puedo dejar un recado? 4 Quisiera cambiar la (hora de la) entrevista. 5 ¿Puede pasar por la oficina mañana?

3 1 Espere un momento. 2 Disculpe, por favor. 3 Mire. 4 Tenga. 5 Pase por aquí. 6 Perdone

4 1 el encargado/la encargada; 2 una empresa; 3 puesto; 4 las cualidades; 5 una entrevista; 6 una reunión; 7 un recado

5 1 estoy trabajando; 2 Termino; 3 estás haciendo; 4 habla; 5 descanso; 6 está jugando ; 7 llega

6 1 Trabajo todo el día sin parar. 2 Voy a hacer los exámenes sin estudiar. 3 Fui de compras ayer sin comer. 4 Estuve en casa el fin de semana sin salir.

Summary 13

1 ¿Bueno? 2 ¿Puedo hablar con el señor García? 3 ¿Podría hablarle más tarde? 4 ¿Puedo dejarle un recado? 5 Pase por aquí, por favor. 6 Qué estás haciendo? 7 Hola. Soy Paula Soto. Trabajo para Nexus.

Unit 14

2 fiebre ✓ (empezó el lunes), gripa ✓, dolor de garganta ✓ (empezó el miércoles), inflamación de la garganta ✓

3 1 han vivido; 2 ha venido; 3 ha hecho; 4 he comprado; 5 hemos sido.

7 1 V; 2 F; 3 V; 4 F: he's twisted his ankle; 5 F: she tells him to put his leg on a chair

8 El domingo pasado fue terrible. Me torcí el tobillo jugando futbol en la playa. También tengo fiebre y tengo la garganta inflamada. El médico me dijo que tengo que quedarme en el departamento durante el resto de las vacaciones. He estado en cama cuatro días y me duele mucho el tobillo. Quiero regresar a casa.

12 1 no; 2 sí; 3 sí; 4 no; 5 sí; 6 no; 7 no

13 1 c; 2d; 3a; 4b; 5e

14 *Sample answers*: Bebo demasiado. Como demasiadas papas. Fumo. No hago ejercicio. No como fruta. No descanso. He dejado de fumar. He dejado de comer papas. He dejado de beber tanta cerveza.

17 1 kite flying – **cometa**; hiking – **excursionismo**; beach volleyball – **voleiplaya**
2 a **los beneficios**: benefits; b **la ampolla**: blister; c **los reflejos**: reflexes; d **fortalecer**: to strengthen; e **el brazo**: arm; f **las lesiones**: injuries; g **el codo**: elbow; h **la muñeca**: wrist; i **la mano**: hand; j **el estrés**: stress; k **la torcedura**: sprain
3 1 frisbee; cometa; 2 el excursionismo; 3 frisbee; 4 voleiplaya; 5 cometa

18 1 Porque están juntos. 2 En casa de María. 3 Porque no debe vivir sola en el pueblo. 4 Dos. 5 Porque María ganará más dinero en su nuevo puesto. 6 Un edificio muy bueno para la empresa y un departamento. 7 Dentro de seis meses. 8 Las echaba de menos pero no podía regresar.

19 Quiero estar con mi familia. Tengo dos recámaras. Encontré un departamento muy cerca de aquí. Yo creo que podremos empezar dentro de seis meses.

20 9, 6, (3), 1, 2, 4, 8, 7, 5 (No. 3 is the perfect and does not refer to a specific time in the past)

21 Ayer Jorge encontró un edificio muy bueno para la empresa. Dentro de seis meses podrán empezar el trabajo. María tendrá que hablar con su jefe pronto. Hace muchos años Jorge dejó a su familia. Ahora están aquí. Hoy ha sido un día muy especial.

Test

1 1 Me duele la cabeza/Tengo dolor de cabeza. 2 Tengo fiebre. 3 Me duelen los ojos. 4 Me duele el pecho/Tengo dolor de pecho. 5 Me duele la garganta/Tengo dolor de garganta. 6 Tengo tos. 7 Me duelen los brazos. 8 Me duele la espalda/Tengo dolor de espalda.

2 Me siento … 1 bien; 2 mal; 3 muy bien; 4 mal, enfermo/a; 5 muy mal

3　1 Tengo que ponerme una pomada. 2 Tengo que tomar unas pastillas. 3 Tengo que tomar aspirina. 4 Tengo que tomar un jarabe.

4　1 me duelen, me duele; 2 le duele, me duele; 3 les duele, nos duelen; 4 te duele, me duele

5　1 Me he torcido el tobillo. 2 Me he hecho daño en la rodilla. 3 Se ha roto la pierna. 4 Se ha hecho daño en la cabeza. 5 Se ha quemado.

6　1 Pasa; 2 Abre; 3 Haz; 4 pon
　　1 Pase; 2 Levante; 3 Venga; 4 Siga

7　1 demasiado; 2 demasiado; 3 demasiado; 4 demasiados; 5 demasiados; 6 demasiada; 7 demasiado; 8 demasiadas

8　1 Debes trabajar menos. 2 Debe beber menos. 3 Debe ver menos televisión. 4 Debe hacer ejercicio. 5 Debe dejar de fumar. 6 Debe comer más verdura. 7 Debes comer menos. 8 Debes comer menos papas.

Summary 14

1 ¿Qué le pasa? *2* Tengo fiebre. *3* Me duele la cabeza. *4* Me siento muy mal. *5* Abre la puerta. *6* No debes fumar. *7* Dejé de fumar.

Review 4

1　1 cansarse; 2 bañarse; 3 aburrirse; 4 quemarse; 5 acordarse; 6 preocuparse; 7 divertirse; 8 quedarse; 9 sentirse; 10 hacerse daño

2　1 campamento; 2 costa; 3 barco; 4 carne asada; 5 jardín; 6 estupenda

3　1 b; 2 a; 3 c

4　1 Tienes razón. 2 Echar de menos (a alguien). 3 Vale la pena. 4 Para empezar.

5　1 Regresé. 2 Estuvo en Oaxaca. 3 ¿Qué hicieron? 4 Fuimos a la playa. 5 Compraron una casa en el mar.

6　1 Hace buen tiempo. 2 Hace sol. 3 Hace calor. 4 Llueve. 5 Hace frío. 6 Hace mal tiempo.

7　Personalized answers using this model: Hace _____ horas/días/semanas/años, etc.

8　1 Jugaba; 2 Compré; 3 era; 4 viajaba; 5 vivimos/vivíamos; 6 Tuve

9　1 Pase; 2 Abre; 3 Pongan; 4 levanta

10　1 estoy estudiando; 2 están comiendo; 3 estamos viajando; 4 están terminando; 5 estás viviendo

11　1 Me torcí el tobillo. 2 Me hice daño en el pie. 3 Me rompí el brazo. 4 Me quemé la espalda.

12　1 A is going shopping; B is going to the cinema; 2 they're going to meet up in a bar; 3 they're going to dinner at A's uncle and aunt's house; 4 B is going to Venezuela

13　1 Srta. Vázquez; 2 the person trying to reach Beatriz Herrero; 3 Sr. Solano; 4 Sr. Lopez

14　He estado de vacaciones.
Fui a Alicante. Estuve en el departamento de mis papás.
Fui con mis amigos.
Sí, pero también me gusta visitar los pueblos.
Hizo sol todos los días menos el sábado, que llovió todo el día.
Bailé y me divertí.

16　¿Puedo hablar con el señor Solano?
¿Cuándo regresa?
¿Puedo dejar un recado?
Dígale que le llamó el señor García. No puedo asistir a la reunión el viernes.
¿Puedo cambiarla?
El martes de la semana que viene.
A las diez.
Hasta el martes.

Grammar summary

Nouns

Gender
In Spanish, all nouns are identified as either masculine or feminine. Gender can be identified by the form of the definite article – **el, los** (masculine) and **la, las** (feminine) – or the indefinite article – **un, unos** (masculine) and **una, unas** (feminine).

As a general rule, nouns ending in -o are usually masculine and nouns ending in -a are usually feminine:

el zapato shoe   **la camisa** shirt

There are a few exceptions to this rule, for example:

el día day   **la mano** hand

For nouns ending in other letters, the gender has to be learned in each case:

el café coffee   **la noche** night

Plurals
For nouns ending in a vowel, add -s:

el helado ice cream   **los helados** ice creams
la casa house   **las casas** houses
el jitomate tomato   **los jitomates** tomatoes

For nouns ending in a consonant add -es:

el hospital hospital   **los hospitales** hospitals

The definite article

The form is determined by the number and gender of the noun that follows.

	sing.	*pl.*
masc.	**el** carro	**los** carros
fem.	**la** casa	**las** casas

The masculine definite article is contracted when it is preceded by the preposition **a** or **de**:

a + el = al   Voy **al** cine. I'm going to the movies.
de + el = del   el carro **del** mesero the waiter's car

The indefinite article

The form is determined by the number and gender of the noun that follows.

	sing.	*pl.*
masc.	**un** carro	**unos** carros
fem.	**una** casa	**unas** casas

The indefinite article is not used when stating someone's job.

Miguel es **profesor**. Miguel is a teacher.

Adjectives

Agreement

Adjectives agree in number and gender with the noun they describe. Adjectives ending in **-o** change as follows:

	sing.	*pl.*
masc.	el restaurante **caro**	los restaurantes **caros**
fem.	la casa **cara**	las casas **caras**

With the exception of nationalities, most adjectives ending in **-e** or a consonant have the same form in the singular. In the plural, an **-s** is added to those ending in **-e** and **-es** to those ending in a consonant.

	sing.	*pl.*
masc. & fem.	inteligente	inteligentes
masc. & fem.	hábil	hábiles

Adjectives of nationality ending in a consonant change as follows:

	sing.	*pl.*
masc.	el señor francés	los señores franceses
fem.	la señora francesa	las señoras francesas

Position

Adjectives usually follow the noun:

una vista **bonita** a pretty view
un departamento **grande** a big apartment

However, some adjectives precede the noun. The most common are: **bueno** ('good'), **malo** ('bad'), **otro** ('other'), **poco** ('little'/'few'). **bueno** and **malo** change form when they precede the noun:

bueno – buen   Hace buen tiempo. It's good weather.
malo – mal   Hace mal día. It's a bad day.

Comparatives and superlatives

Comparatives

The comparative of adjectives and adverbs is formed as follows:

(1) adjectives: **más** + adjective + **que** or **menos** + adjective + **que**
The adjective agrees in number and gender with the noun to which it refers.

Este libro es **más** interesante **que** el otro. This book is more interesting than the other one.

(2) adverbs: verb/adverb + **más que** or **menos que**

> Mi hermano trabaja **menos que** sus compañeros. My brother works less than his colleagues.
> Este carro **va más** rápido **que** el otro. This car goes faster than the other.

Irregular comparative forms
A number of adjectives have irregular comparative forms:

bueno – mejor (better)	**grande – mayor** (bigger)
malo – peor (worse)	**pequeño – menor** (smaller)

Superlatives
The superlative of adjectives and adverbs is formed as follows:

(1) adjectives: **el/la … más** + adjective or **el/la … menos** + adjective
The adjective agrees in number and gender with the noun to which it refers:

> El restaurante **más/menos** caro de la ciudad. The most/least expensive restaurant in the city.

(2) adverb: **el/la … que** + verb + **más/menos**

> El que trabaja **más/menos** en la oficina es mi hermano. The one who works most/least in the office is my brother.

Subject pronouns

person	sing.		pl.	
	masc.	*fem.*	*masc.*	*fem.*
1st I/we	**yo**	**yo**	**nosotros**	**nosotras**
2nd (informal) you	**tú**	**tú**	**ustedes**	**ustedes**
2nd (formal) you	**usted**	**usted**	**ustedes**	**ustedes**
	(Ud/Vd)	**(Ud/Vd)**	**(Uds/Vds)**	**(Uds/Vds)**
3rd he/she/they	**él**	**ella**	**ellos**	**ellas**

Note: **Ud/Vd, Uds/Vds** are the written abbreviations of **Usted/Ustedes**.

> **Yo** soy mexicano. I'm Mexican.
> **Ellas** son de Chihuahua. They [*fem.*] are from Chihuahua.

Subject pronouns are generally omitted in conversation.

Object pronouns

Direct object pronouns

person	sing.		pl.	
	masc.	*fem.*	*masc.*	*fem.*
1st (I; we)	**me**	**me**	**nos**	**nos**
2nd (you)	**te**	**te**	**los**	**las**
3rd (him/her/it; they)	**lo**	**la**	**los**	**las**

Lo vi en la tienda. I saw it in the store.

La carne. ¿**La** quiere? The meat. Do you want it?

Indirect object pronouns

person	sing.		pl.	
	masc.	fem.	masc.	fem.
1st (I; we)	me	me	nos	nos
2nd (you)	te	te	les	les
3rd (you/him/her/it; they)	le/se	le/se	les/se	les/se

Mi mamá **nos** dará café. My mother will give us coffee.

Te daré este libro. I'll give you this book.

Position of object pronouns

Object pronouns are usually placed immediately before the verb:

Carmen **me** invitó a su boda. Carmen invited me to her wedding.

When the verb is in the infinitive, imperative, or gerund ('-ing') form, the object pronoun is attached to the end of the verb:

Quiero **comprarlo**. I want to buy it.   **Cómpralo**. Buy it.

Está **comprándolo**. He's buying it.

Disjunctive pronouns

sing.	pl.
mí	nosotros
ti	ustedes
él/ella/usted	ellos/ellas

A disjunctive pronoun is an emphatic form of pronoun used in certain situations, which include:

(1) after a preposition:

Para **mí**, la sopa. The soup for me.

Voy sin **ella**. I'm going without her.

(2) for emphasis with the verb **gustar**:

Le gusta a **él**. He (in particular) likes it.

Note that the pronouns **mí** and **ti** change when used with **con**:

conmigo with me   **contigo** with you

Demonstrative adjectives and pronouns

	sing.	pl.
masc.	este anillo	estos carros
fem.	esta blusa	estas chaquetas

Two other kinds of demonstrative adjectives are used to indicate comparative distance of objects. For something that is not very far away: **ese / esa / esos / esas**:

Quiero **ese** anillo. I want that ring [*e.g. just there*].

For something at a greater distance: **aquel / aquella / aquellos / aquellas**:

Vivo en **aquella** casa. I live in that house (over there).

In the pronoun form an accent is added:

Quiero **éste**. I want this one.

Possessive adjectives and pronouns

Possessive adjectives ('my', 'your', etc.) and pronouns ('mine', 'yours', etc.) agree in number and gender with the noun to which they refer, rather than with the possessor.

Possessive adjectives

	sing.	pl.
my	mi	mis
your [*sing.*]	tu	tus
his/her/its/your [*formal sing.*]	su	sus
our	nuestro/a	nuestros/as
their/your [*pl.*]	su	sus

Mi trabajo está cerca de **mi** casa. My work is near my house.
Nuestros papás están en Oaxaca. Our parents are in Oaxaca.

Possessive pronouns

	sing.	pl.
mine	mío/a	míos/as
yours [*sing.*]	tuyo/a	tuyos/as
his/hers/its/yours [*formal sing.*]	suyo/a	suyos/as
ours	nuestro/a	nuestros/as
theirs/yours [*pl.*]	suyo/a	suyos/as

Mi trabajo está cerca de mi casa. My work is near my house.
El mío está lejos de mi casa. Mine is a long way from my house.

Questions and exclamations

Questions are indicated by an inverted question mark at the beginning and a normal question mark at the end: ¿ ... ?

Questions are formed in three ways:
(1) by using the same word order as a sentence but with a rising intonation:

¿María trabaja en el centro de la ciudad? Does María work in the centre of town?

(2) by inverting the subject and verb in the sentence:

¿Estudia Juan todas las noches? Does Juan study every night?

(3) by using a question word:

¿Cuándo vas a visitar a tu mamá? When are you going to visit your mother?

Numbers

0 cero	16 dieciséis	32 treinta y dos	600 seiscientos/as
1 uno/una	17 diecisiete	33 treinta y tres	700 setecientos/as
2 dos	18 dieciocho	40 cuarenta	800 ochocientos/as
3 tres	19 diecinueve	50 cincuenta	900 novecientos/as
4 cuatro	20 veinte	60 sesenta	1000 mil
5 cinco	21 veintiuno	70 setenta	
6 seis	22 veintidós	80 ochenta	
7 siete	23 veintitrés	90 noventa	
8 ocho	24 veinticuatro	100 cien	
9 nueve	25 veinticinco	101 ciento uno/a	
10 diez	26 veintiséis	111 ciento once	
11 once	27 veintisiete	125 ciento veinticinco	
12 doce	28 veintiocho	200 doscientos/as	
13 trece	29 veintinueve	300 trescientos/as	
14 catorce	30 treinta	400 cuatrocientos/as	
15 quince	31 treinta y uno	500 quinientos/as	

Ordinal numbers

el primero/la primera	first	el sexto/la sexta	sixth
el segundo/la segunda	second	el séptimo/la séptima	seventh
el tercero/la tercera	third	el octavo/la octava	eighth
el cuarto/la cuarta	fourth	el noveno/la novena	ninth
el quinto/la quinta	fifth	el décimo/la décima	tenth

Ordinals are normally placed before the noun.

Viven en el cuarto piso. They live on the fourth floor.

Two ordinal numbers, **primero** and **tercero**, modify their form when they appear before a masculine noun:

el primer piso the first floor   **el tercer piso** the third floor

Adverbs

Most adverbs are formed by adding **-mente** to the feminine form of the adjective.

rápida – rápidamente   quickly

The following adverbs are irregular:

bastante	quite, enough	**menos**	less
bien	well	**mucho**	a lot, much
demasiado	too much	**muy**	very
mal	badly	**poco**	a little
más	more		

Verbs

The infinitive
The infinitive is the basic form of the verb found in the dictionary.
In Spanish, the infinitive has one of three possible endings: **-ar**,
-er, or **-ir**. Examples of regular verbs are: **trabajar** ('to work'),
comer ('to eat'), **vivir** ('to live').

Regular verbs within each group take the same endings.

The present tense
The infinitive endings are replaced as follows:

trabajar		**comer**		**vivir**	
trabaj**o**	trabaj**amos**	com**o**	com**emos**	viv**o**	viv**imos**
trabaj**as**	trabaj**an**	com**es**	com**en**	viv**es**	viv**en**
trabaj**a**		com**e**		viv**e**	

Radical-changing verbs
Radical-changing verbs are verbs which are regular in their
endings (taking the endings of **-ar**, **-er**, or **-ir** verbs as appropriate),
but which undergo a change in the stem in certain persons of the
verb.

• Verbs that undergo a vowel change:

e – ie = querer ('to want') – **quiero**
Verbs that follow this pattern are: **cerrar** ('to close'), **empezar** ('to
begin'), **pensar** ('to think'), **comenzar** ('to begin'), **divertir** ('to
enjoy'), **preferir** ('to prefer').

o – ue = poder ('to be able') – **puedo**
Verbs that follow this pattern are: **costar** ('to cost'), **doler** ('to
hurt'), **dormir** ('to sleep').

u – ue = jugar ('to play') – **juego**

e – i = vestir ('to dress') – **visto**
Verbs that follow this pattern are **seguir** ('to follow'), **repetir** ('to
repeat').

• Verbs that undergo a consonant change in the first person
  singular:

c – zc = parecer ('to appear') – **parezco, pareces**
Verbs that follow this pattern: **ofrecer** ('to offer')

c – g = hacer ('to make, to do'): **hago, haces**
l – lg = salir ('to leave'): **salgo, sales**
n – ng = poner ('to put'): **pongo, pones**

• Irregular changes to spelling:

Verbs that change by adding **g** to the first person only, and
change a vowel in the second and third person singular and third
person plural:

tener ('to have')		venir ('to come')	
tengo	tenemos	vengo	venimos
tienes	tienen	vienes	vienen
tiene		viene	

Verbs that change in the first person singular: **e – ig**:

traer ('to bring')	
traigo	traemos
traes	traen
trae	

Some verbs are completely irregular in all persons:

ir ('to go')		ser ('to be')		estar ('to be')	
voy	vamos	soy	somos	estoy	estamos
vas	van	eres	son	estás	están
va		es		está	

Reflexive verbs
A reflexive verb is one whose subject performs the action of the verb upon himself, herself, or itself. In Spanish this idea is conveyed by the use of a reflexive pronoun ('myself', 'yourself', etc.), although the pronoun is not normally used in English, e.g. **levantarse**, 'to get up' [*literally* 'to raise oneself']:
Reflexive verbs take the endings of the relevant verb group (**-ar**, **-er**, or **-ir**).

(yo) **me** levant**o**	(nosotros/as) **nos** levant**amos**
(tú) **te** levant**as**	(ellos/as/ustedes) **se** levant**an**
(él/ella/usted) **se** levant**a**	

In the infinitive (**levantarse**) and the imperative (**levántate**), the reflexive pronoun is added to the end of the verb.

Other reflexive verbs: **acostarse** ('to go to bed'), **bañarse** ('to have a shower'), **peinarse** ('to comb one's hair'), **vestirse** ('to get dressed'), **lavarse** ('to have a wash').

Use of the present tense
The present tense can express an action that is happening at the moment, or habitual actions:

Voy a la oficina. I'm going to the office.
Voy a la playa los veranos. I go to the beach in the summer.

The present continuous
The present continuous describes an action taking place at the moment of speaking. It is formed with the present tense of the verb **estar** + a verb in the gerund. The gerund is made up of the stem of the verb + the endings **-ando** for **-ar** verbs, and **-iendo** for **-er** and **-ir** verbs.

Estoy trabajando. I'm working.
¿Estás comiendo? Are you eating?
Está viviendo en México. He's living in México.

The present continuous can also be used to describe an event in the present which continues over a period of time.

Mi hermana **está estudiando** en la universidad. My sister is studying at the university.

The future tense
The future tense expresses an action that will happen in the future.

Jugaré futbol mañana. I'll play/I'm going to play soccer tomorrow.

Regular verbs are formed by adding the appropriate future suffix to the infinitive, as follows:

trabajar	**comer**	**vivir**
trabajar**é**	comer**é**	vivir**é**
trabajar**ás**	comer**ás**	vivir**ás**
trabajar**á**	comer**á**	vivir**á**
trabajar**emos**	comer**emos**	vivir**emos**
trabajar**án**	comer**án**	vivir**án**

The following verbs are irregular:

- Verbs that change the stem by adding **d**:

  tener: tendré, tendrás, tendrá, tendremos, tendrán

Other verbs that follow this pattern are: **venir (vendré)**, **poner (pondré)**, **salir (saldré)**.

- Verbs that drop the **e** from the stem:

  saber ('to know'): sabré, sabrás, sabrá, sabremos, sabrán

poder ('to be able') also follows this pattern: **podré, podrás,** etc.

- Verbs with irregular forms:

decir ('to say')		**hacer**		**querer**	
diré	diremos	haré	haremos	querré	querremos
dirás	dirán	harás	harán	querrás	querrán
dirá		hará		querrá	

The construction **ir + a +** infinitive can also be used to talk about the future, in much the same way as the English construction ('going to').

Voy a jugar futbol mañana. I'm going to play soccer tomorrow.

The simple past
The simple past is used to describe finished or completed actions that happened in the past:

¿Adónde fuiste ayer? Where did you go yesterday?
¿Qué hiciste anoche? What did you do last night?
Bailé. I danced.

It is often used with **ya** to describe events in the recent past, where English would use the perfect tense ('I have finished')

Ya comí. I've (just) had lunch.

The simple past tense is formed as follows:

bailar ('to dance')		comer		salir	
bailé	bailamos	comí	comimos	salí	salimos
bailaste	bailaron	comiste	comieron	saliste	salieron
bailó		comió		salió	

Note that -er and -ir verbs are formed in exactly the same way. Note also that the first person plural in -ar and -ir verb types is the same as for the simple present.

The following are irregular in all persons.

- Verbs that change the stem vowel to **u**:

  poder: pude, pudiste, pudo
  saber: supe
  poner: puse

- Verbs that change the stem vowel to **i**:

  decir: dije, dijiste, dijo
  hacer: hice
  querer: quise
  venir: vine

- Verbs that add the consonant **j**:

  traer: traje, trajiste, trajo
  decir: dije
  conducir: conduje

dar ('to give')		ser		estar	
di	dimos	fui	fuimos	estuve	estuvimos
diste	dieron	fuiste	fueron	estuviste	estuvieron
dio		fue		estuvo	

The imperfect

The imperfect tense is used to describe:

- things that used to happen:

  Cuando **era** pequeña **vivía** en el campo. When I was young I used to live in the country.

- places, objects, and people in the past:

  Era alta y delgada. She was tall and slim.

- background information that is secondary to the main action:

  Preparaba la cena cuando llegó mi tío. I was preparing dinner when my uncle arrived.

The imperfect tense is formed as follows:

bailar		comer		salir	
bailaba	bailábamos	comía	comíamos	salía	salíamos
bailabas	bailaban	comías	comían	salías	salían
bailaba		comía		salía	

Irregular verbs in the imperfect:

ser		ir	
era	éramos	iba	íbamos
eras	eran	ibas	iban
era		iba	

Perfect

The perfect tense is used to describe events in the recent past, in much the same way as the English perfect tense ('I have finished', etc.). It is generally used in the negative or in questions.

No he hecho mucho esta semana. I haven't done much this week.

¿**Cuántas veces has jugado** futbol este año? How many times have you played soccer this year?

The perfect is formed using the present of **haber** ('to have') + the past participle of the verb. The past participle is made up of the stem of the verb + the endings **-ado** for **-ar** verbs, and **-ido** for **-er** and **-ir** verbs. The participle does not vary in gender or number.

bailar		comer	
he bailado	hemos bailado	he comido	hemos comido
has bailado	han bailado	has comido	han comido
ha bailado		ha comido	

salir	
he salido	hemos salido
has salido	han salido
ha salido	

Many verbs have an irregular past participle, e.g.:

abrir ('to open'): **abierto**   hacer ('to make, to do'): **hecho**
escribir ('to write'): **escrito**   poner ('to put'): **puesto**

The imperative

The imperative is used to tell or order someone to do something. The distinction between the informal **tú** and the formal **usted** disappears in the plural form **ustedes**.

	tú	usted	ustedes	
	[*informal sing.*]	[*formal sing.*]	[*pl.*]	
hablar	habla	hable	hablen	speak
comer	come	coma	coman	eat
escribir	escribe	escriba	escriban	write

Habla más despacio. Speak more quietly.

The formal 'you' form (**usted**) is used in polite conversation in stores and other formal situations:

Deme dos kilos, por favor. Give me/Could you give me two kilos, please.
Siga esta calle. Follow this street.

235

ser and estar
Spanish has two verbs meaning 'to be': **ser** and **estar**.

ser is used:
– to describe a permanent state:

> **Soy** profesora. I'm a teacher.
> La casa **es** grande. The house is big.
> Mi jefe **es** simpático. My boss is nice.

– to tell the time:

> **Son** las dos. It's two o'clock.

estar is used:
– to describe position or location, or a temporary state

> ¿Dónde **está** tu pueblo? Where is your town?
> **Estoy** enfermo. I'm ill.
> La casa **está** limpia. The house is clean.

See under the tenses in the verb section of the Grammar Summary for details of how **ser** and **estar** are formed.

Verbs followed by the infinitive
Certain verbs, such as **poder** ('to be able'), **querer** ('to want'), and **necesitar** ('to need'), are followed by the infinitive:

> ¿**Puede traer** la cuenta? Could you bring the check?
> **Quiero salir** esta noche. I want to go out tonight.
> **Necesito cambiar** el boleto. I need to change the ticket.

Note these other constructions which also take the infinitive:

> **Tengo que estudiar** esta noche. I have to study tonight.
> **Hay que limpiar** esta casa. This house has to be cleaned.
> **Fui a** bailar. I went dancing.

Other verb constructions

- **hacer**
  To describe the weather:

  Hace calor. It's hot.

  To describe when you did something:

  Lo vi **hace** cinco minutos. I saw him five minutes ago.

- **gustar** ('to like')
  The verb gustar is used with an indirect object pronoun:

  Me gusta el teatro. I like the theater. [*literally* The theater is pleasing to me.]

- **se** in passive constructions
  se is often used in passive constructions or where there is no specific subject. It is followed by a verb in the third person singular or plural:

  Se toma con crema. You eat it [*literally* it is eaten] with cream.
  Se puede comer frío. You can eat it/It can be eaten cold.
  Se cortan los ingredientes. You slice the ingredients.

Vocabulary

A

	a la plancha	grilled
	a pie	on foot
	a veces	sometimes
	a ver	let's see
	abierto	open
	abril	April
	abrir	to open
la	abuelita	grandmother
el	abuelito	grandfather
	acampar	to go camping
	aburrirse	to get bored
el	accidente	accident
el	aceite	oil
	acordarse	to remember
	acostarse	to go to bed
la	actitud	attitude
	actual	current
	acudir	to gather in a place
	adecuado	adequate, necessary, suitable
	adelgazar	to slim, to lose weight
	adiós	goodbye
	¿adónde?	where (to)?
las	afueras	outskirts (of a city)
la	agencia	agency
	agosto	August
el	agua [fem.]	water
	ahorita	right now
	ahorita viene	he/she is just coming [answering the telephone]
	alegre	happy, joyous
	alemán	German
	Alemania	Germany
	¿algo más?	anything else?
	alguien	someone
	allí	there
el	almíbar	syrup
el	almuerzo	mid-morning snack; lunch [not Mexico]
	alto	tall
el/la	amigo/a	friend
	añadir	to add
	ancho	wide
	andar	travel
el	andén	platform, bus bay
	angosto	narrow
el	anillo	ring [jewellery]
el	año pasado	last year
	anoche	last night
	antier	the day before yesterday
	antiguo	old, antique
	antipático	unpleasant, unfriendly
	anular	to annul, cancel
el	anuncio	advertisement
	aquí	here
	Argentina	Argentina
	argentino	Argentinian
el	arroz	rice
el	artículo	(newspaper) article
	asistir	to attend
	atrás	behind
	Australia	Australia
	australiano	Australian
el	autobús	bus
la	autopista	freeway
la	avenida	avenue
	ayudar	to help
el	azúcar	sugar
	azul	blue

B

	bailar	to dance
	bajo	short [stature]
el	balcón	balcony
	bañarse	to take a shower
el	banco	bank
	barato	cheap
la	barbacoa	barbecue
el	barco	boat
la	barrera	barrier
	bastante	quite
la	bebida	drink
la	biblioteca	library
	bien	fine
	bilingüe	bilingual
	blanco	white
la	blusa	blouse
la	boca	mouth
la	boda	wedding
el	boleto	(travel) ticket
(el	boleto de) ida y vuelta	round-trip (ticket)
	bonito	pretty
la	botana	bar snack
el	bote	jar
la	botella	bottle
	buenas noches	good evening, good night
	buenas noticias	good news
	buenas tardes	good afternoon
	bueno	good
	¿bueno?	hello [answering telephone]
	buenos días	good morning
	buscar	to look for

el	caballero	gentleman
el	cacahuate	peanut
el	café con leche	coffee with milk
el	café negro	(black) coffee
la	cafetería	cafeteria/bar
la	caja	box
los	calamares	squid
el	caldo de pollo	chicken broth
	calentar	to heat up
la	calidad	(personal) quality
	calificado	qualified
la	cama	bed
	cambiar	to change
el	camión	bus
la	camisa	shirt
el	campamento	campsite
el	campo	countryside
	Canadá	Canada
	canadiense	Canadian
la	canción	song
	cansado	tired
	cansarse	to get tired
	cantar	to sing
las	caricaturas	cartoons
la	carne asada	barbecue
la	carnicería	butcher's store
	caro	expensive
el	carro	car
la	carta	letter, à la carte menu
la	cartera	wallet
la	casa	house
	casado	married
	casi nunca	hardly ever
la	catedral	cathedral
la	cebolla	onion
	celebrar	to celebrate
el	cementerio	cemetery
	cenar	to have dinner
	centro comercial	shopping mall
	cerca	near
el	cerdo	pork, pig
	cerrar	to close [store, museum]
la	cerveza	beer
la	chamarra	jacket
la	champaña	champagne
el	champiñón	mushroom
la	chica	girl, chickpeas
los	chícharos	peas
el	chico	boy
	chino	Chinese
el	chocolate	chocolate
el	choque	collision, crash
el	chorizo	*spicy sausage*
la	chuleta	chop (of meat)
el/la	ciclista	cyclist
	cien	hundred
	cinco	five
	cincuenta	fifty
el	cine	the movies/movie

		theater
la	ciudad	city, town
el	cocido	stew [*with meat and chickpeas*]
la	cocina	kitchen, cooking
	coger	to catch
el	collar	necklace
	Colombia	Colombia
	colombiano	Colombian
el	comedor	dining room
	comer	to eat
la	comida	lunch [*México*]
la	comida fuerte	main meal
	como	like [*similar to*]
	¿cómo es?	what's it like? what does it consist of?
	¿cómo está usted?	how are you?
	¿cómo se llama?	what's your name?
el/la	compañero/a	colleague
	comportarse	to behave
	comprar	to shop, to buy
las	compras	shopping
la	computación	information technology
la	computadora	computer
la	comunidad	community
	con	with
el	concierto	concert
el	concurso	competition
el/la	conductor(a)	driver
el	conejo	rabbit
	conmigo	with me
	conocer	to know, to meet
el/la	contador(a)	accountant
	contagiar	to pass on [*germs, an illness*]
	continuar	to continue
la	conversación	conversation
	corear	to chant
el/la	corredor(a)	runner
	correr	to run
	cortar	to cut
	corto	short (hair)
la	costa	coast
	costar	to cost, to take (time)
	crecer	to grow
	creer	to think, to believe
el	cristal	glass
	¿cuánto cuesta?	how much does it cost?
	¿cuánto	how much is it?
	¿cuánto tardas?	how long does it take (you)?
	¿cuántos años tienen?	how old are they?
	cuarenta	forty
el	(cuarto de) baño	bathroom
el	cuarto doble	double room
	cuatro	four
	cuatrocientos	four hundred
la	cuchara	spoon
el	cuchillo	knife
la	cuenta	check

	cuidar	to look after
el	cumpleaños	birthday

D

	dar a la calle	to face the street
	de	from, of
	de acuerdo	fine
	de nada	that's OK, that's fine, it's a pleasure
	debajo	underneath
	decidir	to decide
	decir	to say
	dejar	to let, leave, give, lend
	dejar de fumar	to give up smoking
	delante de	in front of
	delgado	thin, slim
	demasiado	too much, too many
	dentro de	within
el	departamento	apartment
el/la	dependiente/a	salesman, saleswoman
los	deportes	sports
	derecha	right [*direction*]
	derecho	straight ahead
el	derecho	(legal) right
	desayunar	to have breakfast
	descansar	to relax
el	descanso	rest, relaxation
	después	afterwards
	detrás de	behind
el	día	day
	diciembre	December
	diez	ten
la	dieta	diet
el	dinero	money
	dirigir	to direct, to manage
el	disco	record
	¡disculpe!	excuse me
el/la	diseñador(a)	designer
el	disquete	floppy disk
	distinto	different
	divertirse	to enjoy oneself
	doblado	dubbed
	doblarse	to be dubbed
el	documento	document
	doler (me duele)	to hurt (it hurts)
el	dolor	pain
	domingo	Sunday
	¿dónde?	where?
	dos	two
	doscientos	two hundred
	durante	during
	durar	to last
el	durazno	peach

E

la	edad	age
el	edificio	building
el	efecto	effect
los	ejotes	green beans
	él	he, it

	el/la	the
el	elevador	elevator
	ella	she, it
	ellos/ellas	they
	emitir	to broadcast
	empezar	to begin
el/la	empleado/a	employee
la	empresa	company
el/la	empresario/a	company director
	en	in
	en venta	for sale
	en seguida	immediately
	encantado	pleased to meet you
	encantar	to love
el/la	encargado/a	person in charge
	encima	above, on
	encontrar	to find
la	energía	energy
	enero	January
	enfermo	ill, sick
	enfrente de	opposite
	enojado	angry, annoyed
	enrollar	to roll
la	ensalada	salad
	enseñar	to show
	entender	to understand
	enterarse	to find out
	entonces	then, in that case
	entre	between
	entrenar	to train
la	entrevista	interview
	equilibrado	balanced
el	equipaje	luggage
el	equipo	team
	equivocado	wrong, mistaken
	escocés	Scottish
	Escocia	Scotland
	escribir	to write
el	escritor	writer
los	espaguetis	spaghetti
la	espalda	back
	España	Spain
	español	Spanish
el	espectáculo	show
	esperar	to wait
	esta noche	tonight
	esta	this [*fem.*]
	ésta	this one [*fem.*]
la	estación	station
el	estacionamiento	parking lot
	estacionarse	to park
los	Estados Unidos	the United States
	estar	to be
	estar retrasado	to be delayed
el	este	east
	este	this [*masc.*]
	éste	this one [*masc.*]
el	estilo	style
	estudiar	to study
	¡estupendo!	great! terrific!
	exactamente	exactly

el	examen	exam
	explicar	to explain
el	extraño	stranger
	extrañar	to miss

F

la	falda	skirt
	faltar	to lack, to be missing
la	familia	family
	febrero	February
la	fecha	date
	¡felicidades!	congratulations!
	feliz	happy
la	fiebre	temperature, fever
la	fiesta	party, festival
el	fin de semana	weekend
	físicamente	physically
el	flan	*crème caramel*
	flojo	lazy
la	florería	flower store
la	forma	form
la	foto	photo
la	fotocopia	photocopy
el/la	fotógrafo/a	photographer
	francés	French
	Francia	France
	freír	to fry
la	fresa	strawberry
	frío	cold
	frito	fried
la	fruta	fruit
la	fruta del tiempo	seasonal fruit
la	frutería	fruitstand
los	fuegos artificiales	fireworks
	fuera	away, outside
	fuerte	strong
los	fumadores	smoking section
	fumar	to smoke
el/la	funcionario/a	clerk, civil servant

G

	ganar	to earn, to win
el	garbanzo	chickpea
la	garganta	throat
	generoso	generous
la	gente	people
	gord(it)o	fat, plump
	gracias	thank you
el	gramo	gramme
	grande	big
	grave	serious
	gravemente	seriously
la	gripa	flu
	gritar	to shout
el	grito	shout
el	grupo	music group
el	guajolote	turkey
	guapo	beautiful, attractive
	Guatemala	Guatemala
la	guayaba	guava

el	guisado	stew
	gustar	to please

H

	hablar	to speak
	hace buen tiempo	it's good weather
	hace calor	it's hot
	hace frío	it's cold
	hace mucho	a long time ago
	hace poco	recently, a short time ago
	hace sol	it's sunny
	hacer	to do, to make
	hacer ejercicio	to exercise
	hacerse daño	to hurt oneself
la	hamburguesa	hamburger
la	harina	flour
	hasta	until
	hasta luego	see you later
	hay	there is, there are
	hay que …	it's necessary to …
el	helado	ice cream
	herido	injured
la	hermana	sister
el	hermano	brother
el	héroe	hero
	hervir	to boil
el	hielo	ice
la	hija	daughter
el	hijo	son
	hispano-hablante	Spanish-speaking
	histórico	historic
	¡hola!	hello!
	hongo	mushroom
	honrado	honest
la	hora	hour
el	horario	timetable
el	hospital	hospital
el	hotel	hotel
	hoy	today
el	huachinango	*red snapper*

I

la	idea	idea
	importante	important
	incómodo	uncomfortable
la	independencia	independence
	inflamado	swollen, inflamed
la	influencia	influence
la	información	information
la	informática	computing.information technology
la	ingeniera	engineer [*female*]
el	ingeniero	engineer [*male*]
	Inglaterra	England
	inglés	English
la	iniciativa	initiative
la	instalación	installation
	inteligente	intelligent
	interesante	interesting
	ir	to go

ir bien	to go well	
Italia	Italy	
italiano	Italian	
izquierda	left [*direction*]	

J

el **jamón**	ham	
el **jarabe**	syrup [*e.g.cough syrup*]	
el **jardín**	garden	
el/la **jefe/a**	boss, head	
el **jitomate**	tomato	
la **joyería**	jeweler's	
el **jueves**	Thursday	
el/la **jugador(a)**	player	
jugar	to play [*games, sport*]	
el **jugo (de naranja)**	(orange) juice	
julio	July	
junio	June	
junto	together	
la **juventud**	youth	

K

el **kilo**	kilo	

L

lado (al lado de)	next to	
largo	long	
la **lata**	can	
lavarse	to wash	
la **leche**	milk	
leer	to read	
lejos	far away	
la **letra**	lyrics	
levantarse	to get up	
la **ley**	law	
la **libertad**	freedom	
libre	free [*time*]	
ligero	light [*weight*]	
el **limón**	lemon	
limpiar	to clean	
la **línea**	line	
liso	straight	
el **litro**	liter	
llamar	to call	
la **llave**	key	
llegar	to arrive	
lleno	full	
llevar	to take, to carry, to give a lift, to wear	
llevar a cabo	to carry out	
llover	to rain	
luego	then, afterwards, at once	
el **lugar**	place, spot	
el **lunes**	Monday	

M

el **maíz**	maize, corn	
la **mamá**	mother	
malo	bad	
la **mañana**	morning	
mandar	to send	
manejar	to manage, to operate, to drive	
el **mango**	mango	
el **mantenimiento**	maintenance	
la **manzana**	apple	
el **mapa**	map	
el **marido**	husband	
los **mariscos**	seafood	
el **martes**	Tuesday	
marzo	March	
más o menos	more or less	
mayo	May	
mayor	old [*person*], older	
la **medianoche**	midnight	
medio	half	
el **mediodía**	midday	
mejor	better	
el **melón**	melon	
menos	except, less	
el **menú del día**	menu of the day, set menu	
el **mercado**	market	
el **mes**	month	
el **mes que viene**	next month	
la **mesa**	table	
el/la **mesero/a**	waiter/waitress	
el **metro**	subway	
mexicano	Mexican	
México	Mexico	
la **mezcla**	mixture	
mi	my	
mientras	while	
el **miércoles**	Wednesday	
el **minuto**	minute	
mirar	to look	
¡mire!	look!	
moderno	modern	
la **mojarra**	*Mexican fish*	
el **moment(it)o**	moment	
la **montaña**	mountain	
montar	to ride, to get on (a train, bus, etc.)	
el **monumento**	monument	
morado	purple	
el **motivo**	reason, motive	
mucho	much, a lot	
mucho gusto	pleased to meet you	
muchos	many	
los **muebles**	furniture	
muerto	dead	
la **muralla**	wall	
el **músculo**	muscle	
el **museo**	museum	
muy	very	
muy bien	very well	

N

	el nacimiento	birth
	la nacionalidad	nationality
	nada más	nothing else
	nervioso	nervous, excited
	la nevería	ice cream store
	la nieve	sherbet
	la niña	little girl
	el niño	little boy
	no importa	it's not important
	la noche	night
	las normas	regulations, rules
	el norte	north
	nosotros/as	we, us, ourselves
	las noticias	news
	la novela	soap opera
	noventa	ninety
	noviembre	November
	nueve	nine
	nuevo	new

O

	obligado	obliged
	la obra	play, work
	observar	to observe
	ochenta	eighty
	ocho	eight
	octubre	October
	ocupado	busy
	ocurrir	to occur, to happen
	el oeste	west
	la oficina	office
	la oficina de correos	post office
	ofrecer	to offer
	el ojo	eye
	olvidar	to forget
	otro	other, another

P

	el papá	father
	los papás	parents
	el palacio	palace
	el pan	bread
	la panadería	baker's
	el pantalón	pants
	los pantalones	pants
	el pañuelo	handkerchief
	la papa	potato
	las papas fritas	potato chips
	el paquete	parcel
	para	for
	para empezar	to start with
	la parada de camión	bus stop
	parar	to stop
	parecido	similar
	los parientes	relatives
	el partido	(soccer) game
	el pasaporte	passport
	pasar	to spend, to pass (time)

	pasar (una película)	to show (a movie)
	pasear	to walk, to stroll
	el paseo	walk, stroll
	el pastel	cake
	la pastelería	cake shop
	la pastilla	pill, tablet
	la patria	homeland, fatherland
	el pecho	chest [body]
	pedir	to ask for
	peinarse	to comb one's hair
	pelear(se)	to quarrel, to fight
	la película	movie
	la película cómica	comedy movie
	peligroso	dangerous
	el pelo	hair
	pequeño	small
	perder	to lose
	perder peso	to lose weight
	perdón	I'm sorry
	perdone	excuse me
	perezoso	lazy
	el perfume	perfume
	el periódico	newspaper
	el/la periodista	journalist
	permitir	to permit, allow
	pero	but
	la persona	person
	personal	personnel
	la personalidad	personality
	pesar	to weigh
	el pescado	fish
	los pesos	pesos
	el pie	foot
	la pierna	leg
	el pimiento	pepper [vegetable]
	la piña	pineapple
	pisar	to step on
	el piso	floor (of a building)
	la pizza	pizza
	a la plancha	grilled
	el plato	plate, dish, course
	el plato fuerte	entrée
	la playa	beach
	la plaza	(town) square
	pobre	poor
	el pollo	chicken
	la pomada	ointment
	ponerse en contacto con	to get in touch with
	por aquí	around here
	por favor	please
	por lo menos	at least
	el postre	dessert
	precioso	beautiful
	preferir	to prefer
	preguntar	to ask (a question)
	el premio	prize
	preocupado	worried
	preocuparse	to worry
	primero	first

el/la	primo/a	cousin	el	retraso	delay

el/la primo/a — cousin
la procesión — procession
el programa — television program
prometer — to promise
pronto — early, soon
la propina — tip
próximo — next
el pueblo — town, village
la puerta — door
pues — well
el puesto — (work) position
el puesto callejero — street stand
el puesto de abarrote — grocery stand
la pulsera — bracelet

Q

que — which
¡qué casualidad! — what a coincidence!
¿qué desea? — what would you like?
¡qué envidia! — I'm so envious/jealous!
¡qué lástima! — what a pity!
¿qué quería? — what would you like?
¡qué suerte! — you lucky thing!
¡qué susto! — what a shock!
¿qué te parece? — what do you think?
quedarse — to stay
quemado — burnt
quemarse — to get sunburnt
querer — to love, to want
la quesadilla — tortilla filled with cheese
el queso — cheese
quiero … — I'd like …
quince — fifteen
quince días — two weeks
quinientos — five hundred
quizás — perhaps, possibly

R

rápido — fast
la raqueta de tenis — tennis racket
raro — strange
rebozar — to cover in batter
el recado — message
la recámara — bedroom
recetar — to prescribe
el recibidor — entrance
recibir — to receive
recomendar — to recommend
recordar — to remember
el recuerdo — memory
el refresco — soft drink
el regalo — gift
el régimen — diet
regresar — to return
el/la representante de ventas — sales representative
la res — beef
reservar — to reserve
el restaurante — restaurant
retrasado — delayed

el retraso — delay
la revolución — revolution
el ritmo — rhythm
rizado — curly
la rodilla — knee
el rollo de fotos — roll of film
romper — to break
la ropa — clothes
rosa — pink
rubio — blond(e)
el ruido — noise

S

la sal — salt
la sala de conciertos — concert hall
la salchicha — sausage
la salchichonería — delicatessen
salir — to leave, go out
el salón — lounge
la salsa picante — spicy sauce
¡salud! — cheers!
los saludos — greetings
las sandalias — sandals
la sandía — watermelon
la sardina — sardine
la sección — section
el/la secretario/a — secretary
el secreto — secret
seguir — to follow
segundo — second
los seguros — insurance
seis — six
la semana — week
sencillo — simple
el señor — Mr
la señora — Mrs, Ms
la señorita — Miss
sentirse — to feel
septiembre — September
ser — to be
serio — serious
el servicio al cliente — client service
sesenta — sixty
la sesión — performance
setenta — seventy
siete — seven
el siglo — century
el silencio — silence
la silla — chair
simpático — likeable, friendly, pleasant
sincero — sincere
sino — but
el sitio — space, place
sobre — about
el sobre — envelope
la sopa — soup
sospechar — to suspect
su — his, her
subtitulado — subtitled

243

el	subtítulo	subtitle	
	suceder	to happen	
	sucio	dirty	
la	sucursal	branch (of a company)	
el	sueldo	salary	
la	suerte	luck	
el	suéter	sweater	
el	supermercado	supermarket	
el	sur	south	

T

	también	as well, also
el	Támesis	Thames
la	tarde	afternoon
la	tarjeta	postcard
el	té	tea
el	teatro	theater
la	telenovela	television soap
el	temperamento	temperament
la	temporada	(sports) season
	tener	to have
	tener hambre	to be hungry
	tener prisa	to be in a hurry
	tener razón	to be right
	tener sueño	to be sleepy
	tenga	here you are
el	tenis	sneaker
	tercero	third
	terminar	to finish
la	tía	aunt
la	tienda	store
la	tienda de electrodomésticos	electrical appliances store
el	timbre	stamp
el	tío	uncle
el	tobillo	ankle
	tocar la campana	toll the bell
	todo derecho	straight ahead
	todo tipo	all kinds
	todos	all, every
	tomar	to have (food or drink)
	torcer	to twist
el	toro	bull
la	torre	tower
la	torta	sandwich
la	torta (de jamón)	(ham) sandwich
la	tortería	*store selling torta*
la	tortilla	tortilla
la	tortillería	*store selling tortillas*
la	tostada	toast
	trabajador	hardworking
	trabajar	to work
el	trabajo	work
	traer	to bring
el	tráfico	traffic
el	traje	suit
	tranquilamente	quietly, without fuss
la	tranquilidad	calmness, peacefulness
	tranquilo	calm, peaceful

	trasladar	to move
el	trayecto	route
	treinta	thirty
el	tren	train
	tres	three
	trescientos	three hundred
el	trigo	wheat
	triste	sad
	tú	you [*informal*]

U

	último	last
la	universidad	university
	uno	one
	urgentemente	urgently
	usar	to use
	usted	you [*formal, singular*]
	ustedes	you [*formal, plural*]
	utilizar	to use
la	uva	grape

V

las	vacaciones	vacation
	vale la pena	it's worth it
	varios	several
el/la	vecino/a	neighbor
	veinte	twenty
	vender	to sell
	ver	to see
el	verano	summer
la	verdulería	grocery
la	verdura	vegetables
	versión original	original version
el	vestido	dress
	vestirse	to get dressed
	viajar	to travel
el	viaje	trip
el	video	video
	viejo	old
el	viernes	Friday
el	vino	wine
el	vino blanco	white wine
el	vino tinto	red wine
	violento	violent
	visitar	to visit
la	vista	view
	vivir	to live
la	vuelta	roundtrip (journey, ticket)

Y

	yo	I

Z

la	zanahoria	carrot
los	zapatos	shoes
el	zapote	sapote [*type of fruit*]

Glossary of grammatical terms

Adjective: A word used to give information about a noun.

una casa **grande** a big house
mi carro es **nuevo** my car is new

Adverb: A word used to give information about a verb.

Maneja **rápidamente**. He drives fast.
Estoy **bien**. I'm well.

Article: In English 'the' is the definite article (in Spanish **el/la/los/las**) and 'a' and 'an' are the indefinite articles (**un/una/unos/unas**). See *Definite article, Indefinite article.*

Comparative: The form of an adjective or adverb used to express higher or lower degree. See also *Superlative.*

El anillo es **más/menos caro** que el collar. The ring is more/less expensive than the necklace.

Conditional: A verb form often used to say what you would like to do or to give an invitation.

Me gustaría ir a Acapulco de vacaciones. I'd like to go to Acapulco on vacation.

Definite article: In English, the definite article is 'the'. In Spanish, the definite articles are **el, la, los, las.**

Direct object: The noun, pronoun, or phrase directly affected by the action of the verb.

He comprado **una chamarra**. I've bought a jacket.
Las quiero. I want them

Disjunctive pronoun: A form of pronoun used after a preposition or for emphasis.

Para **mí**, la sopa. The soup for me.
Le gusta **a él**. He (in particular) likes it.

Ending: A letter or letters added to the stem of the verb to show the tense, subject, and number; also to nouns and adjectives, to show the number and gender.

Trabajar**é** mañana. I'll work tomorrow.
las cas**as** grand**es** the big houses

Feminine: One of the two genders in Spanish. See *Gender.*

Future tense: The form of a verb used to express what will happen in the future.

El tren **llegará** pronto. The train will arrive soon.

Gender: In Spanish, all nouns have a gender, either masculine or feminine, although a very small number can have both. The gender of a noun is indicated by the form of the definite or indefinite article used (**el/la; un/una**). Gender also affects the form of accompanying words such as adjectives, possessive pronouns, etc.

masculine: **el carro, un pueblo bonito**
feminine: **la casa, una blusa roja**

Gerund: A form mainly used in the present or past continuous tense. It corresponds to the '-ing' form in English. See *Present continuous.*

Estoy **estudiando**. I'm studying.

Imperative: The form of a verb that is used to express orders or instructions, or to suggest that someone does something.

Pase por aquí, por favor. Please come this way. [*formal*]
Pasa por aquí. Come this way. [*informal*]

Imperfect tense: The form of a verb used to express a continuous or habitual action in the past.

Antes **vivía** en Guadalajara. Previously, he used to live in Guadalajara.

Indefinite article: In English, the indefinite articles are 'a' and 'an'. In Spanish they are **un**, **una**, and in the plural form **unos**, **unas**, the equivalent of 'some' in English.

Indirect object: The noun, pronoun, or phrase indirectly affected by the action of the verb.

Le voy a escribir. I'm going to write to him.

Infinitive: The basic form of a verb which does not indicate a particular tense or number or person.

trabajar, 'to work'
comer, 'to have dinner, to eat'
vivir, 'to live'

Intonation: The pattern of sounds made in a sentence as the speaker's voice rises and falls.

Irregular verb: A verb that does not follow one of the set patterns and has its own individual forms. Many common verbs such as **venir** ('to come'), **ser** ('to be'), and **ir** ('to go') are irregular.

Masculine: One of the two genders in Spanish. See *Gender*.

Noun: A word that identifies a person, thing, place, or concept.

hermano brother
Sr. García Sr. García
carro car
libro book
jardín garden
vida life

Number: Indicating whether a noun or pronoun is singular or plural. Number is one of the factors determining the form of accompanying words such as adjectives and possessive forms.

singular: **un hombre** a man
una mujer a woman
plural: **dos hombres** two men
dos mujeres two women
unos carros some cars

Cardinal numbers: numbers used to count – one, two, three/ **uno**, **dos**, **tres**, etc.
Ordinal numbers: numbers that show the position or order of something – first, second, third/**primero**, **segundo**, **tercero**, etc.

Object: The noun, pronoun, or phrase affected by the action of the verb.

See *Direct object, Indirect object.*

Past participle: The form of a verb used either on its own as an adjective:

Estoy **cansado**. I'm tired.

or in combination with the verb **haber** in the perfect tense:

He hablado con Miguel. I have spoken to Miguel.

Perfect tense: The form of a verb used to talk about the recent past, very like the English perfect tense (e.g. he has eaten).

No he terminado mi trabajo. I haven't finished my work.

Person: A category used to distinguish between the 'I'/'we' (first person), 'you' (second person), and 'he'/'she'/'it'/'they' (third person) forms of the verb. The person is reflected in the verb and/or in the pronoun accompanying it, although in Spanish the pronoun is often omitted.

(Yo) hablo. (first person singular)
Ella trabaja. (third person singular)

Plural: Denoting more than one. See *Number*.

Possessive forms: Adjectives and pronouns used to show belonging.

Él ha perdido **su** libro. He has lost his book.
Ese carro es **mío**. That car is mine.

Preposition: A word (e.g. 'at', 'by', 'from') or phrase (e.g. 'to the left of', 'next to') used before a noun or pronoun to show its relationship to the rest of the sentence.

Estaré **en** la escuela **a** las nueve. I'll be at school at nine.
Tus libros están **en** la mesa. Your books are on the table.
El hospital está **al lado del** hotel. The hospital is next to the hotel.

Present tense: The form of a verb used to express something that is happening or in existence now, or as a habitual occurrence.

Hablamos todos los días. We speak every day.
Tengo un trabajo bueno. I have a good job.

Pronoun: A word used to stand for a noun. Pronouns may refer to things or concepts ('it', 'them'), or people ('she', 'him'), and may be indefinite ('someone', 'something').

Yo creo que **tú** tienes razón. I think that you are right.
A mí me gusta **éste**. I like this one.
¿**Algo** más? Anything else?

Radical-changing verb: A verb which has regular endings, but which undergoes a change in the stem in certain persons.

Reflexive verb: A verb whose object refers to the same person as its subject. The verb form contains an pronoun to indicate this reflexive action:

Su mamá **se levanta** a las siete. His mother gets [herself] up at seven.

Regular verb: A verb that follows a common set pattern.

Simple past tense: A tense used to describe an action which occurred once in the past at a defined moment and which is now complete:

Fui al cine ayer. I went to the movies yesterday.

Singular: Denoting only one. See *Number*.

Stem: The part of a verb to which endings showing tense, number, and person are added.

hablar: (yo) **hablo**, (tú) **hablas**

Subject: The noun, pronoun, or phrase that performs the action indicated by the verb.

Mi mamá está enferma. My mother is ill.
Ella tiene quince años. She's 15.

Subjunctive: A form of the verb used for formal imperatives or polite enquiries or requests.

Pase por aquí. Please come through.
Quisiera hablar con el Sr. García. I'd like to speak to Sr. García.

Superlative: The form of an adjective or adverb used to express the highest or lowest degree. See also *Comparative*.

Su carro es **el más rápido**. His car is the fastest.
Juan es **el mejor** de la clase. Juan is the best in the class.

Syllable: A unit of pronunciation which forms either the whole or part of a word.

sol (one syllable)
jar/dín (two syllables)
co/mi/da (three syllables)

Tense: The form of a verb which indicates when the action takes place, i.e. in the past, present, or future.

Verb: A word or phrase used to express what is being done or what is happening. It may also express a state.

Miguel **está comiendo**. Miguel is eating.
El tren **ha salido**. The train has left.
Pablo **tiene** dos hermanos. Pablo has two brothers

Index

In addition to the Language Building pages listed below, see also the relevant section of the Grammar Summary.